FEEDING
WELLINGTON'S ARMY IN THE PENINSULA

FEEDING WELLINGTON'S ARMY IN THE PENINSULA

THE JOURNAL OF ASSISTANT
COMMISSARY GENERAL TUPPER CAREY
VOLUME I
1804–SPRING 1813

Edited by Gareth Glover

With a Foreword by Emeritus Professor Charles Esdaile

Pen & Sword
MILITARY
AN IMPRINT OF PEN & SWORD BOOKS LTD.
YORKSHIRE – PHILADELPHIA

First published in Great Britain in 2023 by
PEN AND SWORD MILITARY
An imprint of
Pen & Sword Books Limited
Yorkshire – Philadelphia

Copyright © Gareth Glover, 2023

ISBN 978 1 39904 141 6

The right of Gareth Glover to be identified as Author of this work has been asserted by him in accordance with the Copyright, Designs and Patents Act 1988.

A CIP catalogue record for this book is available from the British Library.

All rights reserved. No part of this book may be reproduced or transmitted in any form or by any means, electronic or mechanical including photocopying, recording or by any information storage and retrieval system, without permission from the Publisher in writing.

Typeset in Times New Roman 12/16 by
SJmagic DESIGN SERVICES, India.
Printed and bound in the UK by CPI Group (UK) Ltd.

Pen & Sword Books Limited incorporates the imprints of Atlas, Archaeology, Aviation, Discovery, Family History, Fiction, History, Maritime, Military, Military Classics, Politics, Select, Transport, True Crime, Air World, Frontline Publishing, Leo Cooper, Remember When, Seaforth Publishing, The Praetorian Press, Wharncliffe Local History, Wharncliffe Transport, Wharncliffe True Crime and White Owl.

For a complete list of Pen & Sword titles please contact
PEN & SWORD BOOKS LIMITED
George House, Units 12 & 13, Beevor Street, Off Pontefract Road,
Barnsley, South Yorkshire, S71 1HN, England
E-mail: enquiries@pen-and-sword.co.uk
Website: www.pen-and-sword.co.uk

or

PEN AND SWORD BOOKS
1950 Lawrence Rd, Havertown, PA 19083, USA
E-mail: uspen-and-sword@casematepublishers.com
Website: www.penandswordbooks.com

Contents

List of Plates — vi

Foreword — vii

Introduction — xii

Acknowledgements — xxii

Recollections & extracts from letters written at the time, of campaign events in the life of Commissary General Tupper Carey during the years 1808 to 1818

Formative Years — xxvi

1st Campaign: September 1808, Corunna, Orense [Ourense] & retreat to Vigo, embarkation and return to England — 1

2nd Campaign: 1809 February. Embark at Lisbon, Passage of the Douro at Oporto, Talavera and retreat — 36

3rd Campaign: French sieges of Ciudad Rodrigo and Almeida, Battle of Busaco and retreat to lines near Lisbon and advance 1810 — 99

4th Campaign: January 1812. English Sieges of Ciudad Rodrigo and Badajoz, Advance into Spain. Battle of Salamanca, Entrance into Madrid, Burgos and Retreat. — 164

Index — 250

List of Plates

1. A Portuguese ox cart, by George Hunter
2. Camp life, by William Pyne.
3. A Commissary circa 1812.
4. A Portuguese cacadore.
5. The retreat to Corunna.
6. General Sir John Moore.
7. Marshal Sir William Carr Beresford.
8. General Sir Rowland Hill.
9. General Sir John Gaspard Le Marchant
10. A view of Lisbon, by Landmann.
11. A view of Oporto, by Henry Smith.
12. Aqueduct of Segovia.
13. A view of Coimbra, by St Clair.
14. The Inquisition Building, Coimbra.
15. Don Julian Sanchez.
16. General Sir John Doyle.
17. General Howorth's Peninsular War medals.
18. Fort La Lippe.
19. The Retiro fortifications – a contemporary map.
20. Le Marchant's heavy dragoons charging at Salamanca.
21. *Marching the French Prisoners into Salamanca after the Battle 1812*, published by E. Orme.

Foreword

It was with great pleasure that I agreed to write a few words of introduction to this work. As for the reasons for this, first and foremost is the immense respect I have for its editor, Gareth Glover. Someone whom I have been proud to count as a friend for many years, Gareth has been indefatigable in digging out personal accounts of the Peninsular War and Waterloo that have never before seen the light of day and have frequently been of immense use to me in my own writings: their progenitor being one of the great unsung heroes of Napoleonic historiography, his efforts deserve far greater recognition than they have ever received and I sincerely hope that one day something will be done to put this right. However, even had this new memoir been the fruit of the labours of someone completely unknown, I would still have been delighted to undertake the task. Thus, I have always been convinced that the Commissariat was one of the key factors – indeed, possibly even *the* key factor – in the military success enjoyed by the Duke of Wellington. There were times, certainly, when the tasks which it faced were beyond its powers, just as there were individuals in its ranks who proved either incompetent or dishonest, but without its efforts no British army could have kept the field, and certainly not for the length of time that British troops had to in the desperately inhospitable conditions afforded by the Iberian peninsula. To my mind, then, the more we know about the work of such men as Tupper Carey the better, and I am therefore genuinely very pleased to see the publication of his memoirs.

Moving on, what is there to be gleaned from Carey's recollections? At the head of the list, of course, must come the myriad details that they offer with respect to the workings and procedures of the Commissariat and the many travails to which its members were subjected. Conscious, perhaps, that his status as a non-combatant might lead to him being viewed with a certain cynicism, Tupper was naturally anxious to stress the disadvantages with which he had to contend. As he wrote, then:

> It is the first duty of the Commissary General and his officers to obtain provisions and forage for every man and horse in the army ... This duty is full of difficulties to the commissary; he can never please in an active campaign whatever may be his exertions. The magistrates and inhabitants do all they can to mislead him and the troops are never satisfied, and what he cannot provide is immediately attributed to cupidity and a desire thereby to deprive them of their right; in short, nothing less than turning stones into bread will suffice, and no one unacquainted with this profession in countries like Spain and Portugal, with indifferent roads, bad transport and no inland water communication, can form the slightest idea of the harassing nature of providing [i.e. supplying] a British army always ready to eat and drink of the best.

All this is true enough, but what really strikes the reader is the sheer drudgery of the work that had to be put in by Carey and his fellows, the pages of the memoir being littered with accounts of endless days and nights spent buried in paperwork in the most spartan of surroundings, and that all too often with little in the way of company and comradeship.

Setting all this aside, what do we learn of the campaigns in which Carey served? In so far as this is concerned, we must not expect the author to be other than what he was, namely a young Englishman of the Anglican faith who found himself operating in the most alien of environments. That being the case, it is no surprise to find much

FOREWORD

disparagement of Spain and Portugal and their inhabitants. Thus, for the most part – the one place of which Carey approved was Madrid – the towns and cities were mired in filth, the villages collections of miserable hovels, the roads terrible, the inns comfortless and the countryside a barren wilderness overrun with wolves. As for the inhabitants, they were lazy, ignorant in the extreme and arrogant beyond belief, as well as seemingly but little interested in the war that was being waged on their behalf and organized in armies that were barely worthy of the name, the best that Carey could say of them being that they might make good soldiers if only they were properly fed and given British officers. And as to why all this was so, the answer was obvious: Spain and Portugal being Catholic countries that were overrun with priests and subject to the rule of the Inquisition, they could not be anything other than backward and uncivilized. What we have, then, is a classic restatement of the 'Black Legend', and one that readers should take with a pinch of salt, and all the more so given the formulaic nature of some of the commentary, Carey having clearly been influenced very heavily by the eighteenth-century travelogues produced by such visitors to the Peninsula as William Dalrymple and Henry Swinburne. Indeed, on occasion the author cannot be described as anything but either wilfully prejudiced or downright ignorant: his claim, for example, that no books were available in Spain other than such things as lives of the saints has no basis in reality, the second half of the eighteenth century having seen educated Spaniards become conversant with the literature of the Enlightenment in considerable numbers, while the idea that the press was limited to news-sheets in the style of the old *Gaceta de Madrid* is beyond laughable. That said, however, Carey's remarks are not entirely to be dismissed, the archival evidence suggesting, for example, that popular support for the war against Napoleon really was little better than minimal. Nor, meanwhile, is there any reason to doubt the various mentions to be found of bitter clashes between British soldiers and the inhabitants that in more than one instance ended in murder and may have contributed to the havoc unleashed on the unfortunate cities of Ciudad Rodrigo, Badajoz and San Sebastián in the wake of their capture by assault.

If Carey does not escape from stereotype, he was yet an acute observer who was not afraid to engage in criticism of the British army and its superiors, a good example here being the candour with which he describes how many of Moore's troops not only strayed from the ranks in the course of the famous retreat to La Coruña, but fell to plundering the countryside and, on occasion, murdering the inhabitants. For this, meanwhile, it is quite clear that Tupper placed a good part of the blame on Sir John Moore, and, in particular, the undue haste with which he all too clearly conducted the retreat. As he wrote, then,

> Retreat, and such a one as we were then making, seemed to have rendered the officers careless of consequence, and the soldiers insubordinate and unmanageable and under no discipline, the sole object appearing to be to get as soon as possible on board ship and out of the reach of the enemy; and it is inconceivable when a panic of that nature has once taken root in an army, how soon a disorganisation follows and is taken immediate advantage of by the men.

What made the matter still worse, moreover, was that the terrain through which the army had to make its way was such as to make it all but impossible for the French to catch it. Thus:

> Sir John Moore's distrust of Spanish exertion and co-operation . . . saved the army under his command from falling into the hands of Bonaparte while in the plain of Castille. But that same distrust acting on his mind when in the strongest country in the world as Galicia is, and impressing thereon an idea that the enemy were turning his

FOREWORD

flanks, which they could not do as was afterwards proved, turned at last what should have been an orderly retreat into a disorganised run, during which every disorder was committed.

What, finally, do we learn of the many battles that Carey witnessed, these including, among others, Talavera, Salamanca, Vitoria and Waterloo? Invariably stationed in the rear of Wellington's troops, he is clearly not to be relied on as a guide to the military movements of the days in question and in fact makes no attempt to provide anything of the sort: indeed, he confesses that for the most part he could see nothing but clouds of smoke and dust. What does come over very well, however, is the chaos that invariably beset the area behind the lines, with wounded men staggering to the rear, convoys of ammunition being hurried to the front, camp-followers searching for their menfolk, columns of French prisoners being marched off to captivity, dispatch-riders galloping to and fro, and more-or-less numerous crowds of fugitives and deserters crowding wood, field and road alike. As if all this the hustle and bustle was not enough, matters were further enlivened by shot and shell in the form of the many rounds of enemy artillery fire that overshot their targets and an all-consuming air of fear and uncertainty: we know that Wellington never lost a battle, but Carey was not possessed of such hindsight, and, as he is candid enough to admit, on at least one occasion took to his heels in panic-stricken flight.

To conclude, then, this is a most welcome publication which I am very glad to add to my collection of British Napoleonic memoirs, and cannot but be one more feather in the editor's cap, always assuming, of course, that said item of headgear can find space for yet one more among the many with which it is already so rightfully adorned. Well done that man!

Charles Esdaile,
Professor Emeritus,
University of Liverpool

Introduction

Some of the finest memoirs written from the Peninsular War (1808–14) have actually emanated from one of the civilian branches, the Commissariat Department. For those already cognisant with at least some of these memoirs, one is immediately drawn to the astonishing account of that inveterate womaniser August Schaumann,[1] the travelogue of William Graham,[2] or the more prosaic memoirs of John Daniel[3] and Richard Henegan,[4] but these memoirs often fail to fully explain the role they performed in much detail or how they achieved it in such a hostile environment.

Commissary General Tupper Carey may also be known by some for his short but interesting and very honest account of his service during the Waterloo campaign with General Sir Henry Clinton's 2nd Division,[5] but unfortunately that is all we have had of his memoirs. To be strictly accurate, that is not true, because the early part of his

---

1 Published as *On the Road with Wellington: The Diary of a War Commissary in the Peninsular Campaigns*, London 1924.

2 Published as *Travels through Portugal and Spain during the Peninsular War*, London 1820.

3 Published as *Journal of an Officer in the Commissariat Department: 1811-1815 and a Short Account of the Army of Occupation in France during the years 1816-18*, London 1820.

4 Published as *Seven years campaigning in the Peninsula and the Netherlands from 1808-1815*, London 1846.

5 A truncated version of his Waterloo campaign journal was published as 'Extracts from "Reminiscences of a Commissariat Officer"' in volume 79 of *The Cornhill Magazine* of June 1899 and republished in the editor's *Waterloo Archive Volume VI*, Barnsley 2014.

INTRODUCTION

Peninsular War recollections was published in an obscure magazine in a small series of articles,[6] but they never even reached as far as the Battle of Talavera in 1809 before they stopped, hinting perhaps that the rest was already lost forever.

Then, a few years ago, I received an email from Dr Juliet Carey, a direct descendant, stating that the family had the entire memoirs of Tupper Carey and wanted someone to publish them in their entirety – I need hardly say that I jumped at the chance.

Tupper's memoirs are contained in four large, tightly handwritten journals, covering from his first moment as a junior office clerk, through to the end of the Army of Occupation when he was arguably the most important Commissary then working for the Duke of Wellington. The manuscript unfortunately does not cover his later career in the West Indies and eventually Malta, but what it does contain is a vast amount of detail on the role he carried out, giving us a truly unique window into the life of a Commissary, thankfully without ever over-doing the sheer drudgery of the role at times. However, although a civilian and greatly discouraged from putting himself in mortal danger, Tupper was often to be found watching the fighting from some nearby (and hopefully safe) vantage point and often describes the actions he witnessed, particularly where it affected his own charge, whether a battalion, a brigade or even later an entire division. Interspersed with these primary roles, he was often seconded to form supply bases in the rear of the army, or to hastily remove or destroy stores when threatened by enemy advances. He also talks freely about fellow officers, and being a private journal written simply for the eyes of his immediate family, he is not shy in giving his honest opinions of both his subordinates or indeed his superiors.

---

6   A series of articles entitled 'Recollections of my Public Life from the period of entering the Commissariat to the Close of the Campaign in France in 1818' was published in *The Clan Sandeman Family Magazine* in four excerpts between March 1899 and January 1901. I can only find one copy of this publication anywhere and that is in the National Library of Scotland.

Indeed his memoirs are so voluminous (nearly 180,000 words), that they have had to be published in two volumes. This the first volume, covers his early life, joining as a clerk and his early years as a Commissary up until the spring of 1813, just before the Duke of Wellington launched his troops on that memorable campaign, designed to drive the French back out of Spain, across the Pyrenees.

* * *

Tupper was born on 16 April 1788 and was baptised on 25 April 1788 at the Town Church.[7] He was apparently sent away to school – all efforts have failed to discover where – and in 1804 he returned home at the age of 16 and was immediately put to work as a clerk and so started his career in the Commissariat.

So let us look at where he served, in what capacity and what major events this volume covers within the very varied career of Tupper Carey in his own words, taken from his statement written in Malta in the early 1840s.

> Services of Commissary General Tupper Carey officially called for by the Lords Commissioners of Her Majesty's Treasury while at the head of the Commissariat Department in the Island of Malta and dependencies
>
> He entered the Commissariat at the age of 16 at Guernsey in December 1804 as clerk to the Assistant Commissary General Rawlings, during whose continued and protracted absences in England in 1807 until August 1808 [he] carried on in great measure, the duty of that island and was entrusted with the custody of the public money in Bank of England notes, often times to the amount of £1,000 and upwards,

---

7 Reference DSCN 9115 Town Church Registers. The Town Church is now known more readily as St Stephen's, St Peter Port.

INTRODUCTION

intended to operate the reduction of the existing discount on public bills.

He left that station for more active service and on the recommendation of Lieutenant General Sir J Doyle, under whom he had been serving, was immediately afterwards appointed by Commissary in Chief Erskine, to the army of Sir David Baird, proceeding in September 1808 to the Peninsula. On landing at Corunna, [he] remained some time at Deputy Commissary General Cooper's office and was sent in November to form a department at Orense [Ourense] on the frontiers of Galicia, intended for the supply of the two armies in effecting their junction; which depot, on the retreat of Sir John Moore, was distributed to the Marquis of Romana's army and to the Light Division of the British Army retiring to Vigo, afterwards was attached as Commissariat Officer to the rear guard and embarked with them for England.

He continued in Mr Erskine's office [at] Whitehall until he re-embarked for Portugal in April 1809 and then had the Commissariat charge of two brigades [of artillery] and [the] reserve artillery during the operations of the passage of the Douro, Battle of Talavera and subsequent retreat.

Was employed at Elvas, in the Superintendent of Transport [Office] attached to the extensive General Hospital at [the] depot there; afterwards in Commissary General Murray's office at Badajoz, for some months and returned to the Reserve of Artillery, at the express request of Major General Sir W [E] Howorth who commanded the artillery in its march to the north of Portugal in December 1809 and [he] was then made [an] Acting Assistant Commissary General.

In January 1810 [he was given] the additional Commissariat charge of the extensive depot of Coimbra; in

July that of Pinhanços at the time of movement of the army near the frontier, while the French were besieging Ciudad Rodrigo and Almeida. [He] broke it up upon the approach of the enemy, subsequently in September established that of Espinhal and for the same reason abandoned it. Was actively employed in the retirement to the Lines of Torres Vedras near Lisbon, in removing stores from several points on the line of movement and on the Tagus, to avoid their falling into the hands of the enemy. Immediately after joined Sir William Erskine's Brigade of infantry [in the 1st Division] in the Lines of Torres Vedras and remained with it until March 1811.

Went ill to Lisbon from fatigue and was then employed in the Deputy Commissary General Vaux's office examining accounts until July, when he rejoined the army at Portalegre and took charge of the depot of Castelo Branco in August and was confirmed Assistant Commissary General on the 10th of that month.

In November [1811, he] was transferred to the 3rd Regiment of Heavy Dragoons as Senior Commissariat Officer of the brigade of cavalry under the command of the late Major General Le Marchant, with which he continued during the sieges of Ciudad Rodrigo, Badajoz, Battle of Salamanca, entrance into Madrid and siege of Burgos until the retreat from there in November 1812. From thence in November 1812, he joined the [4th] Division of infantry under Lieutenant General Sir Lowry Cole, as Senior Superintending Commissariat Officer with which he continued during the many arduous campaigns of the years 1813.

The dates of his seniority are:
Acting Assistant Commissary General December 1809
Deputy Assistant Commissary General 23 May 1810
Assistant Commissary General 10 August 1811

INTRODUCTION

The rest of Tupper's incredible career will be covered in the second volume.

The Commissariat

Junior Commissaries were generally employed initially as clerks, checking the paperwork and invoices from the contractors who supplied the soldiers with virtually every store required, from food and drink to their fuel for cooking. More senior Commissaries were given the more demanding role of overseeing the actual supply of provisions and stores to the units they were seconded to, whether a battalion, a brigade or a division depending on their seniority. When their units were constantly on the march, this role became particularly vital and infinitely more difficult to achieve and it often became a very stressful and thankless role; if you fed the troops it was merely what they expected and if you failed to feed them they were very quick to complain bitterly. Commissaries were dressed in a blue coat as a uniform but they were civilians and should be looked upon as Treasury officials overseeing the money spent by the army and had a rank structure until 1810 of only Clerk, Assistant Commissary General, Deputy Commissary General and Commissary General, with no equivalent status to a rank in the Army.

From March 1810 it was expanded by including two further ranks and was given equivalent status to:

- Clerk (equivalent to an Ensign).
- Deputy Assistant Commissary General (looked after a battalion – equivalent to a Lieutenant).
- Assistant Commissary General (looked after a brigade – equivalent to a Captain).
- Deputy Commissary General (looked after a division – equivalent to a Major).

- Commissary General (looking after an entire corps or army – equivalent to a Brigadier General).

And in Whitehall at the very top were a Principal Deputy Commissary General and above him a Commissary in Chief.

Being independent from the Army, the Ordnance Department, which particularly controlled weapons and ammunition, had its own Commissaries, known as the Field Train Department with a different rank structure.

Around 130–140 Commissaries were operating with Wellington's army in the Peninsula at any one time. Pay rates in 1812 were:

Commissary General	£3 per day
Deputy Commissary General	£1 10 shillings per day
Assistant Commissary General	15 shillings per day
Deputy Assistant Commissary General	10 shillings per day

As can be seen from his service record above, Tupper Carey served throughout almost the entire Peninsular War in a multitude of roles and saw regular promotion. He appears to have been scrupulously honest and extremely diligent and capable in his job and certainly many senior officers sought his employment with their corps, a sure sign of his abilities and high reputation. He was not, however, unique in these qualities and the publication of his recollections will hopefully do much to counter the ill-founded but dire reputation of the Commissariat Department. It cannot be denied that a number of Commissaries were court-martialled and dismissed from the service for illegal practices, designed purely to line their own pockets; with stories of Commissaries making a fortune by buying back privately the receipts issued to the farmers for their crops at a vastly deflated value; altering the numbers on the official receipts to over-claim on payments; or illegally charging to process payments more expeditiously. Even apocryphal stories abound of Commissaries

INTRODUCTION

being threatened by senior officers with hanging if they failed to provide rations for their troops.[8] Elements of this were true of some, but most if not all were eventually caught and dismissed, while the vast majority of Commissaries diligently carried out their incredibly difficult jobs with complete honesty and integrity. Indeed S.G.P. Ward wrote in a lengthy article on 'The Peninsular Commissary'[9] that in his great work *Wellington's Headquarters*,[10] having only touched briefly on the role of the Commissary, he had opined that with only some exceptions, they 'tended to come from the very worst elements of the commercial world'. His conclusion on the Commissary was, however, much changed 40 years later, when he stated:

> The closer study which I have been able to give him since has convinced me that I misjudged him. There were some rogues, there were some commissaries that made money on the side; but I am sure that most of them were honest men by their lights and that among their number there were men of great ability, enterprise and business acumen.

It is hoped that having read the accounts of Tupper Carey in full, who undoubtedly was one of those of great ability, that the reader will be persuaded to fully endorse this more enlightened view of the more typical Peninsular Commissary.

---

8 The famous claim that General Picton threatened to hang his Commissary is stated to be wholly untrue in all of the memoirs of Commissaries including Tupper Carey. Certainly the Commissary (George Head) attached to his particular division at the time it is claimed to have occurred denies it ever happened.

9 *Journal of the Society for Army Historical Research* Vol. 75 No. 304 (Winter 1997) pp. 230–9.

10 S.G.P. Ward, *Wellington's Headquarters: A Study of the Administrative Problems in the Peninsula 1809-14*, Oxford University Press 1957.

The Careys of Guernsey

The Carey or Careye surname is believed to originate from the *Manor de Carrey* in Lisieux, Normandy, with the first reference in Guernsey to Johan Caree who was a *Coustoumier* (lawyer) in St Martins, Guernsey in 1288. The name seems to have been spelt mostly Careye, until anglicized to Carey in the Town Church Register by Laurent Carey in 1756. The family prospered, with members serving the island as Bailiffs, Jurats and Deans of Guernsey. Indeed, the Careys can be seen as one of the great families of Guernsey, alongside those of Le Mesurier, Saumarez, Brock, Le Marchant, Dobree, Tupper, De La Rue and De Lisle, most of whom have had strong connections to the British military for centuries.

Tupper Carey was the third surviving son of Isaac Carey Esquire of Hauteville[11] and Vallon[12] (1758–1828) and Marguerite Carey (née Tupper) (1760–1837) who had married at the Town Church of St Peter Port on 16 April 1788. Isaac was Constable of St Peter Port, Jurat of the Royal Court and Colonel of the South Regiment of Royal Guernsey Militia. He also owned a cutter in 1780 named *Hero* which acted as a privateer (William Le Chour commanding) and in 1780 alone she captured thirteen prizes at a total value of £28,497, 1 shilling and 6 pence.[13] On 3 December 1781 she captured *Le Gourmand* of Lorient (90 tons, five men) on voyage from Nantes to Brest and took her into St Michael's Mount harbour, Cornwall.[14] There is a further

---

11 He bought No. 16 Hauteville on 14 May 1785 from one Abraham Naftel. The house was later known as 'Mesnil Careye'. The house description of 1785 consists of 'A house, a laundry, garden and a building in the garden'. Isaac paid 38 quarters, 2 bushels of wheat, or about £765 (about £60,000 in modern terms). Nearby Hauteville House was later owned by Victor Hugo. Information from *Buildings in the town and parish of St Peter Port*, published by C.E.B. Brett in 1975 for the National Trust of Guernsey.

12 The property of Le Vallon, St Martin, was purchased from one Nicholas David, which apparently consisted of 'A house, barn, cowshed and a garden'.

13 Worth around £3 million today.

14 National Archives reference HCA 32/338/8.

INTRODUCTION

record of a *Hero* capturing the *Auguste* on 11 April 1803 and taking her prize into Falmouth, however by this stage she would appear to be in other hands.[15]

Isaac and Marguerite had thirteen children in total, eleven of whom survived into adulthood; they are as follows:[16]

No.	Name	Birth–Death	Marriages
1	Thomas	1780–1853	m.1 Mary Le Mesurier
			m.2 Barbara Jackson
			m.3 Caroline Lauga
2	Henrietta	1780–1863	m. John Carey
3	Elizabeth	1782–1815	m. Albert Foster
4	John	1784 died 5 weeks old	
5	John	1786–1850	m. Matilda Priaulx
6	Tupper	1788–1867	m. Anne Le Mesurier
7	De Vic	1790–1876	m. Frances Priaulx
8	Maria	1792–1881	m. John Connell
9	Sausmarez[17]	1794–1879	m. Elizabeth Dobree
10	Isaac	1796 died 4 months old	
11	Frederick	1798–1886	Died unmarried
12	Havilland	1799–1870	m. Augusta Dobree
13	Adolphus	1802–34	m. Frances Walters

A number of his siblings do appear within Tupper's Recollections and it appears that they were a close-knit family.

---

15 Jersey Archives Reference HCA 34/64, the captain then being John Tilly.

16 From the *History of the Careys of Guernsey* by W.W. Carey, 1938. Reference StB/1/Library/B/4 in the Island Archives, Guernsey.

17 This unusual spelling is confirmed by the records.

Acknowledgements

Any project of this size and complexity requires the aid of a great number of people to bring everything together and I must offer my heartfelt thanks to them here.

First and foremost, I must thank profusely the descendant family of Tupper Carey for giving me the opportunity to work on these incredible Recollections and trusting me to produce them in the functional way for a modern audience. I must particularly thank Dr Juliet Carey, Senior Curator of Waddesdon Manor, who initially contacted me on behalf of the family and who is the current custodian of Tupper's papers. Thanks are also due to Caroline Carey, who arranged for the digitisation of a typescript of the Reminiscences[1] and to Benjamin Carey for allowing me to illustrate his portrait. Juliet also kindly allowed myself and wife Mary to invade her London home to photograph and inspect all of the original Tupper journals and other family correspondence regarding them. I must also in this vein offer my deepest thanks to the historian Munro Price who suggested contacting Professor Charles Esdaile about the journals. He has long been a fervent supporter of my work and kindly suggested me as the best man to tackle these memoirs to Juliet.

A posthumous thank you must also be given to the current generation's grandfather, Captain Peter Charles Sandeman Tupper

---

[1] This transcript was, overall, surprisingly well done, but the transcriber not being au fait with early nineteenth-century language or the personalities of the period has erred in a number of instances. The entire transcript was checked against the original by the editor and corrected.

ACKNOWLEDGEMENTS

Carey, Royal Navy, who served throughout the Second World War and began the work of researching the career of Tupper Carey. Also, to their father Simon Henry Dundas Carey, who continued the painstaking work of compiling Tupper's life from records, in an age when personal attendance or interminably lengthy postal correspondence with numerous archives across Europe were the only resources available to them. Their work answered many of the questions that arose during Tupper's convoluted career and their meticulous research and voluminous correspondence was of inestimable value to me in preparing his story. A number of questions still remained unanswered, however, and their correspondence clearly shows their understandable frustration at not being able to complete their research to a point where they were fully happy. My further research, greatly helped by the aid of the internet and the much more ready correspondence available via e-mail with various institutions, has I am pleased to record finally answered all of their outstanding questions and I hope that they would have approved of the final outcome.

I must also offer my sincere thanks to Michael Hyde who freely shared his extensive knowledge of the Commissariat Department and is actively working on producing a book on the subject. Nathan Coyde, Archives Manager of the Island Archives, Guernsey and Chris Le Tissier of Channel Island Books, for kindly supplying gratis, excerpts from *The History of the Careys of Guernsey*. Also to Mr Ellis Bebb, Vicar's Warden at St Stephen's Church in St Peter Port, for kindly providing photographs of the stained-glass window and brass plaque dedicated to Tupper situated within the church and to gravestonephotos.com for agreeing to allow me to use their photo and details of those buried in the Carey Mausoleum at the Candie Cemetery in St Peter Port.

Further thanks must also be offered to Robert Burnham and Ron McGuigan who as always, have helped enormously in identifying certain obscure characters, or unravel odd incidents mentioned in the Recollections.

Last but not least I must offer grateful thanks to my long-suffering wife Mary and my adult daughter Sarah, for putting up with my constant ramblings regarding the process of bringing such a book to publication and very annoying habit of asking them to help decipher difficult passages of text at the most inconvenient moments. Your never-failing (although regularly tested) support and love is remarkable and fully appreciated and reciprocated.

Recollections & extracts from letters written at the time, of campaign events in the life of Commissary General Tupper Carey during the years 1808 to 1818

My professional career has been a short one, owing to its trying nature having so far affected my health that at 35 years of age, I was become so nervous, at any exciting cause, or required effort of mind for the transaction of the public business, that I declined employment for a while in expectation that my energies might return, which not having been realised after 12 years of retirement it is not likely I shall ever again go on service[1] but that short period having been connected with the great events which led to the downfall of Buonaparte, I am induced at this long distance of time, for my own private amusement, to endeavour to collect together my personal proceedings in the great drama, as a reminiscence to refer to occasionally, in after life.

---

1 From this note it is evident that he actually wrote this journal around 1835, little suspecting that he would again be called to service in Malta from 1837 to 1845.

Reminiscences

Formative Years

With so large a family as my father[1] had, (being 8 sons) and none of them being brought up to any profession, great difficulties arose in placing them in eligible situations and had it not been for the stirring times of that period, it is impossible to tell how so many could have found employment, exclusive of commercial pursuits, or what was analogous, our parents being totally averse to the Army or Navy. Any occurring occupations was therefore seized upon, and the moment I returned from school in 1804 from whence I came back little benefited by two years instructions; the fact was at that time education was not deemed very essential for the generality of the sons of the gentry unless intended for professional pursuits and therefore I was not more defective than my compeers, though I must confess I was not fitted to be very efficient in what I undertook. The trial was however to be made, and Mr Rawlings,[2] then Commissary to the troops in Guernsey, being a

---

1 Isaac Carey.

2 Assistant Commissary Philip Rawlings for the troops on Alderney and Guernsey became Acting Deputy Commissary General in Lisbon in 1808. He is mentioned by Commissary Schaumann in Portugal in 1808 in a less than flattering manner. 'Commissary-General Rawlings, a puffed-up and very uncivil fellow who, bye-the-bye, was cashiered two years later, had set up a large marquee on the beach and provided himself with all his London camp equipment, consisting of camp chairs of red morocco, small mahogany tables, a silk camp bed with steel springs, a canteen of silver knives, forks and spoons and a costly apparatus for his personal ablutions. Several clerks who were appointed at the same time as myself were given a tent. But in the evening the brute Rawlings would not hear of our making up our beds with a little of the hay that had been landed, although two of his own goats were standing up to their bellies in it. As soon as he had fallen asleep, however, we robbed the said goats of their hay and laid ourselves down upon it.' He served in the Peninsula from August 1808 to June 1809, partly with the Portuguese army and

FORMATIVE YEARS

friend to the family and wanting a clerk, I listed in this demi-military capacity, but how he was content with my first efforts, is to me now a matter of wonder. I continued however slowly improving under him for upwards of three years and I suppose became at last useful, for he often went to England leaving me to do his duty, which from having large sums in bank notes always in hand, and which he placed in my charge to operate in the reduction of exchanges against government, made my situation confidential and on one occasion the amount was so great (nearly £10,000[3]) that my father did not feel quite easy at having so large a sum in his house under simple lock and key. The routine of duty was regular and with the exception of going once to Alderney and Serk [Sark] no great variety occurred; there was a large garrison here under the command of Sir John Doyle[4] occupied in drilling, idleness, drinking and amusements, and how the public money was consumed no-one could have the slightest idea of, but those through whose hands it passed; not that there was any speculation, but solely arising from the number of officers on the Staff, expenses of public works to defend the island, number of regiments; posterity will hardly believe it, but the trial was great, for the ascendancy between Buonaparte and the British nation was then being attempted, and no effort was too gigantic to oppose him, his attempt on Spain developed his intention, and the great struggle began which finally led to his downfall.

In the beginning of summer [1808] the troops began to collect in the sea ports of England, and Mr Rawlings received intimation that he might be required to accompany them and when his appointment

---

became a Deputy Commissary General in 1809. In a case of the King versus Rawlings on 13 December 1823, he was charged with owing the treasury £8,849 15 shillings and 1½ pence (about £550,000 today) from his time on Guernsey and at Lisbon. He apparently owned Waltham Place in Berkshire (now a biodiversant farm) worth a living of £600 per annum (about £40,000 today) but was ordered to sell the property to pay his accounts.

3 Worth approximately £500,000 in today's terms.
4 Brigadier General Sir John Doyle had served in the American War of Independence and the French Revolutionary Wars, raising the 87th Foot in 1793. He was appointed Lieutenant Governor of Guernsey in 1803, a position he held until 1813.

came, he mentioned to me that if I wished it, he would endeavour to get me to go. My family were at first averse to it, but at last I was allowed to follow my own inclinations. I found, however that previously to my being allowed to move, I was obliged to remain one month to initiate his successor in his duties, which having done, I repaired to Portsmouth in August, expecting to meet Mr R[awlings] there; but I found he was gone out with an expedition, the destination of which was not then known, so I found myself thrown on the wide world with the person I looked up to, gone beyond the possibility of my reaching him; I was not however dismayed, for having a letter in my favor [sic] from Sir John Doyle, I proceeded up to London, and having presented it to the Commissary in Chief,[5] I was appointed a clerk in the department attached to the expedition proceeding under the orders of Sir David Beard [Baird].[6]

---

5 The Commissary in Chief was Lieutenant Colonel James Willoughby Gordon.

6 Lieutenant General David Baird commanded a force of 12,000 reinforcements for Sir John Moore's army, which landed at Corunna.

1st Campaign

September 1808, Corunna, Orense [Ourense] & retreat to Vigo, embarkation and return to England

I joined at Portsmouth in September, where we were detained some time and in referring to one of my letters written at that time, it appears that the Convention of Cintra gave great dissatisfaction,[1] and with respect to what happened under my own eye to a Portuguese line of battle ship, the officers of which were loud in their murmurs and so troublesome, that they were confined and sent on board their ship in arrest and it was apprehended that the crew might be riotous in a situation dangerous for the country in the heart of the dockyard filled with every material of the most combustible nature; they became however quiet after the first impulse of their feelings. We spent our money and almost became bankrupts from the recurring delays, waiting impatiently to embark and in the meantime, we visited the Isle of Wight. We sailed from thence some days after and reached Falmouth the latter end of the month and ascertained that we were destined for Spain. That small town, generally very dull, was while the army was there, a scene of the greatest confusion and disorder,

---

1 The Convention of Cintra [Sintra] was signed at Queluz Palace on 30 August 1808 by French General Jean Junot and General Sir Hew Dalrymple. The agreement saw all French forces in Portugal surrender and be transported back to France in British ships. However, the reaction of the British public was furious, causing the three senior British officers who had signed the convention to be sent home under investigation.

nothing to be seen but military in the streets, which are not broader than those in Guernsey, we drained the country of every disposable provision for the mess tables &c and the inns were so crowded that it was next to impossible to obtain a bed, or a dinner and I was absolutely obliged to write to my family, standing at the bar of a small inn, for want of better accommodation. Being obliged to lounge about during the day, there being no house room for everybody; at night we slept on board, orders being hourly expected for the expedition to sail; which took place on the 9 October and consisted of upwards of one hundred sail besides the convoying men of war, and we reached Corunna in the incredible short time of 4 days after a beautiful passage across the Bay of Biscay with a north east wind. I felt very sea sick as I did invariably after, but notwithstanding crept up occasionally on deck to enjoy the splendid spectacle of seeing the ocean literally covered with ships crowding all sail in the same direction, with the exception of the men of war who were occupied in forcing on and towing the dull sailers, keeping others from straggling and chasing any strange sail which made its appearance, with now and then an occasional gun to remind the careless and obstinate masters to keep in due bounds and be attentive to the signals making either to shorten, or make more sail.

The harbour of Corunna is a basin almost land locked and in the course of the day of our arrival, the whole fleet was snugly anchored in it, but no orders for our future disposal having reached, we remained some days in inactivity, arising as it was then reported, to the Spanish government being unwilling to admit more of us into the country, or as some would have it to the authorities in the town, which was a fortified one, and they were unwilling to put it in the hands of the English without superior authority, their jealousy being great on that head. Couriers were however flying about and no doubt orders would soon arrive to decide on our future destination, in the meantime we were on the tip-toe of expectation, the scene was most animating, the troops were regularly paraded on board,

1ST CAMPAIGN

drums beating and bands playing. We found the climate extremely mild even at times oppressive and the nights most genial, and I can never forget the harmonic discord which tattoo occasioned when it burst simultaneously from every ship, on every variety of instrument at the same moment 8 o'clock, in the confined space of the harbour, producing reverberations adding to the chaos of sound.

In thus being some days on board the transports in total inaction, it was well we had a short passage and had plentifully provided for being three weeks afloat, as the town and country had little to gratify in the way of comforts to those who had hitherto been enjoying the sumptuousness of a mess table which they were no longer to calculate upon, but in the sorry meal afforded by rations; anything the country afforded being most expensive and its cost most impudently raised and exacted.

At last we were officially ordered on shore and the troops were disembarked by brigades, and thus marched off in[to] the interior, so as not to crowd the town in too great numbers.

Our whole force amounted to *10,000 men* consisting all of 1st battalions,[2] which had been formed for a length of time and were decidedly a superior class of men in height and discipline to any troops which were afterwards sent to the *peninsular* and fought and gained the subsequent great victories.

I had landed an hour before and the result of my observations were not, as may well be supposed, favourable in contrast with Old England, which we had but just left, but the abord[3] for the first time in a totally different country, in manners, climate and religion, could not fail to be original and was intense to a young mind and my whole energies had never been so busy. Filth and dirt were the first characteristics in the street, idle fellows smoking their segars,

---

2 This statement is incorrect, amongst the battalions landed were 3/1st Foot Guards, 3/1st Foot, 2/14th, 2/23rd, 2/31st, 3/27th, 2/59th, 2/60th, 2/81st and 2/95th.

3 Manner.

apparently as indifferent about the state of affairs, as if there had been no enemy in their country, priests in abundance, a perpetual deafening peal from the church bells. The houses though solidly built having few glass windows and possessing no internal comfort to our ideas. The streets presented curious sights; beggary in every shape, fish frying and chestnuts roasting in the open air with their favourite garlic sending forth its odours wherever cooking was going on; the cries and conversation going on to me in an unintelligible language and the only occupation the inhabitants appeared to have was, in listlessly seeing the troops disembark and march off with their bands playing with the accompanying enthusiasm of fiery spirits hot from every comfort and burning to distinguish themselves, but which soon was in a degree cooled by the miserable life which awaited them, even from the first day they put foot on Spanish soil. For after landing they bid adieu to every description of bed; a blanket and bare boards, or earth and now and then some straw was all they had to depend upon, or could expect, even the officers in many instances shared in common with the men. All this was such a medley of the pomp and misery of war, contrasted with a population in poverty, kept under by despotism and misrule for generations past, that I shall never forget the impression it made on me at the time. The town was illuminated for three days in compliment, as some said, to our arrival, and others for some ideal advantage obtained by their armies which were falling back and flying before the French, but were invariably said to be advancing, it being a characteristic of the Spaniard to be the vainest of the vain, and fancying that his degraded country was superior to any under the sun, a feeling which no defect could substantially alter. This illumination was however a fair criterion of their bombast, being but a poor exhibition of a few oil lamps in each house.

 Our official duties at length began and we had soon a surfeit of them, by an uninterrupted and close application in the office of the Commissary General from almost daybreak till ten at night, no intermission but for meals, which were of so indifferent a nature, that the sooner they were over the better. We were a set of raw inexperienced lads as clerks, left to do as well as we could in obtaining lodgings without a knowledge of our rights or allowances, and had it not been for one of us who understood a little Spanish and who arranged everything connected with our lodgings, messing &c we should have been in no enviable situation. Our chiefs took no notice of us or assisted us in getting billets, so that it was only by dint of pushing our way through every obstacle, that we at last found out how to get on, and I may say, I learnt that but imperfectly during this first campaign. It was however no wonder that our superiors did not help us out in our emergencies, as they were in almost every instance as incapable and uninformed as ourselves in campaigning and oppressed to an indescribable degree with their incessant duties, whereas with the troops, these difficulties did not exist, as one of the especial duties of the Quarter Master General's department was to see the officers and men accommodated with lodgings &c when practicable. In short so long as we toiled and fagged there was not a soul to look after or care one button for our welfare, and the total inexperience of my department as well as every other in the Army made the duties much more oppressive to us and to everyone, than if they had been well regulated. As the duties of the Commissariat Department are little understood, underrated and unfairly stigmatized, I shall endeavour in as few words as possible to give a slight outline of them.

It is the first duty of the Commissary General and his officers to obtain provisions and forage for every man and horse in the Army, either by the resources of the country or by extraneous means, that is to say by inducing the holders of what is necessary, to part with it voluntarily on payment, or promise of payment, or through the magistrates by a formal requisition and in default thereof by recourse to main force; it being an axiom with an army either of friend or foe, that it cannot starve in the midst of plenty. This duty is full of difficulties to the Commissary; he can never please in an active campaign whatever may be his exertions. The magistrates and inhabitants do all they can to mislead him and the troops are never satisfied and what he cannot provide is immediately attributed to cupidity and a desire thereby to deprive them of their right; in short, nothing less than turning stones into bread will suffice, and no one unacquainted with this profession in countries like Spain and Portugal, with indifferent roads, bad transport and no inland water communication can form the slightest idea of the harassing nature of providing a British Army, always ready to eat and drink of the best.

Another important branch of duty is obtaining money, not only for the Commissariat duties, but for the pay of the Army, and every other contingency which its wants exact and which though partly provided for from England was required to be rose wherever it could be found; and in many instances from the want of a sufficiency of it, many distressing difficulties were experienced.

Next in the list was the providing of transport or conveyance, of every description of stores following the Army either belonging to Ordnance,[4] Engineers, Medical or its own, which consisted in the formation of depots in the lines of march pursued by the troops, an object requiring great ramifications of arrangement in applying the resources of the country. The conveyance and issue of the field equipment of the Army consisting of innumerable articles, devolved also on the Commissariat and after general actions and at all other times, the sick and wounded must also be provided with conveyance and the hospitals furnished with everything (medicines excepted). In short, with the exception of fighting, nothing could be done without the assistance of this department, which never received a mite of the praise it deserved for its unwearied and never ceasing exertions, as I can confidently assert; a day of rest seldom occurred for the six years and a half [I] passed in the peninsula.

Sometime after our arrival, one of the most splendid brigades of cavalry any country could produce, landed from England under the

---

4 The Ordnance Department supplied the weapons and equipment of the army.

command of the present Marquis of Anglesea [*sic*], then Lord Paget,[5] consisting of three regiments of hussars about 1,600 strong, such splendid men, horses and appointments as could not fail to strike the Spaniards with astonishment; and yet in two short months not one of these horses remained alive; having been destroyed in the manner I shall hereafter describe.

Corunna afforded but little novelty for those stationed in it, which was my case for a time, except the numerous prevailing reports of the advances of the French Armies towards ours, which was evidently true, from the apparent irresolution of our Army's movements, advancing and retreating and advancing again before the junction was actually effected with Sir John Moore's Army. As therefore the retreat was expected, which afterwards took place from the great inequalities of the armies, ours not amounting to more than 35,000 at most exclusive of the Spaniards, who were not yet arranged in regular armies, while the French were hundreds of thousands.

I sent some of my baggage home by a Guernsey vessel which happened to put into the port with despatches from the Canary Islands, reserving what I thought I could do with, but which I afterwards found I could not carry up the country.

In the beginning of December an order came down to the Commissary General to send an officer forthwith to form a depot at Orense [Ourense], on the frontier between Spain and Portugal; and fortunately for me, the senior clerk was at the moment out of the way, and I was fixed upon for that service, and on that account, as well as from having acquired in the office of issuing provisions, an insight in the allowances to the Army, which he had not, I was only allowed three short hours to receive my instructions and close the business I was about.

---

5 Lieutenant General Lord Henry Paget commanded the cavalry. He arrived with the Brigade of Hussars in November 1808, consisting of the 7th, 10th and 15th Hussars.

My preparations therefore, were of the most summary and limited nature. I was provided with a mule and strapped behind me I took two changes [of clothes], leaving the remainder in store with the general baggage of the Army, with the chance of never seeing it again. Such was the want of experience we laboured under and the little insight given to the juniors of the department, that we were totally unprepared for a march into the interior, until ordered to proceed, so that some idea may be formed of the really miserable and uncomfortable way we first commenced our peregrinations in a country totally destitute of inns and without understanding, that we in common with the Army, were entitled to be quartered on private houses, which I never found out till the next campaign, and it may be very confidently asserted that what was experienced and endured could only be borne by young and ardent spirits.

I set off on my journey in the afternoon accompanied by a Spaniard who had undertaken to supply the intended depot and travelled until ten at night through a country entirely new to me, for which nature had done everything and man nothing. We stopped at the foot of mountains at a posada, or lodging house, and made a miserable supper on hard eggs and maize bread, which to persons unaccustomed to it, is not at all palatable, but nothing else whatever could be procured without a knife, fork or spoon to be seen, as every native carries one of the former for his particular use, rendering a supply for general purposes unnecessary. Notwithstanding which, I set to work with my fingers and with the assistance of a voracious appetite contrived to dispose of a fair share of what I would not otherwise have looked at, and which was digested by a gentle exercise all the night long in having to contend with not a flea or two, but myriads of them and other persecutors, which gave me at the onset a tolerable idea of what was to be experienced in that way for the future, until experience and better arrangements in subsequent campaigns enabled us to travel with our own beds. Rising early next morning little refreshed by my nightly pastime, we made a breakfast much in character with the evening meal, after which we mounted our mules and began to ascend the hills at the usual rate of these animals, an amble which the severest of us could not hasten, in the gradual ascent we were making. I was not a little busy with the grand and beautiful scenery, which was progressively developing itself to the view; hills rising above those we had already ascended, which made me almost think we should never reach the ridge we had to cross, so little had I been accustomed to nature in her majestic form. At last, attaining the summit, a flat and open country presented itself below with a few villages scattered here and there. We passed through several, which from their wretched appearance looked more like having been recently pillaged and burnt by an enemy, than of being inhabited, though that was not the case, such was their miserable measure of life and the total want of comfort in their houses without glass or chimnies [sic] to be seen, built of dark granite, un-plastered or coloured but left in its dingy and rough state. After having travelled the whole day without intermission, in winding round the bottom of a hill we were highly delighted with the distant view of the spires of the famed and holy city of St Jago de Compostello [Santiago de Compostela], which to a person fatigued with travelling for 10 hours was a gratifying sight. I observed on the whole of the road, crosses on pedestals conspicuously placed at every winding or turning of it, or stuck upon some rock overhanging the same in passing, [at] which my companion touched his hat and crossed himself. They are, it is said, testimonials of some robbery or murder committed on the spot and erected to commemorate the event.

We entered St Jago [Santiago de Compostela] at five o'clock in the evening having travelled a distance of 15 leagues of Spanish (or sixty English miles) which sharpened our appetites and drew us at once towards the best inn the place afforded, which was not to be compared to the worst public house in England. In going to the room destined for me, I was under the necessity of passing through the kitchen, the floor of which was an inch thick in dirt and the ceiling looked more like one of our smith's forges, with this difference, that it was decorated in profusion with festoons of the principal ingredients of Spanish cooking, garlic and its inmate the cook, looked more like one of the witches in Macbeth performing her incantations over a boiling cauldron, than busy in preparing savoury dishes for human creatures. I occupied the same bed which had received the Commissary of the 1st Division of the Army under General Crawford [Craufurd][6] some time before and for a wonder I forgot Spain and all its uncomforts [sic] during a delicious night enjoyed by the total absence of tormentors. Curiosity made me soon stirring, and it was more than gratified owing to my companion and Conductor getting frightened at the alarming reports circulated of the enemy's movements and advances, which induced him to refuse positively to advance one step further without first communicating with the Commissary General at Corunna. Accordingly, a courier was despatched and I was left to ramble about and amuse myself until his return, conceiving it useless to go on myself, and which I afterwards found to be really the case.

I visited the cathedral of all Galicia,[7] as the first and principal object in a Roman Catholic country, an old Gothic pile very much resembling those in England, but the interior was the principal attraction, displaying the most gorgeous and imposing array of decoration to impress the mind with religious awe, by which I perceived the French armies had not yet paid it a visit; such a blaze of gold and silver candlesticks, ornaments, shrines, images in splendid attire, altars decorated with candelabra, hangings of the most costly description, in short everything laid out to produce a most brilliant coup d'oeil [a grand view], and to one totally unaccustomed to such a religious display it is no wonder it was not easily forgotten. I observed to my companion what immense resources the country would derive,

---

6 Colonel Robert Craufurd (known by the troops as 'Black Bob') commanded the 1st Flank Brigade, acting as a Brigadier General.

7 The cathedral is renowned as the last resting place of St James.

were it to appropriate to its defence the great riches thus displayed here and elsewhere, in which he coincided, but observed that were the churches stripped of the valuables they contained, it would so exasperate the clergy that it would lead to the withholding their powerful support, and he pointed out to me what I had already begun to perceive, that they were the very soul of the war by their unbounded influence on the minds of the most bigoted and intolerably ignorant race of people. I came to the conclusion that such a display spread over the country had no doubt much more influence with its spiritual ramifications than an equal value of the precious metals. The one would have soon been spent while the other acted most effectually and powerfully throughout the war.

After having feasted my eyes with this display of catholic superstition, we proceeded to the richest of the convents,[8] a huge pile and among the paintings I was most attracted by those representing the different deaths of the 12 Apostles, but I do not recollect who painted them. As usual every place and corner was crowded with costly ornaments and I could not but wonder at the degree of security in which these religious orders seemed to live, with all these valuables exposed, with as rapacious an enemy as ever overran a country at no great distance from them, but the fact is, they must have had secure and hidden recesses into which in a few hours the most precious articles were deposited, and as it was afterwards found, the clergy always possessed the very best and earliest information of what was passing, by which they were always prepared for any occurring emergency.

I was also shewn some engravings which were much prized, but as far as I could judge they were very inferior to what I had seen in England. Their library appeared very extensive but as I thought little of books at the time, I cannot say if the contents were valuable.

---

8 He calls it a convent, but later referring to a women's convent would indicate that he actually referred to a monastery. It was almost certainly the Monastery of San Martino Pinario, the second-largest monastery in all of Spain, after San Lorenzo de El Escorial.

In the library, they had only one English work, Sir Isaac Newton's *Principia and Fluxions*,[9] at least it was the only one pointed out to me; in descending the staircase the friar mentioned that the English troops amounting to 2,000 had remained for three nights on the ground floor of their convent from which some idea may be formed of the immense size of this building.

Not having sufficient knowledge of the language to enable me to transact business with the authorities where I was going to carry on my Commissariat duties, I hired a French emigrant priest to accompany me as interpreter, who had been driven out of France by the Revolution and was living here in great poverty. With his assistance I expected to make a more general survey of the interior of other large buildings, such as the women convents &c as well as of the town, but the courier arrived and brought me the first philippic[10] I ever received, and such a one as made me depart instanter to my destination, leaving my affrighted Spaniard behind to do as he pleased.

We left St Jago [Santiago de Compostela] in the afternoon and proceeded without intermission the whole night and the following day, by which I accomplished my journey and after all hardly lost any time by the effort I made, nor was the service I was on in any way affected by it.

At about 3 leagues from the place of our departure, we came to the banks of the small river Ulla over which a bridge had been begun but remained unfinished, so that we were obliged to have recourse to the ferry which was unfortunately on the other side.[11] We hallooed and made as much noise as possible but the ferryman was gone to bed

---

9 In *Principia Mathematica*, Sir Isaac Newton formulated the laws of motion and universal gravitation, which was published in 1687, his work on *Fluxions* or Calculus, was not published until 1736. This apparent combined book must therefore have been published after this latter date.

10 A bitter criticism or denunciation.

11 The old road from Santiago de Compostela to Ourense crosses the Ulla River near Reboredo.

and he was in his first sleep, so that we had to wait for a good hour, and it was only by alarming the whole neighbourhood that we at last succeeded in rousing him. At this time the country was so much on the qui-vive that disturbing at that hour of night gave them an idea that the enemy might be approaching. Though the weather was cold it was a clear moonlight night which enabled me to examine the bridge, which appeared beautifully began [sic], and as most bridges both ancient and modern are built in Spain rising in the middle to an extraordinary height, making the ascent and descent very rapid so as to allow a wider span for the centre arch, by which the water course was very much increased in a mountainous country subject to occasional extraordinary over-flowings by heavy rains which by their sudden rise come with such impetuosity as to bear down every obstruction and must inevitably sweep away any structure built on different principles, however inconvenient to the traveller.

After bestowing on the ferryman through my interpreter, a few oaths which I perceived the language of the country was most fertile in, we proceeded on and observed as usual a plentiful distribution of crosses which my present companion had learnt to salute, but if they were all memorials of highway misdeeds, we fortunately were not alive to the idea that an additional one might be erected on our account, though certainly we went through dismal forests and the most lonely spots of mountain road alone and at times during the night so bewildering that had not the country been under great excitement and wholly absorbed in their struggle we might perhaps have run some risk. But as it was, none was anticipated nor experienced; we found the people of the villages civil and wondering at what was going on, unaccustomed as they had before been to the sight of a stranger, Galicia being in an out of the way corner of Spain and seldom visited by any but its natives.

The latter part of the journey was through a very mountainous country, and having stopped some time at a cottage to refresh ourselves and mules, I was struck with the total want of comfort it afforded. No chimney, the smoke escaping through the roof, and as the fuel was wood, the smoke was of so pungent a nature that I could not remain any time in it, though the inhabitants bore it with unconcern, but it led to premature blindness, the old people being all affected by it.[12]

Just before entering the city of Orense [Ourense] we crossed at dusk the Minho River over a very high Roman bridge, built on the principle I before alluded to; it was plain, but so narrow that only one vehicle could have crossed over it at one time.

Though twilight was almost over when we arrived, the inhabitants soon found out I was not of their nation and having learnt that I was an Englishman belonging to the army, the poor inn I put up at, in the anxiety of being quickly accommodated after a night and day of uninterrupted exertion on mule back, was absolutely crowded with priests, monks and Spanish officers to see and converse with a complete *rara avis* [rare bird], and for that night and the next day there was no intermission in answering through my interpreter, the numerous and anxious questions put to me, and shewing myself to these good people whose curiosity seemed insatiable for some days. And no wonder, in their anxiety to know and prepare for the worst, with yet a lurking confidence of national conceit that the united efforts of such an immense country as theirs, must eventually succeed, an impression which appeared to animate and lead them to suppose that though supine individually, the country was making gigantic efforts, which feeling was the cause that little was actually done, and what was done from want of combination, was mismanaged.

So little accustomed were the people of this country to strangers that three days after I had arrived, an officer and two soldiers of the 95th Rifles dressed in green uniform, out on some reconnaissance, passed through and mentioned that at a small village 14 miles distant, it was stated to them that an English Commissary of war had arrived

---

12 Smoke particulates can damage the eyes and cause blurring, while continuous damage can permanently degrade vision.

in Orense [Ourense], and described my dress most minutely, which by the bye was nothing more nor less than plain clothes, the clerks of the Commissariat not being dressed *en militaire* in the beginning of the Peninsular war. But as I was accompanied by an interpreter, and the magistrates knew I was soon to commence business, I had acquired more importance in their eyes than I was aware of, or really should have occasioned. The people were however, getting accustomed to me, but the arrival of this detachment quartered in the same house renewed their thirst of seeing something new, and positively the door of no puppet show was ever so crowded as ours was from morning to night, not by rabble, but with the most respectable part of the community.

At length the little I had to do commenced and the purport of my journey being connected with the contemplated movements of part of the army, I shall now allude to it. An opinion must have been entertained by the general [Sir Henry Paget] that a retreat might possibly take place, either on Vigo or the north of Portugal, to prepare for which this town was fixed upon as a station through which the cavalry might pass and save their horses into the latter country. The ports of this province not being eligible for an embarkation of that nature, in the precipitate manner it was likely the enemy might oblige us to effect it, my duty was therefore to cause, or see stored in suitable magazines, forage, that is rye or oats or chopped straw as a substitute for hay, besides flour and live cattle for three day's consumption for three thousand cavalry; but which was for some days slowly advanced in from my first *compagnon de voyage*[13] not having as yet got over his panic.

I had therefore a considerable portion of time on my hands which I occupied in seeing the town and its environs, but I could not be absent for long, not daring to leave my post without it being known where I was, as affairs were looking very gloomy and the people

---

13 Travelling companion.

more and more anxious and impatient; to calm which feelings, as the only stranger among them, I was obliged to appear much more knowing than I really was.

I found this a very small city with nothing interesting excepting its possessing mineral hot springs, which the Romans had made use of, though I did not see any baths either ancient or modern. The spring heads were grated with iron to prevent persons from being scalded and the waters were accumulated in a large basin which was the general wash tub for the city. The water bubbled up as if it boiled and it was said that eggs or any small thing could be cooked in it. Rising as I did early in the morning, I saw in the valley into which these streams flowed a long line of fog for a considerable distance occasioned by the steam or exhalation of the cooling waters.

There was a detachment of Spaniards in the place which from my windows I saw parade every morning, who though fine able-bodied men, did not impress one from the looseness of their discipline and the indifference of their officers, with any great hope of their ever being able to cope with the French troops in the open field. Their personal comforts were not attended to impress them with confidence and the manner they were fed resembled pigs more than men. They were formed on the parade ground in squads at the dinner hour and near each squad was placed a large copper pan or cauldron filled with cooked beans and a very small piece of beef or pork for each man at the bottom of it. They then formed themselves into a circle of about two yards distance round it, each man being provided with a large wooden spoon with which he advanced in his turn filling it and retiring to his place, his left-hand man following him and so on till the vessel was emptied when the meat was shared and eaten. A most frugal meal, but which rendered them indefatigable and light in marching, being able to perform what was impracticable to either the English or French troops.

There was a nunnery in this town, and as I had not yet seen any of the sisterhood, my interpreter and myself in one of our peregrinations, paid it a visit. When we arrived, we were told they were performing some religious ceremony and could not then be seen. We rambled about for an hour and returned and from the receptions we received we were led to think that they had merely made the excuse to prepare themselves, for on again presenting ourselves, instead of its being as usual at the wicket, when stranger and acquaintances were received, the upper part of the inner great gates was thrown open leading to the interior from about 3½ feet upwards, the lower part being shut. The nuns to the number of 20 or 30 with the Lady Abbess at their head, formed a circle and stood to welcome us. They were of different ages, pale and no one remarkable for their beauty. They obliged us to take some bon-bons of their making and conversed with me through my interpreter upon the war, being very anxious to know, as everyone was, whether they would have to fly. They also asked me how, young as I was, could leave my family and follow the army on so dangerous a service.

Having at last satisfied mine and their curiosity, we left them, much amused with the novelty of the scene, and as I was afterwards informed that in thus opening their doors, a very great compliment was intended, and which was only paid to their great men.

After a few days more of comparative quiet without a book to read and strictly confined to the town with the most perplexing reports of the advances of the French armies, without a person to speak to in English, not having seen any followers of the army for some time to give me any news of what was really passing. An express reached me on the 22 December[14] directing me to proceed to the seaport of Vigo and bring up fifty thousand rations of provisions, which I was to obtain from the transports there.

I was not long making my arrangements and after what had occurred on a former occasion by the inertness of my former *compagnon de*

---

14 The date of the receipt of this order is very interesting, it probably having being sent at least two days before, the retreat to Corunna only having been ordered by Moore to start from Sahagun three days later.

voyage, I was not long in reaching my destination, but a few hours on the road soon convinced me that those who had given orders for carrying this business into effect, had not travelled that way, or been aware of its nature; and the difficulties which presented themselves were such that, had time or distance permitted it, I should have at once pointed out to the higher powers what appeared to me almost an impossibility. But a burnt child dreads the fire and I proceeded to face what might happen, having yet to learn that nothing was to be deemed impracticable which had not been tried.

My route was not by a highway, but by a crossroad over such a country of mountains as I had no idea of, at one time on their ridges and the next down into deep vallies [*sic*]. It was nature in its grand features, like huge waves as it were arrested in their progress, and when on the top of some of them higher than the others, the view was indeed magnificent and extending over an apparent chaos divided by the deep bed of the river Minho and overlooking a portion of the mountain frontier of Portugal. Over such a country an unfrequented road could not be of the best description, and though I have since seen a great variety of them, I never passed over a worse one. In some parts the mules had to clamber over blocks of granite which only such sure-footed animals and the peculiar carts of the country (which I shall hereafter describe), could do.

In short, young as I was and totally unpractised in such an undertaking, I felt it as a great trial, the uncomforts [*sic*] on the road were unheeded and I reached Vigo without any occurrence of moment. I found the cargo was at Pontevedra, on an arm of the sea a few miles off, and to which I proceeded without delay and set about the business in good earnest. The weather was dreadful, the rain was pouring in torrents and with but short intervals never ceased the whole time, until I again reached Orense [Ourense].

In a despotic country oppressed with war, force and threats have the ascendancy, and the means of every individual are without ceremony applied to the public service, though the higher classes by their influence escaped occasionally the burden at the expense of their poorer neighbours.

I took with me a small sum of money and not having been provided with any conveyance, I made, as was usual in such cases, a requisition on the magistrates for the necessary transport and in a day or two, it came in from the different villages and consisted of small carts taken from the different farms; drawn by two bullocks without any covering whatsoever, and no one unaccustomed to such primitive carriages can form the slightest idea of their inadequacy, and the little protection afforded to any perishable article conveyed on them. They could not carry above 800 lbs [363kg] weight and were constructed as per the image and the holes receiving stakes to keep the load from falling off and the wheels were two solid cylinders of about 3 feet in diameter and five inches thick, firmly connected by a wooden axletree, on which the simple described body was put and confined by two pieces of wood underneath, much resembling children's toy carts. As it revolved, a sound was produced like the drone of a loud hurdy-gurdy, grease not being allowed, which being different in its squeak to the others, produced a most distressing and overwhelming discordance when a large convoy was moving; which the peasantry would by no means abate as they firmly believed and asserted that it stimulated the oxen in their efforts.[15]

Upon this sort of conveyance then, were the supplies to be conveyed, consisting of biscuits, puncheons of rum[16] and barrels of salt meat, and with regards to the two latter the loading went on satisfactorily, but I was much puzzled to arrange for the former, which a quarter of an hour's rain would destroy. I was, however, put out of my dilemma by a patriotic individual lending hides to cover the biscuit carts, and at last the convoy started, with some spare ones in

---

15 It was also believed to ward off evil spirits.

16 A large cask containing between 70 and 120 gallons (318–546 litres).

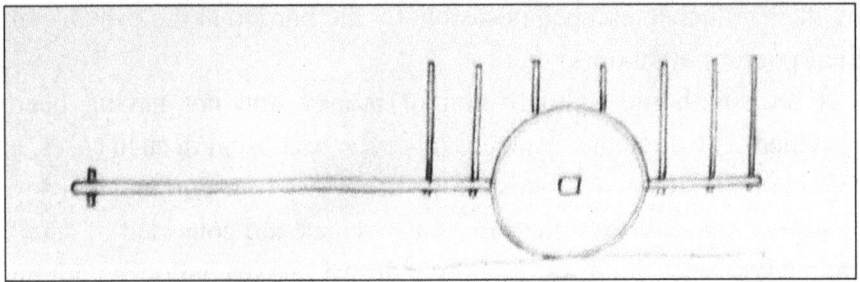
Drawing of a cart by Tupper Carey.

case of any breaking down, as was expected from the badness of the road, the heavy rum puncheons and the unskilfulness of the drivers.

The scene was striking and wild as the train wound up the road ascending the mountains, the men dressed out to protect them from the rain, in their grass cloaks ending in a peak on the head and as it were covered in as with a thatch, hollowing to encourage their cattle, which with the discordant creaking of the carts, altogether created an unusual effect on the mind, unaccustomed to such barbarous civilization. For really neither the road, the cart or the inhabitants seemed to have improved or altered one jot since the time of the Romans.

As this means of transport was, as I said before, impressed in the service they could not be forced to proceed beyond a day's march, so that at the end of the day's toil I was obliged to go through the additional trouble of paying each man his pittance, get others from the neighbouring villages, see the carts loaded and ready for departure for the next day, and as the interpreter and myself had alone all that to attend to, our labour was incessant; no escort or other person beside the stupid cartmen accompanying us to render any assistance. We succeeded however, at last in spite of every obstacle and after several accidents to reach our destination bringing up everything, but notwithstanding the trouble taken the hides turned out but a partial preservative to the biscuit exposed to the incessant rains and when deposited in store was totally unserviceable, and but for occurring events might have got me into trouble, though there did not exist a shadow of blame, but to those who had ordered the operation without well considering its practicability.

One circumstance I cannot but remember with satisfaction as redounding much for the honesty of the peasant cartmen, that not one case of theft occurred throughout the journey; indeed the people of Galicia expatriated all over Spain and Portugal, wherever they are met, are proverbially the most active, persevering and trustworthy porters, being without scruple, trusted with any amount of bullion to be conveyed from one place to another.

January 1809

In the course of this harassing duty the first Christmas and New Year's Day from home passed unheeded and forgotten. I had hardly rested from this duty when the retreat of the army burst like a thunderclap upon us, and though its distant murmurs had been heard in numerous reports, it was not thought so near. The main army took the road to Corunna and the Light Brigade[17] on their way to Vigo, came to Orense [Ourense], so, as it was said, to divide the attention of the enemy.[18] They halted only one day and proceeded on, and I received an order from the Commissary who accompanied them to deliver the supplies to a ragged body of fellows, called the Marquis of Romana's Army,[19] and then join the last British detachment consisting of the sick stragglers and the rearguard.

The Spaniards arrived and their Commissariat at the first refused to take the biscuit which was then in a state of fermentation, but when they saw the puncheons of rum and salt meat in another magazine, their

---

17 Craufurd's brigade was not then designated the 'Light Brigade' but the '1st Flank Brigade'.

18 The troops were sent to Ourense to ensure that the French could not use this road to advance around the flank of the retreating army and cut off their retreat.

19 Don Pedro Caro y Sureda, 3rd Marquis of Romana.

scruples vanished and they gave me a receipt in full for everything, so that I got out of an otherwise disagreeable business.

Immediately afterwards we commenced our march for the sea in anything but an orderly way, following the footsteps of our main force both by the same road and in misconduct. The soldiers, particularly the Germans of the King's German Legion, forming a part of the brigade,[20] straggling from their respective corps and plundering in every direction so that we found the peasantry much exasperated and inclined to wreak their vengeance on the last of us, when before that the inhabitants of that part of the country and indeed everywhere else when treated with kindness, had shewn a disposition to make every sacrifice for the mutual cause we were engaged in. But a retreat, and such a one as we were then making, seemed to have rendered the officers careless of consequence and the soldiers insubordinate and unmanageable, and under no discipline, the sole object appearing to be to get as soon as possible on board ship and out of the reach of the enemy; and it is inconceivable when a panic of that nature has once taken root in an army, how soon a disorganisation follows and is taken immediate advantage of by the men.

We soon perceived, though we were not aware of the extent of the disorder, that our common safety depended on our keeping together, but I compromised as nearly as possible the safety of the detachment under the following circumstance. It was my duty to give a receipt to the magistrate in the morning for what the troops had been provided with overnight. We had the day before quitted Orense [Ourense] and were in the small town of Rivadavia [Ribadavia]. I went up with my interpreter to the Junta house and in the courtyard the rearguard was waiting, being the last to leave the place. I sat down and was in the act of writing when the Alcalde[21] began complaining to him of the

---

20 The King's German Legion (1st and 2nd Light Battalion) were commanded by Brigadier General Charles, Count Alten. This brigade was also ordered to Vigo.

21 The Magistrate or Mayor in Spanish and Portuguese towns.

improper conduct of the troops under apparently great excitement; which on being translated to me, I endeavoured to explain, but he not appearing satisfied, I unconsciously made several remarks in French to my interpreter in the course of writing, reflecting on the Spanish character, thinking they did not understand that language, and I continued in my occupation but several times perceived my companion apparently very uneasy and looking pale at what the Spaniards were saying, and he at last, with much impatience, told me to make haste as we should be late.

Having settled the account we got on our mules and marched off, myself perfectly unconscious of what might have occurred, but when out of the town and in the open country, he stated that he had perceived one of the magistrates understood French and was highly indignant at what I had said, calling me a young fool for my impudence and that they had only to give a signal and the whole detachment would have been destroyed under the irritating feeling which then existed but which I was not then fully aware. In short, he considered from what he overheard that a trifle more would have occasioned something very serious.

As we proceeded on, the soldiers were at their work right and left of the road, firing at and plundering what came in their way, and on several occasions our party bringing up the stragglers and sick had to shew demonstrations of being ready for an emergency and fire at the assembled peasants working up to attack us. And I can very justly say that things were arriving at a crisis that led me to apprehend we should not reach our destination in safety. Fortunately, the distance we had further to march was not great, and as we got towards the sea coast the men were more orderly and we reached Vigo without any further occurrence of moment.

We found the troops already embarked and under orders for sailing, so that no time was to be lost to get on board and as the department connected with the Transport Service had also left, I could get no information of the vessel on which I was to embark and therefore took a boat and went about the small fleet, and at last found the one appropriated to the Commissariat; the smallest of the whole, a brig measuring 130 tons, but it had the advantages of being exclusively appropriated to our department and consequently not crowded. I embarked just as I stood, without a stitch of baggage, having lost the little I had on the road, and my clothes which had now been in constant use for six months and so often wet and dry and laid down in, at times began to shew evident signs of being worse for wear. But appearances were then little attended to, everyone being pretty well on a par and only anxious to get back home.

With the exception of what I have related, the retreat of our part of the army was not accompanied by any very trying event and its acceleration was induced under the delusive idea that the French armies might make parallel movements and get to the seaports before us. A most unfounded notion which the nature of the country must have at every step contradicted. But as it also regards the movements of the principal part of the army under the immediate command of Sir John Moore, I shall hereafter allude to it from the information afforded by those of our officers who were in it, and with whom I was in daily intercourse when in London immediately afterwards.

The small fleet weighed and were about putting out to sea on the 19 January 1809, when a very heavy gale of wind obliged us to anchor almost outside and consequently in some measure under its influence, and as it increased towards night the vessels began to drive, and a much larger one being on the point of running foul of us, the captain of our vessel was put to the only alternative to save his ship, that of cutting away the cables he had out, and which were the only ones he had on board and afterwards put to sea, which we did and got safe outside, having the gale only to contend with.

Having had no time to lay in stock or make any arrangement to provide any comfort for the passage, I was necessarily forced to depend on the ship's allowance and the scanty fare of my brother officers who had neither time or opportunity to obtain much, and they therefore grudged me the indulgence, particularly the senior officer, who for some reason or other took a dislike to me, but fortunately for them all, I served them a turn soon, which got them out of a snare they might otherwise have fallen into without one.

Having come last on board and the cabin being very small, I was obliged to lay on the floor during the passage in my clothes with only a very thin mattress to lay upon and small blanket for cover, and the weather having been though fair, most boisterous, I was in the midst of most dreadful sickness, tossed about the cabin with nothing to steady by. No one can form an idea of such a situation without having experienced it, and I must say for the few days it lasted it was indeed a state of wretchedness.

Next day at dawn we went in the open ocean, and nothing in sight and the weather such that we could not make Vigo. The captain therefore opened his secret instructions which had been given him in case he should be separated from the fleet, and by them he was directed to proceed to Corunna, for which port we shaped our course and arrived off it in two days.

We were steering for the harbour which is landlocked, when getting rather near but considerably out of gunshot, an unusual degree of quiet appeared to exist and not a sail outside, struck the captain's mind as singular when expecting to meet the large fleet which had left Vigo for this port some days before to embark the main army, whose destination seemed to have been to the former port first and then been altered, but very lately and unexpectedly to the latter, which it only reached in time to prevent the most dire consequences.

The harbour being landlocked, as I said before, and never having been there himself or any of his crew, the captain thought the fleet must be inside, but not visible; and being moreover lulled into security by seeing the Spanish Flag flying at the port, he was on the point of obeying his instructions, when getting pretty close during breakfast, curiosity led us of course on deck to have a nearer view of the place, which we had only looked at early in the morning; and he then for the first time expressed his doubts to us and wished to know if any of us had been there before. I was the only one who had and having been stationed there some weeks and perambulated the environs, I knew the tongue of the land on which the lighthouse was and which screened the harbour, was low enough for the masts of ships inside to be seen over it, and as there were no such indications, his suspicions increased and he at once put about ship and a consultation was held to know what was best to be done, and the only reason he gave in favour of going in was that if anything serious had occurred, some men of war would have been left plying off and on, to warn off any single ship bound for the place, but there was none. My evidence staggered him, joined as it was by everybody's solicitations to proceed for England and at last he consented to our wishes, binding us and me in particular in the event of his having done wrong to come forward in his justification, which events that had occurred rendered unnecessary, and well it was that he so decided, as Corunna was then in possession of the French, but they had continued to hoist the Spanish flag as a decoy; which was more dangerous in consequence as we afterwards learnt of the warning ships having been blown off the coast by the same tremendous weather we experienced at Vigo.

Joyfully then did we turn our backs to the land of our national disasters, the extent of which at the time, we had no idea of, and steered direct for home without convoy or protection from numerous French privateers, through whom a single unarmed vessel had to run the gauntlet. It gave us however, a sort of uneasiness but we gave a wide berth to every sail that was seen and before we had got half across the Bay of Biscay another gale arose, in our favour certainly, though it soon rose to such a pitch that danger was apprehended, and no observation could be made for two or three days to know where we were, and the captains of transports had been so accustomed to move with convoys that ours did not seem very *au fait* in that essential part of his duty, and which was exemplified immediately afterwards. For just about dawn on the day we got into Falmouth, we were astounded by a tremendous noise on deck, and of course we all rushed up the companion and found to our dismay that before they had put the ship about we had been running right upon the Lizard or Land's End, and if the darkness had continued another ten minutes we should have gone bump on shore on rocks that would have destroyed the vessel almost instantly. Dismay was on every countenance. The men were with their hair dishevelled and almost naked from having been ordered up on deck in the emergency, and for some minutes a doubt existed if we could weather the breakers, having carried away the fore topsail and shipped a sea in rounding to, which swept away everything on deck, boats &c. Fortunately we were soon put out of suspense by getting clear of the lee shore, and shortly after found ourselves steering direct for the inlet in which Falmouth is situated and we reached in the course of the 26 January 1809.

But a new dilemma awaited us from no anchor being on board, having cut away all we had at Vigo, the captain stated it as his intention to run aground or alongside any vessel which might be anchored and grapple her and which he requested us to assist him in. He accordingly singled one out and we quietly and as gently as possible ran alongside and made fast to her and immediately afterwards were supplied from her with a cable and anchor which enabled us to secure the vessel, and thankful we ought to be for having as it were escaped the battle and the breeze.

We had no clothes but those we stood in and not having changed linen or undressed for a month at least, we immediately sent on shore for a change, but determined to remain in our clothes until we reached London to get a new rig. When I shifted my shirt and drawers, from having been so often wet and dry, were become the colour of the clothes through which the rain filtered, added to which no small number of vermin had already generated in all the plaits [*sic*], so that it was such an exhibition when we stripped on board, that not one of the sailors would take them and they were in consequence unceremoniously thrown overboard.

We were not long getting on shore and to describe the happiness felt by us all in exchanging all at once every un-comfort and misery for the enjoyment of clean linen, a warm fireside, a good dinner and a comfortable bed, is beyond the reach of my feeble pen to describe and must be experienced to be understood and felt, and which was greatly heightened by the universal sympathy evinced by every individual who met us at Falmouth and on the road to London.

This gratification was next day for a moment alloyed by my superior officer ordering me to go with the vessel by sea to Portsmouth as he would not sanction my travelling expenses by land to London, but I put an end instanter to the arrangement by declaring that I should stand by the loss if disallowed and that I would not at any rate go on board again, knowing well there was no necessity for it, and that his resolve was mere caprice, without any act of duty requiring it. Finding me firm and determined not to be put upon, he left me to do as I pleased, and I got my expenses paid.

On our way and in passing through Truro we saw Lord Paget accompanied by the French General Lefebvre-Desnouettes[22] of the French Imperial Horse Guards whom he had made prisoner in the skirmish which had taken place near Sahagun and which had been so creditable to the British cavalry.

We proceeded on to Bath, visiting the pump room and every other place, dressed as we had landed, in our dingy blue coats and velvet cuffs and collars, gilt department buttons, blue pantaloons and red Spanish cockades in our hats, stared at by everybody eager to know particulars of our adventures.

After which, we reached London without further incident than that of receiving the commiserations and answering the numerous interrogations of everyone who met us.

---

22 General of Brigade Charles, Comte Lefebvre-Desnouettes was taken prisoner at the Action at Benavente. He broke his parole in 1811 and escaped to France.

1ST CAMPAIGN

We all expected to be turned adrift in a week or two, but the government having other views, I was lucky enough to get into the Audit Office at Whitehall[23] and was there employed making up accounts most pleasantly until something more stirring was again in agitation.

Many of those who had gone out in the last expedition were frightened at what they had undergone and left the profession for something more to their ideas, but I got among a knot who were yet determined to face more difficulties if the opportunity occurred, nothing daunted at what they experienced in their march to *Corunna*, and though numerous journals have been published, many circumstances which occurred in that celebrated retreat remain untold.

Sir John Moore's distrust of Spanish exertion and co-operation (though goaded by Mr Frere's[24] traitorous taunts, as he must have sold himself to the French party who preponderated in the councils of the Spanish Junta) saved the army under his command from falling into the hands of Buonaparte, while in the plain of Castille. But that same distrust acting on his mind when in the strongest country in the world as Galicia is, and impressing thereon an idea that the enemy were turning his flanks, which they could not do as was afterwards proved, turned at last what should have been an orderly retreat into a disorganised run, during which every disorder was committed. For such was the recklessness of the soldiery that at *Lugo* when the order came for our department to destroy the rum which could not be consumed, the heads of the casks being knocked out, the liquor ran down the streets filled with ordure[25] &c and yet the men bailed

---

23 The Audit Office was based at No. 5 Whitehall Place.

24 John Hookham Frere was an English diplomat and author, contributing to the pages of the *Anti-Jacobin*. He was sent to Spain in 1808 as Plenipotentiary to the Central Junta. He had vociferously encouraged Moore advancing to Madrid and strongly criticised the retreat to Corunna. The British public were strongly against him after this.

25 Dung.

it up in their caps and drank it, and when coming in from the march barefoot and bleeding, no sooner had they received a pair of shoes to go on with, in many instances they were sold to get more liquor.

All was confusion in the administration of the several Staff departments of the army, neither the Adjutant, Quarter Master General, Commissariat, Paymaster General and Medical Departments knew their duty or understood the language of the country, so that no wonder things went wrong and that the mind of the commander-in-chief must have been overpowered and distracted by the multiplicity of detail which should not have fallen on him to draw his mind and energies from the high and responsible duty of manoeuvring the army and attending to its preservation. No doubt that the Military Chest[26] could have been saved had not inexperience failed in procuring other transport. The rear guard got a picking at it, the cavalry soldiers putting the bags of dollars in their nose bags and carrying them on the pommels of their saddles, but a short ride soon wore a hole and the dollars dropped out one by one and strewed the road as they went along, the men not perhaps saving a third of what they had picked up.

The cavalry, however, soon felt the effect of the march and the loss of horses was indeed melancholy and allowing to loss of shoes which could not be replaced, 10 guineas having in several instances been offered for a shoe and refused, and of course a valuable horse was rendered no longer useful and was accordingly destroyed.

In and about Lugo nearly the whole of [the] horses of the splendid Brigade of Hussars, the landing of which I had witnessed at Corunna, were destroyed from want of shoes or otherwise knocked up, but the closing scene of the poor animals consisting of the officer's horses, artillery trains, mules and every other draught beast was truly melancholy, as few if any could be taken on board on the arrival of the troops for embarkation, not being longer required they were ordered to be delivered into a large enclosure outside the town and to

---

26 The coin carried by the army for purchasing supplies was known as the Military Chest.

prevent their falling into the hands of the enemy were all destroyed by shooting and having their throats cut, and it was even mentioned that guns were brought up and fired with grape upon them, every individual officer being afterwards remunerated for his loss by government. These were of course the remains of the animals which reached Corunna, as it must be observed that when the retreat became rapid, the road almost rendered impassable by dreadful weather; for many miles was strewed at every step with broken down waggons, carts, trunks broken open and baggage dispersed, dead mules and horses laying almost buried in the mud, occasioning scenes which eye witnesses could hardly describe to do justice to the scene.

And yet, in the midst of such confusion, with the army almost disorganised and the men savage from not having justice done them, as they said because they had not been made to face the enemy. When it was mentioned that there was about to be made a stand against the French, they became perfectly orderly, tractable and immediately formed and joined their ranks and even the stragglers without officers shewed on several occasions the stuff they were made of, by repulsing the enemy. England never sent a more splendid, though comparatively small army abroad, being composed of first battalions highly disciplined and certainly finer men than he was able to furnish in subsequent campaigns. But unfortunately the false confidence of a minister and the want of experience in the generals and departments, together with the overwhelming numbers of the enemy, added to the total inertness and traitorous despotism of the ruling powers of Spain, nullified the devoted *desires* of that gallant little band, which when overwhelmed by its sufferings, shewed with its last effort what it would have performed had it met the enemy in the meridian [*sic*][27] of its organisation and strength.

---

27 This would appear to have been used in error, presumably he meant something like 'zenith'.

The embarkation was of course done in the greatest hurry and consequent confusion, which was greatly added to by the French unexpectedly opening fire from one of the tongues of land which forms the harbour before the transports could get out; and one of our Commissariat clerks who had been brought up to the sea was the means of saving one. He had got on board when the firing commenced and found a motley crowd of men from almost every regiment and the captain on shore on duty, and no one competent to take directions of the vessel in such an emergency. He ordered the cable to be cut, took the command and being a cold and resolute fellow he was immediately obeyed and succeeded in getting out, but after effecting that object he found there were not provisions sufficient for those on board, so that in the midst of a gale of wind then blowing, he was obliged to obtain some from the first man-of-war he could communicate with at the hazard of his life. He however, succeeded and brought her safe to Plymouth; many of the men landing in twisted straw shoes and some with raw hides cut as sandals which they had supplied themselves with on the march. Even some of the officers made their appearance in that town in the same guise.

On going up in the interior of Spain from Corunna, I unavoidably left behind me nearly the whole of my clothes in a large and new leather portmanteau[28] which I gave in charge of a brother officer with a promise that he would take care of it, but of course I gave it up for lost when informed of the confusion which had occurred in the embarkation. On meeting him in London he told me it had been put on board some transport but did not know the name of the vessel, captain, [n]or could he give me any clue by which I might recover it. What to do puzzled me at first, considering that there were more than 150 transports in the fleet, and on applying at the Transport Office,[29]

---

28 A large travelling bag.

29 The Transport Office was located at Somerset House.

I could obtain little satisfaction, though promises of enquiry were made and upon which I depended for some time.

Happening however, one day to dine at Dr Saumarez at Newington,[30] his brother Sir James (late Lord de Saumarez[31]) was at table and having mentioned the circumstance of my dilemma he offered to assist me, and next day called on the Transport Commissioner, a captain of the Navy and his friend, who at once gave orders about it, and after some time I found it in a store in a back place in Thames Street[32] where it had been laying some time and where it would most likely have remained unclaimed had not this interference brought it to light.

Corunna

The following anecdotes were communicated to me by my friend Colonel Bambridge,[33] which being true, and connected with the retreat of Corunna, I have been induced to annexe them.

As Ensign he carried one of the Colours of the 20th Regiment from Lisbon to Corunna. Colonel Ross,[34] who commanded the regiment (afterwards killed as a major general at New Orleans,[35] United States) was a very able officer & his corps in conjunction with several others formed the rearguard of the army under Sir John Moore, and it became of great importance to keep the men from straggling & falling into the hands of the enemy.

---

30 Richard Saumarez was a younger brother, he was a Surgeon.

31 Admiral of the Red James Saumarez, 1st Baron de Saumarez. He died in October 1836, hence the 'late' comment.

32 Thames Street still exists, but ran closer to the river in earlier times.

33 Colonel John Hankey Bainbrigge had served in the Corunna campaign as an Ensign in the 20th Foot. He was later appointed Fort Major and Adjutant at Guernsey and probably met Tupper when serving in this capacity.

34 Lieutenant Colonel Robert Ross 20th Foot.

35 He is mistaken here, Robert Ross was mortally wounded at North Point during the Battle of Baltimore in 1814 and died soon afterwards.

One of these stragglers found his way into camp in a very mutilated state and mentioned that being half intoxicated on the road the advance of the French cavalry came on, he flourished his musket & threatened them, when one of them cut him down. Rising up again & nothing daunted he did the same to others & thus received several wounds in succession until he was left for dead. Having, however, recovered he succeeded during the night in reaching the British bivouac and completely exhausted with sixteen wounds about his head and body. Colonel Ross thought it a good opportunity to exhibit him as a specimen to his men of the treatment which they might expect from the enemy if they wandered from their corps & accordingly had him paraded just before marching through the ranks, a sight which so exasperated the men that they vowed vengeance and the effect produced was that only 16 men were missing at the conclusion of the retreat, unavoidably taken prisoners from exhaustion and sore feet. These men were subsequently marched into France and every endeavour made to induce them to enter into the French army. They resisted, being determined never to serve against their countrymen, but having heard of a fire brigade which had particular duties, 12 of them entered it in hopes of finding an opportunity of deserting but not having succeeded, they accompanied the Grand French Army into Russia, fell into the hands of the Russians in the retreat & were subsequently attached to the British Rocket Brigade[36] in the campaign of 1813 at the Battle of Leipsic [Leipzig] &c and at the termination of the war they returned to the regiment in England wearing the medals they had earned in their extraordinary career.

During the retreat Ensign Bambridge [Bainbrigge] wore out the heel of the short boots he had on which so affected his marching that he felt under the apprehension of being left behind, for his heel began bleeding & no others were to be obtained; but while in

---

36 'O' Troop Rocket Artillery, under the command of Captain Bogue, served at the Battle of Leipzig.

despair a report reached him that some Spanish stores were in the act of being destroyed, he ran to the spot as fast as he could & on the way fortunately met a brother officer returning with four pairs of shoes which he had picked up, one of which he at once spared him & with it he was enabled to proceed at once, relieved from the dreaded alternative of being made a prisoner.

Immediately after the Battle of Corunna the troops were marched down without delay to be embarked & as they reached the shore they in confusion were hurried in the boats and told the name of the transport on board which they were to be embarked & were directed to proceed in search of it among the innumerable fleet laying in & out of the harbour. Himself and his brother ensign with the two Colours and twelve men got into the boats and started as directed. They rowed in all directions and were sent here and there to find the ship & without succeeding night came on. At last the sailors declared they could pull no longer & advised them to ask to be taken in onboard the nearest ship, which being done the boats crew departed, promising to fetch them next morning & take them to the right vessel, but in the meantime a gale of wind came on. The French brought down guns to annoy the shipping, which obliged some to weigh & others to cut their cables & proceed to sea & thus they started, leaving the regiment without its Colours. The gale was favourable & in a few days they reached Portsmouth, remaining there some days without thinking of reporting themselves (young and inexperienced men as they were) to the proper authorities. In the meantime the regiment put into Falmouth & after some delay proceeded to Portsmouth & these jolly ensigns, having heard of its arrival, went on board to report themselves to the colonel, who on seeing them eagerly enquired where the Colours were & when informed they were safe at the inn, his joy & satisfaction was hardly to be described, for it would have been a most serious affair to have had to report that these emblems of regimental pride & glory were not to be found.

2nd Campaign

1809 February. Embark at Lisbon, Passage of the Douro at Oporto, Talavera and retreat

The sad and appalling accounts which were in circulation of the sufferings of the army frightened everybody and made their due impression on my parents, and as I could not at the time go home, I soon received an affectionate and urgent appeal to consider and weigh well the consequence of continuing any longer a profession likely to be attended with so many difficulties and dangers. But as at that moment there was not any positive appearance of molesting the enemy abroad, I did not give that serious attention to their remonstrances which the anxious desire they had of my returning home evinced, because it could have happened that I might have continued permanently employed where I then was in the Comptroller's Office,[1] Whitehall, instead of returning home to perpetuate habits of idleness, out of which after a time I might perhaps never be able to extricate myself, when accustomed to the comforts of home without care or anxiety for the future.

   A singular occurrence was nearly the cause of my not receiving this parental admonition for as it arrived at my lodgings on Valentine's day, my old landlady told me in the evening that a letter had been brought for me, but as she made it a point to refuse indiscriminately what was brought by the postman on that day, I thought it right to go

---

1 The Office of the Comptroller and Auditor General.

to the General Post Office to see after it, knowing no one in London who was likely to amuse me with a Valentine and I was just in time to rescue it from the destruction, which awaited thousands of love epistles circulated on that anniversary.

After weighing the pros and cons, I had hardly made up my mind to continue or give up the profession I had embarked in, when my resolves were soon tested by the government having resolved to reinforce the few troops existing in Portugal & endeavour to preserve the country and make it the base for keeping up & supporting the opposition of the peninsula against the government which the French were endeavouring to establish.

Having no interest of much weight to depend upon, I was necessarily left to my own resources, though I brought several letters from Guernsey to officers in London, on presenting which promises were made, but I never understood they had been of any assistance, and I therefore saw juniors to me advanced over my head, with no claims but what their friends had made use of by their parliamentary weight with ministers, or those concerned with the management of affairs.

When therefore, in the latter end of March 1809 the Commissary General of the expedition[2] about to be dispatched, came round the offices to ascertain which of the clerks were willing to accompany him, he addressed me among the number, but only offered me the same pay, 7s/6d per diem, which I received on my previous embarkation, but promising to increase it to 10/- on my arrival in Lisbon. Having already been deceived in former promises, I declined the proposal at once & declared that I would not go unless the increased pay was given me, conceiving I was entitled to it by previous services, upon which he stated his inability to do it. Finding me however resolute, he considered for some minutes & then said, 'Wait a little & I will step over to the Treasury and see what can be done for you'. He returned

---

2 The Commissary General of the Peninsula force was John Murray.

soon after and informed me that I was entered as a Treasury clerk at 10/- a day & that I should have to prepare for embarkation, which might take place the beginning of next month; so that I found by a little firmness I got (not what I deserved compared with others who had interest) but sufficient to stimulate me to persevere in the career which had opened to me.

I mention these particulars not exactly as interesting in themselves but simply to shew that I was solely left to my own resources and exertions to get on, having to contend with much neglect & many mortifications before I had such a hold on the service as enabled me to consider myself permanently dependent on it for a future maintenance.

My preparations were soon made for departure & almost immediately after I received orders to proceed to Portsmouth to embark on board the fleet collecting there. I was soon told off with several companions to a ship laden with stores, in a pursuit fraught with trouble & anxiety, and to most of us might be applied the old but vulgar adage, that we got more kicks than halfpence, notwithstanding that our department has the credit of being very fond of money & of making it when the opportunity occurs.

Some days intervened before the weather proved favourable, during which time we amused ourselves in visiting the dockyard, laying in sea stock[3] and seeing the Isle of Wight, which we were about to ride through when the Blue Peter[4] was perceived on board the various ships at Spithead, which obliged us to repair on board on the 14 April 1809.

We had however, hardly got on deck when the wind changed against us & blew a gale of wind, during which we tossed about at anchor in fine style, sick as possible for two days, and of course

---

3 It was necessary to purchase your own supplies of food and drink for a possibly long-extended voyage if the winds were contrary, termed 'sea stock'.

4 The 'Blue Peter' flag was a blue flag with a central white square (used in modern signals as the letter P). It warned crews that the ship was due to sail imminently.

nothing gained by it. Thus, I passed my first birthday away[5] from the paternal roof (excepting those at school) where I wished to be more than once in the midst of the overwhelming feeling caused by sea-sickness.

A day or two after we were more fortunate. The weather cleared, wind fair & soon the whole fleet was in motion going down the Channel and covering it as far as the eye could reach. By the aid of a prosperous breeze, we made considerable progress without anything occurring, but attending to the signals made to shorten or make more sail, accompanied by guns[6] from the men of war which kept the fleet always in a bustle. The sound of drums beating & music added much to the social feeling that we were in company so dissimilar to that loneliness experienced when sailing in a single ship, the picture of which might have been reversed had we met with bad weather, when great danger arises from the compact & huddled manner the vessels sail to keep in company.

We soon crossed the Bay of Biscay & made Cape Ortegal[7] & while going down the coast Lord Wellington (then Sir Arthur Wellesley) joined us in a frigate & after remaining with us a few hours he proceeded on to Lisbon, our destination.

As we were coasting it & when opposite to the great convent of Mafra a projecting rock was pointed out to us overhanging the sea, on which a pole was affixed & when the noble and rich friars were in want of fish, they hung a basket on it, which was a signal for the fishermen of the neighbourhood to bring the produce of their toils for sale, the consumption of which, in such a large establishment, must no doubt have been considerable.

---

5 He had been born on 16 April 1788.

6 The warships used cannon shots to announce to the fleet a new signal.

7 Cape Ortegal is the northernmost point in Spain, situated about 40km north-east of Corunna.

We made the Berlings,[8] which are picturesque rocks, and in passing them it is usual to make preparations on board ship, preparing anchors &c for soon getting into the Tagus which we effected on the 25 April after as short a passage as could be expected considering the large fleet & the great number of dull sailing vessels which abounded in it.

So soon as we had rounded Fort St Julian[9] the entrance to the river burst upon us, and certainly a grander view in nature could hardly have presented itself. The city on the left bank like old Rome on seven hills studded to their tops with buildings, churches with their towers, convents, palaces and batteries in picturesque confusion. In the centre of the river, forming a large basin with innumerable vessels at anchor in the background, the beautiful inland banks of the river & on the right the high bold projection of Almada which, together with our fleet swarming in on a beautiful bland day can hardly be conceived but by those who experienced it.

We were ordered on shore next day and having reported ourselves at the office of the Commissary General received directions to prepare immediately for a speedy departure for the headquarters of the army on the road leading to Oporto.

The appearance of the city from the vessel was most prepossessing and gave us a strong desire to get on shore as soon as possible, but on landing there was a sad falling off, being assailed by the most offensive smells arising from the filth collected in the middle of the streets, and which was worse than can be imagined. But the scene from its extreme novelty was so amusing that we forgot the annoyance of one sense in the gratification of another. Everything wore a new face; the carriages drawn by mules, muleteers leading loaded mules curiously caparisoned, water-carriers, Galicians in pairs & fours, carrying pipes of wine &

---

8 The Berlengas Archipelago is a group of small islands situated about 17km off the Portuguese coast, near the mouth of the Tagus.

9 Fort Sao Juliao da Barra was a Vauban-style fortress on the northern bank of the Tagus controlling access to Lisbon harbour. It is now the official residence of the Portuguese Defence Minister.

other weighty articles, detachments of English cavalry and infantry disembarking, galley-slaves chained together cleaning the streets, Portuguese mounted police cavalry, the clergy with huge broad brimmed hats, friars of all descriptions, numbers of English officers on horseback & on foot, ladies and gentlemen, swarms of beggars, peasantry & townspeople, all diversified in their dress, with dark complexions, all busy in their own way & pursuits, speaking in an unintelligible jargon. The constant rattling of bells together with the novel appearance of the streets & houses formed a picture most entertaining to a newcomer.

In passing by one of the markets, we saw the women shelling peas, which to us just arriving from England appeared very early, but the heat which we found oppressive soon rendered us aware that we were in a more southern climate & that it looked more like an English summer than the first burst of spring.

Previous to our arrival, the most gloomy forebodings existed with the army under General Craddock[10] which was merely keeping on the defensive to protect the capital, but so disposed as to enable the troops to evacuate the country had it been so decided, but the appearance of our reinforcements quite changed the aspect of affairs. The Portuguese who had made up their minds with apparent stupid indifference to receive the French again, expressed themselves with the most enthusiastic hatred of them which they would most willingly have exemplified on any poor defenceless Frenchman who might have become a prisoner, or isolated beyond the protection of their army. Woe be to the straggler of that nation, who for a moment quitted the ground on which it stood.

I brought our several letters of introduction from Mr Sandeman,[11] through while I received as much attention as the very short time

---

10 General John Craddock was appointed commander of the troops remaining in Portugal when General Sir John Moore took his army into Spain in 1808. He handed over the troops to General Sir Arthur Wellesley on his arrival on 22 April 1809.

11 Mr George Sandeman had set up a shipping company in 1790, initially transporting sherry to England and soon expanded into port.

allowed me to remain in the capital would permit, and I shall never forget as long as I live the kindness of Mrs Morrough,[12] the head of an Irish family and Mr Sealy,[13] which was not confined to this instance alone, but subsequently whenever I visited Lisbon.

My preparations were soon made & though somewhat improved upon those I had made in the Corunna campaign, they were still very simple and unpretending & anything but comfortable. Animals were selling at an enormous rate and I therefore chose a large mule, horses being too expensive, and not being able to find an English saddle and bridle, I was under the necessity of putting up with a Portuguese caparison, high stuffed saddle and bridle with blinkers, and my baggage was reduced to a few changes, that I might travel as light as possible & have besides a reserve in case of need.

We soon left Lisbon behind and passing through the various detachments of troops reach[ed] Leyria [Leiria], a city situated at the foot of a picturesque high rock, on the summit of which is the remains of a Moorish or other old castle. The place itself is not large, and in statu[s] quo, as most towns in the peninsula, the inhabitants of which appear to have been fast asleep for two or three centuries, under the iron hand of despotism and priestcraft, and as to comfort in their habitations, the Portuguese away from the capital have little idea of it, and though at this period of the war, they were as attentive as we could expect, their entertainment was limited to providing a bed (such as it was) & lodging.

The mode laid down & followed for quartering troops, including officers in the peninsula was on arriving at the destination for the night, to apply to the magistrate who was *Juiz Ordinans* for a village

---

12 The Morrogh family was originally from Ireland, but had become influential merchants at Lisbon by the late seventeenth century. Andrew and Francis Morrogh were trading there in the early 1800s and there was a company registered there as Morrogh, Walsh and Co. I have been unable to identify Mrs Morrogh.

13 Mr Richard Sealy was a merchant at Lisbon and partner in the Lisbon House of Evans, Offley & Sealy. He died at Lisbon in 1821.

& *Juiz de Fora* for a town, who on ascertaining our rank gave us a billet or order on a private house accordingly. But when attached to troops, the Quarter Master General attached, went forward & performed that duty & in general the Quarter Master and others whose duty it was, chalked the names of the individuals on the doors, so that with our billet in hand, we soon found our habitation for the night, unless the army had taken the field, when the canopy of heaven was our roof.

Another thing that claimed our attention, was how one was to get a dinner or supper, for that was not ready on our arrival. It was necessary therefore, to go to the Commissariat Office, and make out a return & receipt for what we were entitled to, for 3 days in advance, which our servant had to fetch from various parts of the place & if we arrived late, the chances were that we must put up with but a sorry meal, it being seldom practicable to purchase the needful. Experience however, soon rectified many of these little inconveniences & roughing it being the order of the day, we were soon drilled into every privation.

Nothing occurred worth relating [up] to our joining the army moving to *Coimbra* which we reached on the 5th of May, entering which, we were greeted by the loud vivas of the inhabitants, who occupied all the balconies of the houses looking into the main street, the ladies dressed in their best attire & the whole community appearing as on a holiday, waving their handkerchiefs and from time to time, throwing down flowers on the passing troops & no wonder they expressed themselves as they did after having been for a considerable time in the greatest state of anxiety regarding the French Army, which would no doubt have soon occupied their town and commenced the horrors which Oporto had been made to feel two months before, but which our advance had relieved them of for the present.

The access to Coimbra by the Lisbon road, is extremely picturesque. The city on being first perceived appears to occupy the whole face of a projecting hill directly opposite you. From the river side on which it is situated to the pinnacle which is occupied by the cathedral,[14] the university & several convents, the background consists of higher hills studded with trees, and as we descended the hill between groves of orange trees to cross the bridge (said to be an old Roman one[15]) to get into the town, the scene was much enlivened by the road being filled with troops with their respective bands playing.

Hitherto I had performed no duty, but on my reporting myself to the Commissary General & giving in a statement of my services, I was ordered to report myself to Major General Howorth[16] commanding the artillery, with instructions to attend to the provisioning of that corps, moving with headquarters, which I accordingly did & was quartered with them in the Inquisition,[17] a strange place it will be said, but as the accommodation of the troops was of essential importance, little ceremony was made in rendering every available place useful. This building being especially so, from having an extensive enclosure before it, surrounded by walls in which some of the artillery and all the reserve ammunition of the army was safely lodged. The artillery soldiers occupying the extensive corridors of the place and many of the officers & myself living with the Inquisitors, all ecclesiastics, whom we found very superior men & by no means shy in conversing on their duties, which by the bye, were become a dead letter, there having been no prisoners on the premises since the beginning of the war.

One day, when in conversation with them (by means of the little French they knew) Colonel Robe[18] who was the officer under whom I was immediately serving, not himself knowing either French or Portuguese, begged me to request that he might see the interior

---

14 The New Cathedral was built near the University in 1640.

15 No longer extant.

16 Actually Sir Edward Howorth was a Brigadier General in 1809. He commanded the artillery.

17 Off the current Patio da Inquisicao. The cells are still extant.

18 Lieutenant Colonel William Robe, Royal Artillery.

of the Inquisition, more particularly that part connected with their official functions. The Inquisitor General willingly acquiesced, and the following day was fixed upon for the visit, it being necessary to consult his companions whom he said would also accompany us.

Several officers accordingly mustered at the appointed hour to see so extraordinary a place. We walked in procession to the entrance porch, which opened on our approach & on each side of the door we were saluted with reverential bows by two tall men dressed in black, who were the familiars of the establishment & who accompanied us throughout. From the hall which had no particular appearance, we took to the left and were first shewn a flight of steps leading from the door in which prisoners were first introduced from the town to the first apartment in which they were lodged & which certainly must have made appalling impressions on their minds, being all hung with black cloth with a large white cross at the top of the room, and here they were left to meditate for some time ere they were led to their dungeons. Adjoining this was a nice airy room rather richly furnished with a table in the centre, covered with scarlet cloth & provided with silver inkstands, a highchair at the top for the Inquisitor General & lower ones for the Inquisitors, all cushioned & apparently comfortable. This was the apartment in which the delinquents were examined & tried.

While here we perceived each of the Inquisitors apply a key individually to open locks in a small door nearly opposite to the one we entered by, five of them doing the same & when it was opened, we were informed that this deposit contained records of all their proceedings & that it was necessary for all to be present to effect that purpose, and which was the reason we were not shewn in on the day of our application, there being a separate lock for each key.

There were many shelves in the rooms with books on them, but none of us had curiosity to look into them & indeed courtesy forbad it, there being no offer made to open any for our inspection. From thence we proceeded through several corridors to the more dismal part of the building & descending some steps were shewn a succession of small cells or dungeons to which a faint light was introduced by very narrow apertures, hardly the breadth of a finger, every part appeared of solid stone masonry & the only furniture the skeleton of a bedstead, gloomy enough to frighten the stoutest heart when labouring under the conviction that few ever left these abodes who had once entered them.

After seeing more of these wretched receptacles, the Inquisitor General intimated that we had now seen all that was worthy of our inspection, when Colonel Robe desired me in English to observe to him, with as much delivery as possible, that it being the general opinion that instruments of torture had been in use to extort confessions from prisoners, as well as otherwise to punish them, he would if possible like to see them. He appeared at first unwilling to answer, but at last he told us that nothing of the sort existed or had ever been made use of & if such was the understanding in the world it was a vulgar error without foundation.

Seeing no chance of prying further into the secrets of an institution happily now only existing in name, we returned through the corridor, and the gates shut upon us with the same formality as before. No doubt, however exists that many horrible scenes & atrocities have been committed within these walls, for the dread of the inhabitants of getting into its clutches was such, even when we were among them, that even in mentioning the word 'Inquisition' to a Portuguese, he would turn pale & avoid a conversation on the subject & in watching him you might almost perceive a cold perspiration creep over him, strong indications that there was a fearful mystery connected with its proceedings.

The inhabitants of Coimbra shewed unequivocal demonstrations of gratitude at our forward movement & well they might considering the state of jeopardy & much suspense they were in but a few days before. Their kindness to us therefore came from the heart & the convents were not backward in similar attentions, one of them in particular entertained for three days, such officers as were not otherwise accommodated & chose to go there. They were a very rich institution occupied exclusively by scions of noble families & though dressed as friars their clothes were of a much finer texture. It was a singular remark that they always wore spurs out of doors & were never seen less than two together.

Their refectory, or *salle à manger* was very extensive and could accommodate two or three hundred people. On one side in lieu of a sideboard in a large niche was a representation of the Last Supper, the figures (statues coloured) as large as life seated round a table on a platform, and apparently in the act of taking that meal & though not composed by a Phidias[19] yet made a tolerable group, with an effect strikingly bold & analogous to what was temporally occurring in the hall below, though in the present instance the military and sarcedotal [sacerdotal[20]] costume blended together formed a curious & unusual scene, in a monastic building, dedicated to seclusion and meditation. These good people no doubt lived well even when alone, for such was the capability of their cooks, that one of these entertaining days happening to fall on a Friday, a meagre day, the board had only dishes of fish, but there was such a variety & they were all so exquisitely dressed & so savoury & attractive, that no officer felt the loss of meat, or regretted this apology for fasting.

The period of the stay of the army at Coimbra was of short duration & only until it was so united, as that it might attack the enemy with all its strength concentrated for the effort & it was not made in vain. No person who has not seen it, can have an idea of the bustle occasioned by a numerous body of troops, congregating in and round a town with an enemy in the neighbourhood. Everyone appeared busy, some arriving from various directions, others departing with baggage on

---

19 A Greek sculptor whose statue of Zeus at Olympia was one of the Seven Wonders of the Ancient World.

20 Relating to priests.

the move of every description, from the soldier's wife on a donkey to the well-appointed establishment of the general, between which many grades of difference existed which would leave far behind any procession for peculiarity. Groups of officers, of clergy of which the place abounded, both regular and *secular*, of muleteers, soldiers, oxen carts drawn from various parts of the country dressed in their various costumes, composed a medley which crowded the various streets of the place, and shewed from the anxious looks of some & the bold bearing of the others, that something serious was brewing.

We did not wait long, the troops began to move on the 7th and 8th of May & the road towards Oporto, as well as those right and left intended for flank movements were crowded, the baggage, Commissariat and every other description of supply bringing up the rear. I remained some hours behind to settle some accounts & before I left the city it presented a perfect solitude and melancholy contrast to the day before.

The roughing part now began, and with so many wanting accommodation in different quarters for a person of my rank could only be expected, but so long as I had just space enough to lie down wrapped up in a blanket, I was quite satisfied.

The weather was becoming hot, so that a shed was considered in many instances more comfortable and freer of vermin than the interior of many houses, which were often found to swarm with fleas and other insects, to that degree that it was impossible to remain long in a bed furnished by the person on whom we were billeted & it at last became such a nuisance, that most of the officers after the second campaign, carried their own mattresses & trunk beds.[21]

Nothing occurred worth relating during the first two days march, but on the 10th of the month the advance of the army came within sight of the French, and on the road we soon perceived traces of their devastations, and that their foraging parties had been laying the

---

21 A portable metal-framed bed, that folded down into a small chest or trunk.

country waste, leaving nothing in the villages but bare walls, having carried away every portable article which the inhabitants in their flight had not time to secure, by which we were thrown upon our own resources for food and lodging which after a day of toil and great exertion was not over inviting, but there was a good source to it. A youthful & healthy body disposed to put up with anything and to take what happened with cheerfulness.

The next day brought the army in face of the enemy, and we were not long before the booming of the guns announced that the affray was taking place. I rode to the front but it was over, and I only saw the wounded coming in, and a party of French prisoners who had just been taken. Their dress was certainly much more military than ours, well fitted, and their appearance more rough & ready & savage, heightened by moustaches & while we had our waist buttons low in the back, theirs were almost under their arms, which produced a peculiar contrast. The days of many of them were numbered, as they were soon given over to Portuguese escorts to take down to Lisbon, and mercy was not a characteristic trait of either party when either had the upper hand.

Having advanced beyond the enemy's position, which owing to our flank movements not having been so rapid as was intended, had caused their being driven back & not surrounded as was expected,[22] we came upon the worst scenes of war I had yet witnessed. Every house ransacked or burnt, such of the inhabitants as had been bold enough to remain, were found murdered in and about their tenements and in different parts of a pine wood. The peasantry were found hung up on one tree in particular, seven or eight of them were strung up, one on each bough, which was broken off just short enough not to interfere with each other, and a horrible scene it was, as the poor

---

22 The French advance party under General Franceschi stood at the Vouga River. While Wellesley's main force advanced directly towards him, General Hill was sent to collect salt boats at Aveiro and to proceed up the lagoons to land at Vouga in the French rear. Unfortunately the French had retired beyond Ovar before Hill arrived.

fellows were already bloated and their swollen features presenting a ghastly spectacle, which could not be looked at without horror. The road also was here and there strewed with mangled bodies of stripped naked Frenchmen who could go no further and had been in return murdered by the inhabitants worked up to savage despair.

In such a state as the country was left, the troops could obtain no provisions or forage for the horses, and as the Commissariat transport was not at this time well organised, some want was experienced and our labours became harassing, owing to every exertion proving abortive to obtain any; leading of course to discontent on the part of the officers and men, which the best reasons on our part could not satisfy.

The two brigades of artillery with which I was, happened to be detached for a day or two, a day's march from each other & commanded by two Lieutenant colonels[23] & as I could not attend to both at the same time, I remained with the most extensive part of my duty, leaving the other necessarily to go on as well as it could for the time. Next day, coming up with the latter, the colonel was extremely wrath[ful], complaining that his people were without provisions, and that he would report me to the Commander in Chief. I rejoined that I could not help it, having done my best. His wrath continued and so far got the better of him that he declared with an oath, that I must manage to be in two places at once, or the troops must starve; a circumstance I mention to shew some of the unavoidable difficulties our department laboured under.

On the 12th, the army was concentrated on the heights of Villa Nova [Vila Nova de Gaia], overlooking the river Duero, on the other side of which Oporto was in full view before us. The French had destroyed the bridge of boats[24] connecting both banks of the river and

---

23 It is not clear who he means as none of the artillery brigades were commanded by lieutenant colonels at this time. Could he mean Lieutenant Colonels William Robe and Hoylet Framingham who were on the Staff?

24 Twenty boats were moored in the river and planking laid across them to form a bridge.

were, it was said (and they had reason to say so) in perfect security for at least a day, but they had reckoned without judgement, for Lord Wellington was indefatigable and was evidently acting so as to pay them in their own coin, determined not to give them breathing time & as the inhabitants were one & all in favour of our cause, we obtained their assistance in moments of urgency highly advantageous to it, particularly among the lower orders.

The French thought they had secured every boat on the river and that our passage across could not be soon expected, and they remained in fatal security, until too late to remedy it. By degrees and through great exertion some conveyance was obtained,[25] and with apparent inadequate means one of the boldest operations was crowned with success.

Owing to the high ground surrounding Oporto almost every proceeding could be seen, and apart from the pomp of warlike operations, the view on every side was very beautiful and the scenery grand and extensive.

While the first preliminaries were taking place, the city appeared in a perfect state of repose, nothing apparently stirring within it, and on our part such of the troops as were not at the moment employed were quietly filling the main road as well as to the right & left of it in close battalion [columns], among whom were the fine Brigade of Guards and artillery &c concealed from view, and only the officers allowed to look and watch what was passing, so that the enemy might not have too great a suspicion of what was taking place.

An extraordinary stillness for some time reigned around, considering the congregated masses of troops on both sides of the river, while a few of our men were quietly getting across, yet undiscovered by the enemy, owing to an elbow in that part of the stream. But when they at last ascertained the fact, then the whole

---

25 Colonel Waters crossed with some Portuguese in a skiff and released four large barges moored on the north bank. With these the 3rd Foot crossed and established themselves in an unfinished seminary.

scene changed as if by magic, and the most animating and noisy bustle burst upon the senses; the French drums beating to the arms in their peculiar way in the city, then the attack commencing on their part. Our endeavours to send more men across and our guns opening on the heights just overlooking the city produced a grand & imposing prelude to the following operation which enabled us to get into the place and give the French a sound drubbing.

The fight became more complicated, our troops held their ground [at the seminary] & thickened by degrees, and the enemy soon found that they were seriously compromised, though they did everything to restore their fortunes. A great deal of fighting took place, and which from our bird's eye view, [the] situation could be seen in all its details & finding that we were tenaciously holding a building on their side which they could not force, and were getting attacked on all sides, both from the city, by the men creeping over as the boats were obtained,[26] and above it by a force which had crossed some way up, we perceived after some time from where we were, their columns in retreat, and then commenced a bullying scramble after them which made them start double quick. As they were, however, a very active people, and were inured to war, they were quite as alert as ourselves, and were soon out of the reach of the masses, followed up only by the cavalry.

The bridge of boats was soon restored by our engineers and Royal Staff Corps and we entered the city which appeared the picture of desolation, with the few remaining inhabitants still in a state of despair and hardly conscious that they were freed from their oppressors. The houses were left standing, but the population had been ground down and plundered of everything or portable article, and its resources for the supply of our troops were scanty indeed. Such had been the precipitancy of the French retreat that the dinner

---

26 As the French began to abandon Oporto, the residents brought their boats to the southern bank, allowing the Guards to cross.

cooking for Marshal Soult was, it was asserted as a fact, served up to Sir Arthur Wellesley & Staff.

It having been ascertained that all our guns were unnecessary in the pursuit, those I was attached to halted, and I of course remained with them,[27] but the army continued the pursuit next day to drive the enemy across the frontier, and on the way to do them as much injury as possible, and which was fully effected, for it at last became a rout in which they lost all their guns, baggage and almost everything the soldiers could not carry on their backs; though they desolated and laid waste the country in their retreat as before, wreaking their vengeance on the Portuguese in every way with unbridled and sanguinary ferocity, laying aside all discipline and order, until they crossed the imaginary boundary between the two countries, and resuming them immediately on entering Spain by leaving off plundering as if they had returned into their [own] country.

Soult & his army never had such an escape, for owing to the mountainous road by which he had to retreat, he was in several instances hemmed in and must have surrendered but for the daring efforts of his veterans, and the inexperience of the Portuguese Militia & peasantry on the flanks, in not guarding with firmness and resolution passes & bridges which, had they been successfully defended, must have led to the total destruction of their implacable enemy.

As it was necessary for the Commissariat to provide provisions & forage for the troops proceeding forward in a place so completely exhausted as Oporto was, I could not for some time succeed, and had given it up in despair when I got secret information that a certain house contained some. We were soon in it, searching everywhere, but all to no purpose, though every wainscot,[28] door, cranny and every

---

27 As he does not comment on the artillery being German, it is most likely he was attached to two of the three British artillery brigades. As Lawson's 3-pounder brigade was the only one involved in the subsequent pursuit of the French, it is reasonable to assume that Carey was looking after Captain Sillery's and May's brigades of light 6-pounders.

28 Wooden panel.

other corner had been carefully examined, and I was just turning away to leave the upper floor when I perceived a grain of Indian corn jammed between two boards. This again set us on the alert and after more minutely examining the dark wooden ceiling, there seemed to the quickest eye of us all, traces of a trap door. A large piece of wood was instantly procured and the united efforts of several soldiers acting with it as a battering ram, forced it open and we were most agreeably deluged with a shower of Indian corn which enabled the artillery to get what was essentially wanted and freed me from being found fault with for not doing what would have been otherwise impossible but for this discovery, it being well understood that the best disposed inhabitant would not give for the use of the army what he thought was cleverly hid, for probably it might be the only resource on which his family depended for subsistence, and therefore in all cases of difficulty we made a lawful prize of what was thus discovered; for which a receipt was granted to the owner when he made his claim and was eventually paid, but there was such a distrust of the payment that few could get over it during the six years of the campaign. We became, therefore, quite expert in our dilemma in the discovery of false partitions, doorways plastered up & every other device which the poor people had recourse to, to preserve their little stores from the iron and keen grasp of hungry soldiers.

We remained in Oporto some days while the pursuit of the enemy continued, and during that time numbers of the inhabitants returned and the place got again comparatively cheerful. The British factory[29] which had been totally deserted, again swarmed with English merchants, who here were indeed honorables [sic] of the earth, as they enjoyed the special protection of the government, and though subject to the laws of the country, had a native judge wholly occupied in attending to their interests. They have a princely establishment and

---

29 The British Factory (now the British Association) was and still is housed in a building known locally as the *Feitoria Inglesa*.

when unmolested by external enemies must have lived in great style having it all their own way with the authorities.

We had hardly got rid of the enemy on one front when another army threatened us in another direction stronger than we were, and for a time it was apprehended that they might have reached Lisbon before us, having appeared on the frontier nearer than we were to that city.[30] The army consequently decamped for the south as soon as possible and retraced its steps to Coimbra which we reached on the 1 June, without any material want except that the inhabitants on the line of march were returning to their ruined homes, in dismay at the destruction made of their property.

From Coimbra we marched to Leyria [Leiria] and taking to our left passed through Ourem and to Abrantes where we arrived on the 20th of June.

This part of the country had suffered little and was rich in cultivation, and very picturesque, the towns being generally situated at the base of bold rocks or craggy heights (or knolls) on which were the remains of Moorish castles (no doubt originally Roman), with their towers & keeps still standing and mostly in a good state of preservation. The inhabitants were civil to us and my duty comparatively easy.

Abrantes is on the Tagus & has a bridge of boats connecting both sides of the river and was the great depot of provisions & other stores of the army, being supplied from Lisbon in large boats propelled up the stream by men with long poles owing to the shallowness of the water, which must have been most laborious but of the greatest importance to our army. The town is large and beautifully situated on the slope of a hill overlooking the river with its busy scene, which hill was crowned by a castle originally no doubt, Roman, but now of Moorish construction, made use of by us in this war as a defence

---

30 Marshal Victor was probing the Portuguese frontier north of the River Tagus and General Mackenzie with his small covering force based at Abrantes was concerned at reports of the French being at Alcantara.

in protecting so important a point against a coup de main or other attempt.

On arriving there we were under an impression that the operations of the army would be limited to the defence of Portugal, but the success which had attended our last efforts emboldened our chief to more active measures and an early rumour spread abroad that another trial to assist the Spaniards was in contemplation; the reverses of Sir John Moore not having had their weight in dissuading him or our government from the attempt, presuming we supposed, that he could avoid the quick-sands which the former general had got into and that by that dear-bought experience & his superior energies he could overcome difficulties which, since the last effort, had been deemed insuperable. But he soon learnt that the undertaking was surrounded with many difficulties, and that he was nearly committing a more fatal error than his predecessor, and whatever the page of history may state, providence had a great hand in extricating him from a dilemma in which he found himself by a false conception made in putting too much reliance in the efforts and capabilities of Spanish generals.

Our ambassadors with the Supreme government at Seville were also under a delusion with respect to Spanish energies, and acting on that erroneous conception they stimulated every proposal which was made to assist with our army any combined movement having for object to disturb the French government at Madrid but which, when acted upon by us, was found to fail by the combinations never having been carried into effect by the Spanish authorities so that we found ourselves to be principals instead of auxiliaries, and it was only after having given up all reliance on their exertions & our chief acting on his acquired knowledge in after times, untrammelled by the inducements & taunts of ambassadors, unacquainted with military affairs & yet meddling in them, thinking themselves generals, that we were able eventually to influence the affairs of the peninsula & in the end bring about that crisis which freed it from French rule.

Reports got into circulation that the army was soon to move & enter Spain on the northern side of the Tagus, but owing to the mountainous country, between Abrantes and Castello Branco [Castelo Branco], the road of which was impracticable for guns or carriages of any description, it became necessary to make a circuitous [route] round by the other side of the river which was comparatively flat and we accordingly crossed the bridge of boats and entered the province of Alentejo on the 29 June, reaching Gaviou [Gaviao] on that day, and on the next reached the town of Niza [Nisa], our marches being necessarily short to make halts to enable the great number of troops to dribble across the river again at Villa Velha [Vila Velha de Rodao] by a ferry & any other sort of conveyance which at the moment could be obtained, the slow process of which greatly impeded our march.

The roads were by no means good even for our bullock carts, or other wheel [*sic*] conveyance, and it would be impossible to make any comparison between them and the English roads, for they appeared quite neglected, never having in my recollection seen a workman employed on them in their repair. They seemed to be as they had been for centuries before, without improvement and kept commonly even by the strings of mules and the few bullock carts going on them, carriages for the conveyance of passengers being seldom or ever seen; male travellers invariably using saddle horses or mules, and the only mode of travelling for ladies occasionally met with was perhaps as comfortable as any country produced and which was contrived to meet the badness of the roads; it was in general a species of large double sedan chair, the poles of which like shafts were carried by two stout & sure footed mules of the largest size, one before & the other behind, with a man guiding the foremost either on foot or muleback, according to the length of the journey. The animals were regularly harnessed with very gaudy trappings, usually of red worsted, and the coat sheared in imitation of figured drapery, the whole producing a strange but picturesque effect. It was of course, the higher classes only who could afford this mode of travelling.

The high road from Lisbon to Oporto & to Madrid form exceptions to my observations, as they are wider and being more trodden down and used occasionally by royalty, had been put to rights at some period and levelled.

The country near Villa Velha [Vila Velha de Rodao] on both sides of the river being very bold and the descent and ascent necessarily circuitous, on standing on high ground commanding the pass, a very animated scene presented itself from both roads being crowded with troops of every description, baggage &c, with the banks swarming with those embarking and disembarking although under a scorching sun the rays of which were nearly doubled in the hollow confined by the two mountainous sides of the stream. A very great inconvenience having in this instance been felt by the delay occasioned in crossing in this dilatory manner, a flying bridge of boats was subsequently established & so contrived as that it could in part be removed on either side in the event of any emergency, as this was the road in going from north to south of the frontier which was constantly used in defending Portugal during the next three years.

We took two days to reach the city (as it is called) of Castello Branco [Castelo Branco] through a most uninteresting and barren country in many parts overrun by the gum cistus shrub, with trifling cultivation here and there, and the inhabitants in poverty. To give the name of city to such a place was indeed a degradation of the term, but when classed with others having the same denomination in Portugal, it was not absolutely misapplied. Having been quartered in it for some months subsequently, I shall defer making any observations on its locality until I come to that period of my narrative.

We halted here two days to give breath to men & animals and to mature arrangements previous to our eventful entry into Spain, as this was the last station in the country in which provisions & stores of all description had been collected for distribution.

On the 6 July it was our turn to move in the echelon march of the army, the head of which was extended from the rear several days march, not to interfere but as little as possible with the provisioning, and the accommodation needed by the Staff &c of the respective divisions. It being usual for an army to move disjointed, to render the resources of the country more available rather than crowding them all in one point and consuming everything without order or regularity, so long only however as the enemy was [not] at hand who could possibly disturb that arrangement. For when there was a probability even of their being within some days march, then the troops were concentrated and the whole moved in mass either on one or more parallel roads within communicating distance.

We halted near the small village of Fidera [Ladoeiro] and the next day at Zebreira immediately on the frontier [of] both countries, being divided by a small stream which in summer is often dry and only impassable in the rainy season.

The advance of our army for the purpose of driving away the enemy [who] expected to commit devastation in the country through which it passed we always found to be a source of pride and gratification, the inhabitants receiving us with joy and trembling, and doing their utmost to expedite our movements and thereby get rid of their apprehensions in the hope of our success, and certainly the Portuguese in this instance exerted themselves to avoid a second invasion, and placed all their expectations on us, their English allies, in effecting that purpose to whom they consequently were submissively devoted as well as their magistrates in furnishing all that was necessary until successive years of occupation tired every individual, ruined their country and made them almost indifferent to the results of the war.

A Portuguese is cunning in his national character, fawns and cringes when he has an object to attain and if unsuccessful keeps up his cunning most artfully, combined with treachery, his hat is off on every occasion & he bows as low as the importance of the object in view requires. There is no nobleness in his ideas or deportment, though he entertains the opinion that one Portuguese is equal to two Spaniards & that the worst of his nation is better than the best of the other. He is dirty in his habits, and which the heaps of filth accumulated in every town and village attest without contradiction, proving him to be as great a pig as the animal he rears bearing that name. All this must be the result of a total absence of education and knowledge under priestcraft, for he is acute and intelligent and would be clever had not the state of degradation in which the government had fallen, and its despotic sway impeded the development of his faculties. He hates and despises the Spaniard to that degree that he will not copy him in anything either good or bad, and therefore nothing can equal the difference which an almost imaginary line of boundary between the two countries creates in habits, dress, manners, cookery, bread, mode of building & harnessing cattle &c, all is dissimilar and I cannot bring forward one single point of parallel between the two nations in which uniformity might be said to prevail. Even the formation of the letters of the alphabet are different, and their style of address marking the characteristics of each country was an exemplification, for it was oftentimes amusing to me at first coming in Portugal to receive letters addressed 'Illustrious Sir' which I afterwards found to be a commonplace act of courtesy, so that the only way left to distinguish the higher grades was by the more fulsome title of 'Illustrious and Excellent Senor'. Indeed the extent of the complimentary style which prevailed among all classes could hardly be understood by persons who had never visited the country, even the courtesy kept up between street beggars meeting, not only bordered on the ridiculous but was a perfect burlesque on courtly manners. Their hats (which in most cases were cocked) were doffed almost to the ground, and a long string of compliments & enquiries resulted from their interview, which a passing stranger might, if he wished, overhear, without disturbing the parties.

On the 7th of July, we passed (as I may compare it to the Rubicon[31]) the frontier of Portugal into Spain and from that moment our army may be said to have been compromised to act again in conjunction

---

31 'Crossing the Rubicon' is an idiom meaning that one has passed the point of no return.

with the Spanish force in our front & further to establish the fallacy of depending on the promises and efforts of a misgoverned country. We hardly set foot into it and got on a mile before we perceived a total change in every object, and I must say the contrast was decidedly in favour of Spain, more comfort and cleanliness in the houses, a richer country, a finer race of people dressed more nationally & picturesque with a striking change in everything else which the trifling line of boundary rendered almost incredible. As my professional duties threw me at once in contact with the civil authorities, I was not long finding out the difference in character in the two nations.

We halted for the day near Zarza la Mayor, a small town in which there was an alcalde, or magistrate of inferior rank who probably could not write, his business being evidently transacted by his secretary sitting at his elbow. I was ushered into the office and there perceived three individuals with large slouched hats on, seated at table busily occupied; going up to one I mentioned my business, which he hearkened to without moving or taking off his hat, though mine was in my hand, or offering me to sit down and several officers who came in while I was there, were treated in the same grave and haughty manner without further ceremony or courtesy, our respective business being dispatched in a way we had been little accustomed to in Portugal. And yet these men were little farmers; but then they were Castilians, proud & pompous with the idea that they were the first people under the sun.

From this and other circumstances which immediately followed, the commonest observer could not fail to perceive that from principals, we had become or were considered, auxiliaries only in the cause and our contemplated efforts were coupled by every Spaniard, in their ignorance, with the gigantic means prepared by their country to co-operate with us.

As I before alluded, I was attached to the reserve of artillery consisting of a brigade of 5 six pounder guns & an howitzer to throw shells, drawn by horses and a train of all the spare ammunition, gun carriage wheels & every other material required by the artillery which were conveyed on the small bullock carts of Portugal driven generally by the owners, poor fellows, wholly perhaps depending on their yokes of oxen for the cultivation of their small farms, and which in their own country were willing enough to go with us, but when made aware that the interior of Spain was our destination, they were in despair, loudly praying to be relieved and sent back home, and at the same time making every effort which ingenuity could devise to desert with their cattle, which however was prevented by numerous sentries put over the park. It had been the intention to liberate them, if other transport could have been obtained from the Spanish authorities, but they failed in this essential point & it was one of the first indications of their faithlessness in promises made, that we should want nothing. These poor bullock men were therefore unavoidably forced on, but such was their horror at finding themselves among a people they detested & liable to the casualties of war, that they by degrees disappeared leaving their property in our possession. It was really heart-rending to see the struggle previous to their departure of many of these men, it being generally precluded a day or two before by fondling and embracing their cattle and apparently taking a last farewell of them. We commiserated their situation and encouraged them by every attention to continue with us, but the love of home with these simple people was such that very few were induced to persevere, though they were aware of the certainty of receiving liberal pay when their services were no longer required.

Their places must be filled up and as no Spaniard could be found to do it, the artillerymen were necessarily obliged to become bullock drivers, having perhaps never before handled or driven a bullock, and with such awkward and primitive tackle, it is not to be wondered at that they did not acquit themselves very cleverly, and before they got *au fait* at their novel duty many curious scenes occurred, in half choking the cattle when putting on the yoke, and upsetting the carts from the oxen, not understanding their manner of driving. And from the rough construction of their vehicles (which I have before described when in Galicia), the axle tree of which is immovably connected with the solid cylinder wheels like a baby's cart, chafing against the two pegs or bolts fixed in the body of the carriage to confine the forms in the proper place all made of wood, led to their catching fire occasionally, producing many alarms which might have been of serious consequence from these waggons being mostly loaded with gun powder. In short, what with these occurrences and the deafening & discordant noise of every cart producing a wild hurdy-gurdy strain in its own key by the friction above described, unaided by soap, oil or grease, no officer but those on duty would or could remain in their company. This discordant grating music could be heard at the distance of half a mile and the driver affirmed it as a positive fact that the cattle would not travel cheerfully unassisted by it, which was the cause that no remedy was applied.

On the 10th we reached the small village of Moraleja, and on the 11th the town of Coria, which afforded us a still better opinion of the superiority of Spain over Portugal. The country was evidently richer in cultivation and everything was on a larger scale. The town was situated very picturesquely at the first view we had of it, and in entering some of the houses there was such a delicious coolness compared with the burning atmosphere outside that we often panted for a prolonged enjoyment. But alas, the canopy of heaven was now during most nights, our only roof except such as could be produced by the spreading branches of a tree or a blanket thrown over a pole to form an apology for a tent, an article of luxury enjoyed by few only of the superior ranks who could alone afford to carry them. The nights however, passed in this way were not the worst of our endurances for the exposure to the sun during the whole of the day in such a cloudless climate was decidedly the most insufferable and destructive to the troops.

Two days more of marching enabled us to reach the episcopal city of Palencia [Plasencia] in the neighbourhood of which a great part of the army was concentrated and encamped, the Staff of the higher grades only being lodged in the town. It differed little from [what] we had before seen except in its being much larger than the last town we had passed through, numerous convents, friars & other clergy and every other idle appendage of a large Roman Catholic place, it afforded a luxury we had not before enjoyed, that of iced lemonade & other beverages, which its proximity to a range of mountains whose tops were covered with snow, enabled its inhabitants to obtain without difficulty & for a length of time after, the army was accompanied by men hawking iced lemonade in the camp, but it of course was seldom produced so cool as when obtained in towns.

These men were picturesque in their dress, carrying on their back, much as a soldier his knapsack, the vessel containing the liquid, which consisted of a cylinder of cork about 2½ feet long stripped whole from the tree & the seam afterwards sewed up, with top & bottom of same material into which was fitted a tin can with a sufficient space between it & the cork to receive the ice, having a tube at the top from which the carrier could measure our the contents with ease to himself & without deranging the straps which secured the load to the back.

In this town I met with two of my countrymen who had come from Guernsey in the 87th Regiment, Captain McCrea[32] who at the moment commanded the corps, and Ensign La Serre,[33] neither of whom poor fellows were ever to see either family or friends again. The former though of my age only, had already become an old soldier having been in South America in the sanguinary affairs of Montevideo and Buenos Aires under General Whitelock[34] in which

---

32 Captain Rawdon McCrea, 87th Foot. He was severely wounded at Talavera and died of his wounds on 3 August 1809.

33 Ensign Nicholas La Serre, 87th Foot, was killed at Talavera on 27 July 1809.

34 Lieutenant General John Whitelock had commanded a force sent to seize Buenos Aries in 1807, but the attack failed and the British were forced to surrender, but were allowed to return to England, having also abandoned their hold on Montevideo. Whitelock was court-martialled and dismissed the service.

he had distinguished himself & been severely wounded; whereas I had only the year before begun my campaigning profession & he had already past the drudgery of his, but he was unfortunately cut off prematurely in the battle which was soon to follow; and the latter was doomed to fall at the very first onset of his career, though he had already seen a good deal of hard marching during which his regiment from 1,000 men had dwindled down to half without firing a shot, which I mention to shew the casualties of the service, though it is necessary to explain that they were not entirely lost to the service, consisting as they did of men in hospital or on other duties, who mostly might rejoin their corps. Of course, death had swept off some & disease invalided others.

We halted four days, during part of which Sir Arthur Wellesley was at the headquarters of the Spanish Army arranging (as it was supposed) future operations and seeing how matters stood with his allies. We began to experience a want of supplies by their obstinate supineness and as we had brought nothing from Portugal our exertions in procuring them about the country were incessant and most distressing, and had it not been for the corn in the ear, still in the fields, with which the horses were provided, the Commissariat thus early must have been broken down with the multifarious wants it had to meet, which not to exasperate the Spaniards, were ordered to be procured in regular form through the magistrates and not summarily as we were accustomed to do in Portugal when our applications had not been attended to.

All this courtesy had however, no good effect and we soon got into a worse plight. Under fair promises that things would mend as we got further into the country, the army moved to Malpartida [de Plasencia] the 17th over bad and mountainous roads and next day to Mahada [Majadas de Tietar] crossing a river over a bridge which had been rapidly and roughly constructed by the Staff Corps, which corps consisted of a body of mechanics commanded by scientific officers who were employed in erecting every description of field work required by the army & were considered an opposition body to the Royal Engineers only employed in what concerned sieges and regular fortifications.[35] These latter were considered too slow and formal in all their undertakings, submitting their transactions to Boards of respective officers and [the] Board of Ordnance which were independent of the Horse Guards, while the new corps was entirely at the disposal of the commander of the forces who by warrant on the military chest paid their expenses without estimates or any scrutiny, a summary operation which proved in many instances of great assistance in the rapid execution of operations.

On the 19th we reached the neighbourhood of a small place called Casa de Las Lomas [?], and what with the heat of the weather, and the heavy loads which the animals of all descriptions carried during the last marches, one of the greatest scourges to the effectiveness of the cavalry and the comfort of the officers began to be experienced by the appearance of sore backs of the horses, which when under a state of inflammation rendered them unserviceable for days together & if allowed to come to a head the care was most provokingly tedious. Half of the regiments of cavalry were dismounted and the men obliged to lead their horses on foot, though many did so by order when perhaps there was no positive occasion for it, being done that the corps might be more effective on the day of battle. It was a sad trial for them to look after their horse & themselves after a long march & more so when just arrived from England where they had been pampered by every comfort which good quarters and little or no duty offered. And to an officer whose baggage animal was thus disabled nothing could be more distressing for if he could not get anyone to assist him with a lift, or procure another animal, a thing almost next to impossible, he was exposed to great privation, occurrences arising hourly until experience had enabled them and their batman (soldier

---

35 The Staff Corps were engineers working for the Army; the Engineers were separate to the Army, being part of the Ordnance Department.

servant) to arrange the pack saddle & packing with the skill adapted to the occasion.

The line of baggage was rendered therefore more motley in its appearance by these dismounted cavalry men, dispersed here and there, Spaniards and Portuguese with their peculiar dress serving as muleteers, lemonade sellers, sutlers and the various other descriptions of followers which the progress of an army accumulates in its train, all being covered with dust and begrimed with perspiration.

Since the time the army left Oporto a personage in the garb of a man though with the appearance of a woman always accompanied the baggage of His Excellency the Commander in Chief & numerous Staff, and being well mounted & dressed accordingly, was always a conspicuous object though there were many of the same stamp who nevertheless could bear no comparison to her, it was said she had been an appendage of a French general officer & had been captured in the retreat of their army from Oporto. She was re-named by the soldiers Queen Dellollola. No one knew to whom she appertained, but when curiosity was rife to know something of her history, she disappeared and was no more heard of.

When on the march this day, I thought I perceived with some of the officers of the 24th Regiment[36] a face I recognised and going up to him I found he was an acquaintance, Mr William Henry Brock,[37] dressed in the uniform of an officer of the Guernsey Militia (South Regiment).[38] He did not know me, and no wonder. I hardly had the

---

36 The 2nd Warwickshire Regiment.

37 There was no William H. Brock in the South Guernsey Militia in 1809 according to the list of officers. There was however a William H. Brock in the Guernsey Militia Artillery (date as 2nd Lieutenant unrecorded), who became a Lieutenant on 4 July 1822 and Captain on 1 January 1823, when he also became Adjutant until he retired in 1835. Looking at other officers, it seems that promotion from 2nd Lieutenant regularly took up to twenty years, so it is not unlikely that this is our man.

38 During the Napoleonic Wars the Guernsey Militia consisted of four infantry regiments and an artillery regiment. The regiments were simply denoted by the points of the compass, North, South, East and West, however they were also known by their facing colours, North – Vert, East – Blanc, West – Noir and South – Bleu.

appearance of a gentleman, being mounted on a large mule with an unseemly Portuguese saddle & a bridle with blinkers, dressed in a round hat and blue coat, very shabby and bleached by the great heat of the sun. My face was very much sunburnt & scabbed where it had peeled, with my lips scalded in such a manner that any attempt to laugh made them crack & bleed. This description is in no way overcharged and when he found who I was his first exclamation was, did your parents know how you were situated they would not for a moment allow you to remain in such a service. The fact is, it was at this time the most trying period of the department, for it was thrown on its own inexperienced efforts by the Spanish authorities having failed in acting up to their promises in providing supplies.

Mr B[rock] was himself already tired of the inconveniences he was subject [to], though he had nothing whatever to do but to look after his own personal accommodation, having come to the country with the Paymaster[39] of the corps alluded to, to ascertain if the Paymastership would suit him as a profession, and he continued on to Talavera until events that followed & the unfortunate situation in which his friend placed himself, by running away from the army,[40] induced him to return to Guernsey in double quick time quite sick with what he had undergone, and yet it was a party of pleasure to him of a few days duration compared with the six years of toil & trouble which I passed in Portugal and Spain, quite enough to have undermined the best of constitutions.

A species of vessel for the conveyance of wine came first in use with us this day, though it had been seen before, the troops being served with their rations from pigskins, two of which were usually conveyed on a mule and brought into camp, each skin containing upwards of nine gallons. It brought to our recollection one of Don

---

39 The Paymaster of the 2/24th was Isaac Buxton.

40 Buxton is recorded as having absented himself along with seven other officers in General Orders dated 21 August 1809.

Quixote's adventures, but though well calculated to convey the liquid, it served at the same time to render it to our palates almost undrinkable by a very bad taste it had acquired. In preparing the skin for use they have a way of drawing the dead animal through the neck by the smallest aperture that can be made, which with those of the feet are afterwards sewn up, leaving an open[ing] through which the wine is introduced and poured out. Previous however to closing the skin, it is daubed over inside with a composition of tar or pitch, which for a time almost poisons the contents, particularly in the estimation of those unaccustomed to such a tang. Every muleteer and indeed most travellers are provided with a small one containing from a quart to half a gallon, which has the orifice closed by a wooden spout in the shape of a funnel with a plug at bottom, so that when open by squeezing the skin, the beverage rises and can be drunk, which was our mode of satisfying thirst, but the Spaniard never put it to his lips, his invariable manner being that of pouring it into his mouth holding the skin at arm's-length on a slant above his head; a cleanlier operation, but which could only be successfully tried or attained by long experience.

On the 20th [July] we reached the small town of Oropesa, which had nothing to distinguish it otherwise than it was said to be the point at which the junction of the two armies was to take place preparatory to offensive operations, but which of the two was to take the lead had not yet transpired. In the course however of the evening, orders were issued that our army was to halt the next day, the reason given (not by the authorities who of course never gave any explanation for the orders which were issued) that we all required rest, but the real fact was (as was asserted) that the Spanish General Cuesta[41] had already stickled for precedence who might have the honour of first beating up the enemy quarters, another national feature of their consummate

---

41 Spanish General Gregorio Garcia de la Cuesta y Fernandez de Celis was in his late 60s, impossibly arrogant and corpulent. He suffered a stroke in 1810 and died the following year.

arrogance which constant defeats could not obliterate or lessen, and I believe never did during the war.

Accordingly, early on the 21st [July], being encamped in a field contiguous to the high road our attention was drawn to an immense column of dust rising high in the air in our rear, and immediately after the sound of cavalry trumpets and trampling of innumerable horsemen announced the arrival of our ally in all the pomp of war, and certainly as far as that went, the effect succeeded in impressing on the beholders that martial appearance from which better results might have been expected, especially in the cavalry. At a momentary clearing away of the dust the first individual who presented himself at the head of the column was a priest with a long beard in his robes, mounted on a good horse and carrying a large crucifix, immediately followed by the trumpeters, generals & Staff & the different regiments of cavalry to the number of 7 or 8 thousand men, which took [a] considerable time to pass & to observers unaccustomed to it, their numbers appeared prodigious. Their dress in our eyes was singular & imposing and quite different from what we had before seen. They were in general, well mounted on active stallions, but with little bone or size compared with our own geldings or mares. Some of the regiments were lancers, and the faces of the men almost the colour of ebony with immense large moustaches which gave them a frightful cutthroat appearance, especially when compared with the smooth fair faces of our cavalry who did not even carry a moustache.

Part of their artillery next followed, drawn by powerful mules in rope harness, the guns of much heavier calibre than ours, being nine and twelve pounders, with their appendages heavy and cumbersome & in no way to be for a moment put in comparison with the snug compact arrangement of our own ordnance.

The infantry followed, dressed in brown, partly resembling the French uniform, but by no means so rich, the superior officer wearing no epaulets, being distinguished by narrow strips of gold lace round the cuffs. There seemed to be no old soldiers among them and they appeared to be mostly new levies, with the officers little distinguishable from the privates, the greater part of whom did not appear from their apparent discipline and bearing, equal to cope with the veteran armies of France. Had they however been well trained and led, there was in the opinion of our officers, excellent material to form armies, by which their soil might have been relieved from the presence of any foes. After several hours filing by, the whole was completed by the baggage & followers, a fine and easy subject for the painter to delineate, but not for me to describe, being a combination of national costumes from many parts of Spain which the pencil alone could [not] do justice to, and the picture could have been rendered more diversified on our own hereto generous medley, being some days after blended together when a short retrograde movement took place rather unexpectedly.

The Spanish Army having thus acquired the advance, or assumed it in their usual braggadocio way, proceeded on to Talavera de la Reyna, and for a day we remained in inaction to keep clear of the long line of followers & to await results which were not long coming, for we had hardly commenced our march when this mass of hangers-on again made its appearance, hurrying back in the greatest confusion, owing to the enemy having made his appearance, and they were soon followed by their troops who evidently in the hour of difficulty did not consider themselves quite a match for their opponents without our support and until they had got into our rear and placed us between them and their formidable foe, who however again retired and left us to take possession of the town towards which we were journeying.

Their retreat was conducted in their usual atrocious way by the destruction of everything they could lay hands on, setting fire to the cornfields and doing every possible mischief, and such provisions as they could not take away had been heaped up and burned that we might derive no benefit from them.

The French Army again halted in a strong position at the distance of three leagues[42] from which they were to have been dislodged on the 24th, but old Cuesta would not act, either from imbecility or treachery (as it was said) or because it was [a] Sunday and the operation was deferred to the next day. The two armies were then set in motion for the attack, but on nearing the enemy's position it was found deserted and it had been done in such a hurry to avoid a too early contact (as it was presumed) that they left their camp undestroyed and stocked with many conveniences stripped as usual from villages in their neighbourhood, consisting of chairs, tables, provisions &c which we of course turned to our advantage.

The Spaniards again took the advance & followed them, but the French having concentrated their whole force from the capital &c came on at last in earnest with the intention of measuring their strength with us instead of allowing us to take quick possession of Madrid, which we had foolishly hoped would have been the end of our expedition.

The French in their sojourn in Talavera before its abandonment, left it in a miserable plight, not half the houses were inhabited, many had been turned into stables and partly destroyed, the churches and convents were used as barracks & stripped of their ornaments & valuables, saints & images thrown down from their pedestals & nitches [sic], partly burned or left strewed on the pavement, intermixed with organ pipes or tubes forced out of their places, twisted & flung about, with the broken bell ropes which added to the heap of rubbish, presented a scene I had never before witnessed, but which unhappily I became afterwards familiar with. England may therefore thank God that she has been spared these misfortunes.

We had hardly arrived at Talavera when a scarcity of provisions began to be felt by our army. The magistrates made but slight

---

42 Each nation measured the league differently, ranging from 2.4 to 4.6 miles (4 to 7.4km). Here Carey uses the English league which measured precisely 3 miles (4.8km).

exertions to supply it & much that was collected fell into the hands of the Spaniards, besides which their Commissariat drained every town & village in the neighbourhood leaving hardly any subsistence for their allies. This treatment was abominable and must only have been submitted to by Sir Arthur Wellesley not to embarrass the great effort making to endeavour to drive the French out of the peninsula, by striking a severe blow at this their main army. Bread was so scarce in our camp that a dollar worth, 4s/6d[43] was given willingly for a four-pound loaf. The troops were in consequence allowed their full pay without the usual deduction for rations, which however was a mere dead letter for the time, as money could not then procure the necessary supplies & notwithstanding the want of success of the Commissariat in obtaining them in sufficient quantity, this campaign for the short time it lasted, was the most harassing I ever experienced & it knocked up almost every individual in it. It was incalculably worse than slavery, for we were badgered by every famishing party in our hopeless efforts to feed them; the wear & tear of body and anxiety of mind was incessant & almost insupportable, and one poor man in the midst of his perplexities declared that himself & horse were broken hearted and could no longer endure it.

Our duties commenced before daylight. We slept in the fields or under a tree with the troops, for no one under the rank of field officer could be billeted in towns or villages. The cover of a blanket on the bare ground, or on straw when it could be got, was all we could indulge in. Our toilet[44] was consequently soon made and from that to dusk, with a short respite for eating &c we were incessantly at work either on foot or horseback, exposed to a scorching sun which burnt our skins and tanned our faces and hands to the color [sic] of a mulatto[45] if the complexion was dark, or to the colour of a North American

---

43 About £11 today.

44 Washing.

45 An old term for a person of mixed race.

Indian if it was fair. This was not the occupation of a gentleman & required youth and the best of constitutions to withstand it, and had I known beforehand a fraction of what I underwent, I would not for a moment have embarked in it.

At this time an extraordinary man, a Scotchman, joined the Commissariat. His name was Downie,[46] bold and adventuresome, tall, dark and commanding, and he had already been engaged under Miranda[47] in his attempt at revolutionising Central America. He spoke Spanish fluently & was found most useful. To drudge after troops was not to his fancy, he was therefore employed in excursions in various parts of the country to urge the magistrates in collecting supplies & send them to the army, to enforce which he was usually accompanied by two or three dragoons. He was mounted on a very showy black Andalusian charger and when on that service wore the embroidered dress coat of the department with a profusion of gold chains & rings, with an additional epaulette (one only being allowed to his rank as Assistant Commissary General) and thus equipped, his appearance was imposing and adding thereto the knowledge of the language, produced considerable effect on magistrates & people, who were dazzled by outward show and more so when his persuasive manners were exerted.

In one of these excursions he went to Truxillo [Trujillo], the birthplace of Pizarro[48] and residence of his descendants, and having

---

46 Assistant Commissary General John Downie. He transferred to the Spanish Army, forming a private army of 3,000 men named the Legion of Extramadura, of which he was appointed colonel, and he took to carrying Pizarro's sword. He was made a Brigadier General but was wounded (losing an eye) and captured in an action near Seville in 1812. The Duke of Wellington authorized a prisoner exchange for 150 French soldiers. He continued fighting on the east coast of Spain for the remainder of the war. He became a Major General and died in 1826.

47 Sebastian Francisco de Miranda y Rodriguez de Espinoza was a Venezuelan military leader who was the forerunner of Simon Bolivar. His attempt to free Venezuela from Spanish rule failed in 1812 and he died in 1816 in a prison cell in Cadiz.

48 The Conquistador Francisco Pizarro.

been quartered in their house or palace, he so far ingratiated himself in their good opinion as to cajole them to give him a sword which had belonged to their great ancestor. I saw it often by his side in his profession, it was a long rapier with steel guard & handle, more useful than ornamental but most interesting from historical associations. He always wore it and took the greatest care of it.

Finding the duties of the Commissariat not congenial to his views and martial habits he persuaded the Spanish Government to allow him to raise a legion of that nation and our government to clothe & equip it. He assumed the command and did good service with it, but having dressed it with an attempt to revive the costume of the times of Ferdinand & Isabella,[49] the affair turned out so preposterous & ridiculous as to make it the laughing stock of the army & when worn out it was not renewed. He continued to serve with the Spanish army but could never inoculate them with his prowess or chivalry, for when the French rose [*sic* – raised] the siege of Cadiz & evacuated the neighbourhood in 1812 and in the retreat had abandoned Seville, with a mine laid on the bridge over the Guadalquivir River to interrupt the advance; being in pursuit of them, he harangued his men to induce them to make a dash at the bridge and prevent if possible its destruction by the explosion. In the moment of enthusiasm he sprang forward on his steed, the mine exploded and he found himself alone on the side of the enemy, no one having followed him. A discharge of musketry brought him and his horse to the ground, having received with other wounds a ball in his cheek; and though severely hurt such was the veneration he had for his sword that in the act of falling he threw it across the broken arch & being preserved by his men, he wore it to the end of the war. He was of course instantly made prisoner and most wantonly treated by the French who dragged him after them on a cart for a considerable distance though almost dead of his wounds.

---

49 They reigned in the late fifteenth century.

The French having at last concentrated a force reckoned to amount to 45,000 men, made a move forward & came on in earnest on the 27th of July in their usual impetuous manner, and surprised one of our advanced infantry divisions who were cooking at the moment, and though partial, the affair was a sharp one. We suffered much, but it put us on our guard for the future. Young La Serre, Ensign in the 87th Regiment before alluded to was killed on that occasion. The troops then retired to the position fixed upon in front of Talavera & extending from thence to the left to a ridge of hills, the Spaniards occupying the right as far as the River Tagus, our army the centre or key of the position and more Spaniards on the extreme left.[50] I shall not describe the operations which took place as that belongs to the military historian.

The park of artillery to which I was attached was encamped under the walls of Talavera, just in front of it, and consisted as I have said before, of a considerable number of ammunition carts drawn by bullocks and artillery horses. The Spaniards had established a battery of guns on the walls of the town nearly over our heads, the high road being immediately on our left & for a time was a bustling and animated scene, it being the great communication with the troops in front.

Among the passers-by was a great old fashioned lumbering carriage (coach I mean) drawn by four mules going to the front & who should be in it but General Cuesta. It went on a little way further & he then got out and was assisted to mount his horse. Such was the man entrusted to command an army opposed to the most active, warlike and enterprising enemy.

Another character of a different stamp afterwards attracted my attention. He was a sergeant of highlanders, orderly to Major General Campbell,[51] and was on his way by himself to join the ranks, although not required, being in charge of the general's household, but he

---

50 Carey is correct in stating this, but many accounts ignore the Spanish forces on the left.
51 Brigadier Alexander Campbell.

could not forbear joining in the expected fight. He was armed with the general's double rifle and walked on with an air of confidence & determination, quite characteristic of a brave soldier. At such a moment the difficulty was great to find in the midst of the wood any particular corps, and he had not proceeded far on his way before three French dragoons, who had advanced more forward than could be expected, set upon him, and although he made good use of his rifle in killing one and disabling another he was wounded & taken prisoner. Such was the prevailing animus of our men.

After a while the enemy pushed on & gained ground but not sufficiently for what immediately followed, yet little could be perceived at a distance as it was a thick olive wood between them & us. The Spaniards, however, conceiving that there was reason for doing so, commenced firing from the battery. Several of us had got up in a tree to endeavour to ascertain what was passing and whether from the shock, or from being overloaded, it came down with a crash and hurt several of the party, but a scene of confusion immediately occurred which made us think of something else, for the noise had frightened the cattle & horses to that degree that they broke loose, scampering in all directions and upsetting the carts and tents & running over & trampling on men & everything else in their way. It was a moment of danger & it took considerable time to restore order & collect them. In the meantime, a panic seized the Spanish troops & they came rushing by in numbers which rendered it necessary for our park to move to a more secure place in the rear & centre of our army & which was gradually effected as the disorder would permit.

I then got on my mule and went into the town. I found it in indescribable confusion, everyone hurrying out & as many of the generals and Staff of both armies had their quarters in it, their baggage was loading in the greatest haste to get out of the place & in making its way to the high street from the smaller ones the jostling commenced and in reaching the town gate through which the whole had to pass, and there not being space enough, many animals were thrown down with their loads strewing quite unheeded the property of many individuals under foot, and after all there was no necessity for all this confusion, it having arisen from the panic alluded to. My own little kit was safe with the park, I therefore got out of the disorder as soon as I could, not having it in my power to render any assistance, and I proceeded a little way out where I remained looking at the road now covered with fugitives going to the rear. These consisted of the baggage alluded to, Spanish troops & carts of every description.

It was getting dark and the French had commenced their attack on the hill defended by General Hill.[52] We distinctly perceived the discharges of musketry which added to the panic & I am sorry to say it was contagious. I happened to fall into the company of two paymasters, an officer of Civil Ordnance & another person (non-combatants of course) and on consultation we decided on going to the rear as the only place of safety. Indeed we did not know what else to do or where to go, in the occurring confusion & therefore decided on that awkward step.

It was a fine moonlight night if I recollect right, and we reached Oropesa, a distance of 12 miles, to get if possible, some food for ourselves & animals. After that we resumed our retreat, but feelings of hesitation soon came over me and I agitated the question of either remaining where we were at least or going back to our respective duties. No one paid any attention to what I said as they appeared to have made up their minds to continue their flight. Finding them thus obstinately disposed, my better judgement fortunately prevailed. I turned my horse round, wished them good morning and alone I reached the park in time not to have been missed. They (my late companions) persisted in their wrong course and were eventually tried by courts martial and dismissed the service.[53]

---

52 Major General Sir Rowland Hill commanded 2nd Division.

53 This group would appear to include Paymaster Thomas Stott of the 29th Foot and Paymaster Alexander Thompson 53rd Foot.

2ND CAMPAIGN

On my arrival very early on the 28th the action had commenced and the artillerymen were busy delivering ammunition. We were not near enough to see the melee being ourselves in the plain covered with olive trees which impeded the sight & in the midst of which the troops were contending. The cannonade & clatter of musketry was incessant and appeared very near to us. It told of the desperate work going on, and we could perceive the fierce struggle on the hill to our left but were too far to observe it distinctly through the arising smoke. The stream of wounded (such at least as could move) were passing us going towards Talavera where a hospital was establishing to receive them.

Suspense as to the result kept us on the 'qui vive',[54] and we were necessarily obliged to be in readiness to mount or be on horseback in case of a retreat being ordered to take place at a moment's warning. The time passing was one of the most intense anxiety, seeing as we did the unsteadiness of the Spaniards who were abandoning their corps in great numbers & deliberately going to the rear.

The enemy having been repulsed, the action was suspended for a while but recommenced in the afternoon and being tired of a state of inaction, exciting as it was, I rode into Talavera which I found almost deserted of inhabitants & in solemn silence as if a pestilence had swept them away. The only apparent bustle being in the neighbourhood of the hospital, the streets leading to which were encumbered on the shady side with our wounded men who were mostly laying down in rows stretched side by side, a melancholy spectacle, until they came to be taken into the building.

The desolation in the town drove me out again to wander about with several other Commissaries (approaching at times within gunshot & in one instance so near that one of them received a musket ball in his lower stomach of which he died next day) until the action terminated & it having been decided in our favour, it put an end to

---

54 French – On the alert.

all further anxiety, and a proud feeling succeeded in the thought that 18,000 half-starved British had successfully borne the brunt of a contest against 45,000 foes almost singled handed, for the Spaniards did little more than look on & cover the flanks of our army.

Having duties to perform during the night of the 28th to 29th on the road thronged with crowds going the same way, my attention was suddenly called to the approaching footsteps of a large body of men coming in a contrary direction. We could hardly understand what it meant; it was a moment of perplexity, as it might have been an enemy, but [we] were at once relieved from any suspense on finding that it was the Light (Rifle) Brigade consisting of three of the finest regiments of the service (the [1/]43rd, [1/]52nd & [1/]95th) dashing up to join the army in spite of the most desponding reports, which might have alarmed almost any other officer than the fiery General Crawford [Craufurd].[55] They were however, too late for the action, but in the effort made a march [which] was accomplished, unparalleled in modern warfare.[56]

The artillery park to which I was attached moved a little next day after the battle. Fatigue parties were employed around us in burying the dead and conveying to the town such of the wounded as had not been moved before, the sight was melancholy indeed. We remained two or three days there until the stench from the dead horses which surrounded us became insupportable and obliged us to change ground a little. The poor animals when first killed appeared wasted and thin, but in [the] course of putrefaction in so hot an atmosphere, began swelling, turned on their backs and became huge & colossal, with the hide apparently bursting.

Though early, every search was made for our wounded, it was apprehended that many seriously injured had crept into thickets

---

55 Brigadier General Robert Craufurd.

56 It is claimed that the Light Brigade marched up to 52 miles (83.7km) in 24 hours, in a bid to arrive on the battlefield on time. The distance is disputed but the march was certainly a very tough one in the heat.

where they could not be found & died there and that suspicion was confirmed from the effluvia being greater than the horses could produce as it came from all directions.

The chiefs of the Spanish Army, having seen a specimen of what their ally was capable of, relaxed a little of their greediness and the day after the battle issued to us from their magazines a quantity of bread to our famished ranks, which in part was given to the wounded in hospital. Otherwise they and our troops would have starved, for we were still depending on the precarious resources of the country, or what the fields afforded in vegetables, particularly the Garbanzo [chickpea], a sort of vetch pea in general use among the inhabitants who did not cultivate the potato, yet unknown to them.

I must confess the Commissariat were yet without much experience, and being without money, or proper or adequate transport, surrounded by Spanish agents collecting for their own army (which in the opinion of so vain a people were the cream of our union & able to any work notwithstanding their frequent defeats) it could not with all its exertions, remedy the serious evil of want. The central government of Seville had promised Sir A[rthur] Wellesley on his entering Spain, that the British army would want for nothing, a mere subterfuge to entangle or inveigle us in the heart of the country, for there is little doubt that some of its members were in the French interest, the movement of the armies of that nation appearing to have been made in unison with a view to surround us after a defeat which could not but be expected from such a force as we contended with. For though the Spaniards made numbers equal, we bore the whole weight of the fight. It is said an Englishman cannot fight without victuals, yet in this instance it can be proudly asserted that 18,000 men in a state next to starvation remained triumphant masters of a field of battle on which they had been attacked by very superior numbers and whatever may be said to the contrary, no supplies reached the British army which had been provided by the central government until we had in retreat crossed the bridge of [El Puente del] Arzobispo, and then the quantity was ridiculously small. The fact is that Mr Frere, our ambassador to that Junta was an enthusiast in the cause and believed all the delusive accounts given him and would hear nothing to the contrary. He was (it was said by several persons who had been at Seville & seen him there) attending more to his sensual pleasures than to business;[57] & Spanish duplicity and intrigue was lulling him into fatal security. Well was it therefore for the English nation that on this occasion as well as in every other, its sword was better wielded than its pen, for otherwise the flower of its army must have been undoubtedly sacrificed this year as well as the last.

Thus, two days after the action, a rumour spread abroad that another French Army had made its appearance directly in our rear & on our line of communication with Lisbon, under Soult, the most clever and enterprising of the French marshals. The old imbecile Spanish general undertook to pursue the one that had been beaten & cover the hospital containing our wounded and we marched to meet this new foe. We had hardly however, commenced the move when the Spanish army came back in all haste apparently unable to make head even against the dispirited enemy. Talavera was of course, unavoidably abandoned and many of our poor fellows under the apprehension of being made prisoners came to the desperate resolution of endeavouring to follow us, and the scene that ensued was most distressing, for exhaustion under their sufferings soon knocked them up and the road was strewed with them, which occasioned much difficulty & annoyance from there being no disposable transport on which they might be conveyed with us.

In one of the two actions a young acquaintance of mine, an ensign in the 87th Regiment, barely 17 years old was severely wounded in the arm. Amputation was recommended but, wishing if possible to preserve the limb, the operation was delayed until the appearance of worms & gangrene forced him to it. It was done with the army on the

---

57 He was renowned as a womaniser.

move and as the only means of conveyance, he was forced to get on horseback almost immediately afterwards and I met him occasionally afterwards on the line of retreat, and though suffering much he appeared in good spirits, confident that he could go on until out of the enemy's reach, yet he was a slight lad and eventually recovered.[58]

It became evident under existing circumstances that there were too many enemies to contend with. Our army barely amounted to 17,000 effectives, was insufficient and our allies could not now be reckoned upon. They were more [of] an hindrance than otherwise for all they did was to consume every available supply in the country. Our Commander-in-Chief resolved therefore to separate from them and at once adopt the only mode of retreat left open to us, that of making for the bridge of [El Puente del] Arzobispo on the Tagus and placing that river between us and the new enemy.

Our army commenced crossing and until it was accomplished the Spaniards remained behind for the night. From the heights we occupied after the operation, we had a most extensive view of the country beyond the plain we had just left; a blaze of distant fires were discernible which were said to belong to the enemy which had got in our rear.

The Spaniards lost no time in following us & the safety of the allied army was thus secured, but from their want of caution they suffered themselves to be surprised afterwards in endeavouring to hold the bridge. Had we not thus made a timely retreat we might have got into a worst predicament than Sir John Moore, for had the army prevailed against which we fought, we would have fallen into the lion's jaws. It was a warning to Lord Wellington never again to compromise his army in joint operations with such allies, who were totally incompetent to face the Frenchmen with very superior numbers. They were neither commanded properly, disciplined, fed,

---

58 He refers to Lieutenant John Bagenal who was severely wounded at Talavera on 27 July. In 1814 he received a pension of £50 per annum (about £2,500 today) for the loss of his arm.

paid or clothed to ensure success, yet they were fine bodies of men, patient & enduring and capable had it been permitted [for] us to organise & officer them, to have done better things than they did under this corrupt and rotten administration.

We succeeded in bringing away the wounded to the bridge of [El Puente del] Arzobispo but it would have been better had they remained behind with those who could not move, for the French treated them with great kindness. Yet they were prisoners, until assured of kind treatment the contrary was anticipated, and the expedients resorted to secure the little money they had by them from being plundered were curious; among which was that of an officer having put some doubloons in the poultice[59] on his wound and removing them when the alarm was over.

August 1809

From the incessant fatigue and constant exposure to a broiling sun and night air without covering, I was seized at this time with a violent dysentery. And it increased so rapidly that I was almost immediately rendered unfit for duty, and the confusion being great in all arrangements and everyone looking after themselves, I reported the state I was in and resolved at once to go to the rear (that is on the line of road the army was proceeding), aware that no one could take care of me in the retreat [which was] expected to continue on the enemy crossing the river in pursuit. No one was in consequence to remain behind & to facilitate the removal of the sick and wounded all artillery materials & stores & spare ammunition, the two former were set fire to and the latter drowned, by which the principal part of the bullock carts which had hitherto been employed in their conveyance were applied to this new purpose. On the 5 & 6 August they started off

---

59 A soft mass of material, typically of bran or herbs applied to the body to relieve inflammation and kept in place by a cloth bandage.

in two divisions not to encumber the road too much & have a chance of better accommodation on the road, which was very indifferent, being mountainous and in some parts so steep that the carts & guns still marching with us had to be dragged up by the infantry.

I accompanied the 2nd Division and reached Truxillo [Trujillo], the birthplace of Pizarro, and where he is buried;[60] his descendants are grandees and reside there. We visited his tomb in the church and I am sorry to say it appeared much mutilated by the curious, chipping it to carry off souvenirs of having been there.

We reached Merida without any material occurrence, but as I could get no rest or medical assistance to be of use, from the march continuing without intermission, the disease increased to such a degree that it became useless my getting off my mule occasionally on the road, nature relieving itself of its necessities as best it could and I was only taken off his back to be taken to the room in which I was to pass the night. Merida is full of Roman antiquities but all I did see of them as we passed was an aqueduct[61] & the facade of a temple converted into a dwelling house.

The army having halted, the sick proceeded alone on their mournful journey & reached Badajoz where I was almost knocked up and felt unable to go farther. I requested to be left behind but was persuaded to make one more effort & go to Elvas, a day's journey, where a General Hospital was establishing & I arrived there quite exhausted on the 18 August after having suffered most dreadfully from the intense heat of the weather, which I found doubly oppressive from the weak state I was reduced to. Most fortunately I got good quarters and the people of the house, seeing my deplorable condition, were most attentive & by their kindness the disease was stopped in a short time, leaving me however completely deprived of strength and in the greatest state

---

60 Pizarro died in Peru and was buried in the Cathedral of Lima, his remains are still there. Presumably the edifice he saw at Trujillo was to another member of the Pizarro family.

61 Acueducto de los Milagros carried water from 10km away; the house is built in the Temple of Diana.

of debility, but thanks to the Almighty who had given me a good constitution, I rallied by degrees. Many of our poor fellows however, who had not the same comforts or assistance were not so fortunate and sunk rapidly into their graves.

My wardrobe as may be imagined was not abundant and having an only coat which had been on my back since the month of April & had from blue become a dirty grey from exposure to alternate heat and wet, I lost no time in again making myself decent as soon as possible. For as I was, my appearance was really and indeed worse still than shabby genteel.

From the fatigues and privations to which the soldiers had been exposed & their incautious manner of eating grapes to excess from its abundance, the open vineyards oftentimes bordering the roads, the disease alluded to prevailed in the army to an alarming degree and when they were brought into hospital almost exhausted, a few hours of typhus which was equally raging carried them off in a few hours, it not being possible to keep both diseases apart.

Elvas being the General Hospital of the army which was cantoned in Badajoz and neighbouring towns and villages, the sick were sent there to be attended to. They were brought in convoys of bullock or mule carts in a very miserable way, for they had only straw to lay on without cover to keep off the rays of the sun or to lessen the jolting & on removal from the carts after the journey, numbers were in many instances found dead. Added to which from the country thus occupied on the River Guadiana, being low and swampy, subject to continual ague & fever, the casualties were frightfully increased making the inmates in that hospital to exceed 4,000 at times.

Many of the Commissariat as a matter of course, were equally rendered by the prevailing diseases incapable of duty, but such was the want of them to attend to the wants of the troops that on the slightest appearance of convalescence they were called upon to exert themselves. Though hardly able myself to leave my room, I was forced to superintend a park of carts, mules & asses employed in the conveyance of provisions &c established outside the walls of the city to which I almost crawled daily with difficulty, until increasing strength rendered it less troublesome.

From this park, a daily requisition was made on me for transport to convey the dead from the hospital and the mortality increasing, the duty became very irksome to the car[62] drivers for there not being a sufficiency of hospital servants or attendants to perform the duty decently, the dead were merely sewed up in blankets, put on the carts and the drivers directed to carry and deposit their loads in ditches outside the town; no graves or funeral service attending them there, the work of annihilation being completed by wolves, vultures and dogs attracted to the spot by the arising effluvia. It became at last so repulsive, that the cartmen refused to continue the work, and it was only after a strong remonstrance I made to Colonel Mackinnon[63] the Commandant of the town, that these disgraceful proceedings were mitigated, which were however in some measure unavoidable from the nature of the diseases deterring many from having to do or come in contact with those that had died of them owing to their malignity. The aggregate of deaths in this hospital alone were said to have exceeded 4,500 in four months, independently of casualties in the cantonments of the troops, in an army barely amounting to 20,000 men. To a person [who had] scarcely escaped from danger & still suffering from the effects of illness, these daily occurrences were anything but encouraging, but there is in youth a buoyancy of spirits which made me rise above apprehension and I continued gradually to get better, though I felt it would be some time before I could resume active duties.

I wrote in consequence to the Commissary General then in Lisbon to be employed there until I could regain strength, he informed me in reply that he was coming up to the army & would endeavour

---

62 A shortened form of 'carriage'.

63 Colonel Henry Mackinnon of the Coldstream Guards.

to meet my wishes. I continued in the meantime to transact my disagreeable duty.

Elvas is the frontier town of Portugal in the province of Alentejo (Alentejo signifying in Portuguese – on the other side of the Tagus – when in Lisbon) is fortified and stands on part of a ridge of hills overlooking the plain on which Badajoz, the Spanish frontier town is situated with the Guadiana flowing past it. From this ridge there is an extensive prospect towards Spain. The town was then, as all Portuguese towns still are most likely, very filthy with narrow streets and nothing remarkable in it. The citadel called Fort La Lippe situated on a high detached conical hill is considered impregnable[64] & the Portuguese were so jealous of it that no one were admitted into it without a pass which I did not apply for and I could not therefore form an opinion of its merits from having only viewed it from its base.

Elvas is well described in the *Penny Magazine*, of the 19 August 1837 and subsequent numbers.[65] At the time I was there & before, it was a great smuggling emporium for the introduction of English manufactures into Spain, carried on by several English merchants who appeared to make a good business by it, though the war had given a check to its being carried on with the usual spirit.

The parson on whom I was quartered invited me one day to accompany him to a neighbouring convent to see a novice take the veil, which I willingly did, though I could hardly spare [the] time. We entered the church of the convent, already as full of company of the highest classes as could be accommodated, it being a rich community & the nuns of that rank in life. The ceremony commenced by High Mass performed by the Father Confessor and other assistants, in an interior chapel in which alone the Lady Abbess & nuns were,

---

64 The Nossa Senhora de Graca Fort, or Conde de Lippe Fort, is 1km north of Elvas on a high hill (the Monte da Graca). It later became a prison and is now a museum.

65 The *Penny Magazine* of the Society for the Diffusion of Useful Knowledge was published by Charles Knight from March 1832 to October 1845. It aimed at educating the working class.

separated from the body of the church by an open screen through which we could see the ceremony, considered a bridal one, the nun being a bride of Christ. She was dressed accordingly in a most sumptuous manner as if going to an hymeneal[66] altar, and after many genuflections, bowings and ceremonies so abundant in the Roman Church on all occasions, she was declared irrevocably wedded to her saviour & dedicated to his service. The scene was solemn and imposing and the female part of the spectators were much moved and in tears, more particularly when she knelt at the altar, her worldly attire taken off by degrees from her person, and replaced by the habit of a nun, her flowing long hair being cut off and thrown on the floor as if in disdain of all worldly vanity, she was then greeted by the other nuns who appeared to enjoy the addition of another victim to their number. The ceremony then concluded with some fine music in which the nuns joined vocally.

The lady was young but did not appear handsome. The sacrifice thus consummated might seem as great & trying a one as human nature could be subject to, but such is not the case in most instances, for those who usually take the veil are from family arrangements destined to it from the cradle and are accordingly received into the convent at an early age and quit it only at short intervals to see their families, so that to conform to their future life is but second nature. The Portuguese governor of the town was present, an old veteran with one eye only.

The Commissary General came up from Lisbon & Cintra as he informed me it was his intention to do in the beginning of September, where he had been during the whole of our toilsome campaign in quiet repose on account of his health. He was on his way to join headquarters at Badajoz & I thought it a good opportunity to renew my application for employment at Lisbon but got for answer that he could decide nothing until he had reached his destination.

---

66 Hymeaneal – of or concerning marriage.

Approaching as I was to convalescence, with a great scarcity of effective members of the department, I soon received orders from him to proceed to Badajoz and be employed in his office, a duty quite as desirable as I could expect and I arrived there on the 16th of the same month after a short day's journey.

The army was then in a state of inaction and had been so since I left it, until it had moved to its present cantonment in the neighbouring towns and villages where it remained until [the end of] this year 1809, for the enemy had discontinued the pursuit when I left, finding I suppose that we had fairly got out of his toils.

I was soon installed in my duty and liked it, although with hardly a moments interval of relaxation. Lord Wellington and his general and personal Staff were quartered in Badajoz with the Brigade of Guards which occasioned much bustle and gaiety in the latter. We poor subordinates had no participation, the former being our only unceasing portion.

The town is a fine one, but the streets are narrow to keep out the sun. The gentry were numerous but not in affluence, being without equipages or other signs of riches, their principal amusement consisting in appearing every evening on the Prado or public walk situation on the ramparts overlooking the river. It was an indispensable social event, the ladies and gentlemen were dressed in their best, the former in the graceful mantilla and the latter in the everlasting cloak. English and Spanish officers, priests and other inhabitants added greatly to the diversity of the scene, which was amusing and picturesque. Many sweet looks and smiles were interchanged which led to more familiar intercourse and it was to me and my official companions our only source of relaxation thus to mix in the crowd, for as soon as the shades of night made their appearance all began to disperse and we returned to our desk until late at night.

An act of devotion invariably occurred (and which had a singular effect) in this large assembly, for whilst in the act of walking, conversation and pleasure, it suddenly by mutual consent, remained stationary both in person and voice on hearing the solemn toll of the vesper bell[67] of the cathedral, during which momentary suspension of movement, the men took off their hats and all muttered a short ejaculation, after which the walking and gaiety was resumed as if nothing serious had happened.

The town from being fortified has no suburbs & the country round is devoid of interest, without wood and wholly applied to agriculture. There could not consequently be any diversity in our walks, which were limited to the bridge over the river, an old Roman one,[68] almost in its original state, the ramparts and the citadel on the hill, including the public walk just described. I was quartered on [a] bookseller and took my meals alone, unless the dog of the house could be considered company, but there was every evening a reunion of several grave individuals, priests &c over the brasero (a brass pan containing charcoal placed on a broad wooden stand for the foot) in the middle of the room at which I was at times persuaded when at leisure to give them the news of the day about which they were always most anxious. Their literature and newspapers were however at the lowest ebb, for of the latter the only one then published & circulated throughout Spain was the Diaries or Gazette of Madrid,[69] not much larger than a half sheet of foolscap paper, which contained little else than announcements of religious ceremonies and false or stale news, and as for books in use, they seemed to have none other but a few old romances such as Don Quixote and others of the same innocent description, the circulation of which the Inquisition permitted as not likely to prove mischievous to the community, or to enlighten it on points of which it was better to keep it in ignorance.

---

67 Vespers or Evening Prayers are traditionally performed in the Catholic Church at the moment that dusk begins to fall.

68 The Palmas Bridge was actually built in 1460, no bridge having spanned the river at Badajoz previously.

69 The Gazette of Madrid was first published in 1661.

As the clerks of the department were considered little better than non-commissioned officers & wore no actual or distinguishable dress, none joined in the gaieties of the place. There were balls & other parties called Tortullias [Tertulia[70]] and the officers attended them, among whom was one (Captain Mackinnon[71] of the Guards) who was a great favourite of the ladies & added to many accomplishments, he was the most active man in the army and had a knack of climbing to such a degree that no window of bedroom were it ever so high, was inaccessible to him. It led him into adventures which were not on every occasion creditable to him, but as a strict morality was not a proverbial rule in Spain, he was more admired than blamed. The women were in general pretty with a strut or gait peculiar to themselves, considered elegant by some men, but disapproved by others from an appearance of boldness, the characteristic of the race. The ladies had a large green fan as an indispensable article to their dress in walking out, with which they could communicate almost as readily as with their tongues & as it is described in the *Spectator*,[72] parties at a distance had recourse to it to convey each other's thoughts. Education had made no progress among them, but they were more inclined to be sociable than the male part, not knowing the language fluently of course was a great hindrance to familiar intercourse with them.

Time wore on and our army remained in inaction and from occupying an unhealthy district subject to occasional fever, sickness continued, but it was supposed that there was some political object for not moving. His Lordship on the contrary was often absent, at times in Lisbon & at others at Seville & Cadiz, regulating as it was presumed, his plans with the two governments of Portugal and Spain. An instance of his activity of mind in dealing with details, in the midst of objects of great importance, deserves to be mentioned. During the

---

70 A Spanish literary salon.

71 Lieutenant & Captain Daniel Mackinnon, Coldstream Guards.

72 The *Spectator* newspaper began in 1828.

2ND CAMPAIGN

last and former campaign in Portugal, many receipts for provisions &c delivered to the troops had been given to magistrates & other persons by officers & followers of the army and not paid for. They were generally incorrect and could not in consequence be settled by the Commissariat unless authorised by superior authority. They were accordingly copied & filled three or four quires of paper, closely written and having been submitted to him, he had the patience to read every one of them & though many were of the most insignificant description, he marked with his own hand all such as he approved of or rejected previous to liquidation. I had this document to copy afterwards & it gave me employment for a considerable time.

For the [announcement of the] capture of Walcheren in the Netherlands[73] a *feu de joie*[74] was fired by us at Badajoz, more it was said, to keep up the spirits of the Spaniards than as a sign of exultation on our part.

During the month of November I had serious thoughts of quitting the service and return[ing] home from seeing no prospect of promotion, but I deferred it from day to day in expectation that the army might be leaving the country for England and I could be conveyed at the public expense. This feeling was almost universal among the members of the Commissariat from the endless drudgery to which they had been hitherto subject, but as the troops could not well do without them, all retirement was refused unless from serious indisposition. I had therefore no other alternative but that of continuing in the office of the Commissary General, a situation free

---

73 A huge expedition of nearly 40,000 men was despatched to Holland in July 1809, the British government aiming to cause a diversion in aid of the Austrians, who had declared war against France, and to destroy the French fleet at Antwerp. In this it failed, Austria being decisively beaten at Wagram. The British army soon began to suffer badly with a malarial fever and far more men perished by its effects than in actual combat. The expedition left at the end of August having achieved virtually nothing but the deaths of about 4,000 soldiers. Many of those who survived were debilitated for years by constant relapses.

74 A discharge of musketry in a formed group to announce a success.

from pecuniary or other accounts & no responsibility, and therefore the best I could have chosen.

Rumours of some change of cantonments began however to get again in circulation & which drove away all idea of retirement in my situation. I early learnt what was likely to happen. Buonaparte having again overrun Austria, determined to make a more decided effort to subdue Spain and drive us out of Portugal and our army was accordingly ordered to proceed to the north of the latter country to resist any attempt made upon it & I consequently became acquainted with the details of arrangements for the march as regarded the Commissariat.

On the 29th of November, being as usual quietly at my desk in the Commissary General's room, General Howorth of the artillery under whom I had served during the past campaign, came to speak about his corps & have a commissary attached to it. Pointing to me he said that it would afford pleasure to himself & officers were I allowed to rejoin them in that capacity, as they had every reason to be satisfied with me. The compliment was not paid in vain, for he was told that his wishes would be complied with. As I could hardly be sent again on such a duty with my present rank without appearance of injustice, approved as my exertions had been, the Commissary General next day gave me the gratifying information that my name had been sent in to be submitted to Lord Wellington for insertion in General Orders as an Acting Assistant Commissary General & it was soon announced accordingly.[75] There were several clerks in the office besides myself, one of whom was much my senior, and I certainly expected that he would have been included in the promotion. He was not however, although he had served with our chief at the Cape of Good Hope[76] & since. An idea was entertained that he was not right in his mind at all

---

75 It is contained within the General Order of 7 December 1809.

76 The British had successfully gained The Cape of Good Hope [South Africa] from the Dutch in a brief campaign in 1806.

times, and when aware of his having been overlooked, the suspicion was at once exemplified by his taking all the public documents & papers at the moment on his table & flinging them into the street, upsetting the tables and running out of that office bareheaded and in a dreadful state of excitement, slamming the doors enough to bring them down and going where no one could find him. The papers were immediately picked up and we saw nothing more of him that day. He returned however next day, a little more calm (but still labouring under irritation) under some promise it was supposed, that he would not again be passed over, for he again resumed his duties and was afterwards promoted.

When attached to the 4th Division of infantry during the last siege of Badajoz [April 1812] & when the river had swollen & prevented all communication between both banks by carrying away the pontoon bridge to the serious prejudice of the operation & maintenance of the troops, being anxious to cross if possible to look after supplies, he plunged on horseback into the stream to the astonishment & dismay of those who witnessed the mad attempt & was carried a long way down & but for the assistance afforded him & the strength of his horse, both would assuredly have been drowned. He afterwards quarrelled with a major of cavalry and was brought to a court martial but in consequence of his state of mind was not severely punished. The disease increased and he was suffered to go on half pay. I afterwards saw him in the streets of London dressed in the full uniform of one of the Highland regiments, gazed at by the passing throng. He was a Scotchman of the name of McNaughton.[77]

The aversion of the Spaniards to Joseph Buonaparte as their king was quite characteristic of ignorant minds. They believed him

---

77 Alexander McNaughton became a Deputy Assistant Commissary General on 10 August 1811 and was attached to the 4th Division from November 1811 until May 1812. He was court-martialled on 6 January 1813 for bursting into the room of Major Brotherton, 14th Light Dragoons, and threatening him with violence and calling him a liar. He was found guilty of all charges and dismissed the service.

to be affected with leprosy, a disease held by them in the greatest abhorrence & by which they wished to shew in the strongest light their contempt of him. He was also called *Rey Botellias* [*Botella Rey* – King Bottle], indicating his love of the bottle. In their contempt and dislike of strangers, their prejudices extended to us, especially on the point of religion, their idea being that we had none, or at least that we were not Christians & it was usually exemplified on Sundays.

A chaplain being attached to headquarters and to each division of the army, Divine Service was performed in Badajoz in the most convenient open space nearest the barracks of the troops, as the loan of a church could not of course be obtained from such bigots & enthusiasts without pollution, as they conceived. The soldiers were accordingly marched to the spot with their arms and formed into a grand hollow square one face of which was left open, the Brigade of Guards occupying two sides facing inwards and the artillery & other troops the other, with all the officers ranged in front, the chaplain[78] standing in the centre, but nearer the unoccupied space with his books on a large drum, and immediately on each side of him were the general officers and Staff &c. It was an imposing and picturesque sight and the ceremony was performed with great decorum & should have been respected by the inhabitants, but the contrary happened, for many who were present conducted themselves so disorderly that it became necessary to drive them away and as it was done by soldiers employed for the purpose, the duty was on many occasions performed by a hearty kicking as the only effective mode of ridding us of their presence. The disturbance was carried so far that the bells of the neighbouring churches were set a ringing at the commencement of the service, which compelled us to send men to occupy the belfries until it was over. Most of these disorders were occasioned by the lower classes and should have been put a stop to by the superior ones, but it was not & it showed on that point at least the bad feeling towards us.

---

78 Chaplain to the Forces, the Reverend Samuel Briscall.

We had not been long in this city before another annoyance occurred in making good our billets or lodgings on the houses of the inhabitants, who though ordered by the magistrates to receive us in the usual manner, resisted at times and there being no other means than that of force to get possession, a file of soldiers were called in, which of course fanned existing animosities. For it was most provoking to be kept after a hot march in the streets, at times for hours until the difficulty was overcome. So long as there was an appearance of our advancing and entering into offensive operations against the enemy, this feeling was only partial and kept under, but in the beginning of December when the Spaniards found that we were on the point of leaving the country and returning to Portugal, their discontent manifested itself more openly and hardly a regiment passed through the city from the more distant cantonments without some of the men being assassinated in disputes and it became so serious as to induce Lord Wellington to remain in it until every individual of the army was beyond the reach of their murderous *cuchillos* or knives. They became aware, no doubt, that they were about to be left to the mercy of their enemy and that their vain glory so pompously manifested on all occasions, was of little avail unassisted by an ally whom they affected to despise when danger was distant.

Experience having taught us that the system of conveyance hitherto employed with the army in the transport of provisions, ammunitions &c on bullock carts, was very slow and defective and likely to thwart future operations in the field, the Commissary General commenced, while in Badajoz, the organisation of a pack saddle mule transport which eventually rendered splendid service in enabling our army to move almost at the pleasure of its commander over very bad roads and to remain in positions and localities to the annoyance of the enemy. Where it could not possibly have existed without that valuable assistance, little considered or attended to as one of the essential means which led to operations being crowned with success, and but for the want of which they could not have been attempted.

This transport was divided into brigades of fifty mules with a head muleteer called a *Capataz* [foreman], and muleteers having from two to four mules each their property. They were hired from various parts of the south of Spain, each mule carrying from 200 to 250 pounds [91–113kg] weight. They followed the troops wherever they went over good or bad roads by which ammunition was never wanting, nor provisions when they could be collected. Most of these mules came from parts of the country afterwards occupied by the enemy and having become very numerous in the succeeding campaigns, exceeding 6,000, the French authorities became apprised of it, but instead of preventing their employment, which could have hardly been done effectually, they levied a periodical tax on them of a dollar (4/6d[79]) per mule & left the muleteers to come home & return as suited them without molestation.

---

79 About £11 in modern terms.

3rd Campaign

French sieges of Ciudad Rodrigo and Almeida, Battle of Busaco and retreat to lines near Lisbon and advance 1810

My turn of departure from Badajoz into Portugal took place on Christmas day with the troops to which I had been attached viz the Reserve of Artillery and 27th Regiment of Foot amounting together to about 1,400 men, 350 horses & mules & 120 draft oxen being as yet the largest family I had had to maintain.

Our first day's march was crossing the frontier to Campo Mayor [Maior] in Portugal and in succession passed through Arronches on the 27th, Portalegre, a small town where we halted the 29th, Gafete 30th, Gavion [Gavaio] 31st, crossing the Tagus to Abrantes where we had another day's halt, it being customary for troops to rest every fourth day when convenient. This day of rest was the 2nd of January 1810; the 3rd we moved to Punhete,[1] 4th to Tomar, 5th Aldea da Cruz [?],[2] to the city of Leyria [Leiria] on the 6th, a picturesque but poor place; halted on the 7th [at] Pombal, 8th Condeixa [-a-Velha] 9th and entered Coimbra on the 10th, during which march no incident worth relating occurred beyond great professional occupation, which gave me no time to think of anything else.

---

1 Modern-day Constancia.

2 The identity of this place is problematic, as the only Aldeia da Cruz is not on the route from Tomar to Leiria. The place they halted at is likely to be near Ourem.

Being now higher in rank & with more extensive duties, I had a clerk attached to me (Mr George Head[3]) as my assistant. He was older than me, had had a university education & was my superior in those respects, but quite a child in Commissariat services. He was one of Lord Wellington's protegees, having been brought up for a superior pursuit which he could not follow in consequence of his family having fallen into reduced circumstances. We got on notwithstanding, extremely well together & when I was transferred to other duties he succeeded me in those I had left.

Coimbra became our halting place for some time, but found it much changed since I had passed through it in May last. It was then all joy and satisfaction, but now the constant thoroughfare of troops which the inhabitants had to receive in their houses was wearing them out. I was quartered on a professor of mathematics in the upper town near the university; he was very kind and communicative and at first bored me with his problems in which his whole mind seemed to be absorbed, but finding me acquainted with rudiments only, he gave it up as useless. He spoke French tolerably and I suspect had he found me willing to be instructed, it was his intention to turn a penny

---

3 George Head, who was educated at Charterhouse School at Bristol, was promoted to Deputy Assistant Commissary General on 15 June 1811. He was in the Peninsula from May 1810 to April 1814. He remained a lifelong friend of Tupper and in his *Memoirs of an Assistant Commissary General*, London 1837, he states 'Twenty seven years have now rolled over the head of this my former master [Tupper Carey], since the day on which, distinguished by a blue uniform coat with cuffs and collar of black velvet, unbuttoned in easy costume and pantaloons decorated with a stripe of reddish-brown Spanish leather, cut in zigzag Vandyke pattern and extending the whole length of the outer seam, proudly spurred at the heels, a white streaming feather in his cocked hat, massive gold epaulettes on his shoulders; mounted on a long-tailed Spanish charger and accompanied by his clerk aforesaid [Head] on a small mule, both together on a sunshiny morning rode out of the town of Badajoz...

Than the Commissariat officer above referred to, there are few men in the world, either in a moral sense, or in matters of business, of more scrupulous exactitude; indeed at this time, anxiety feverishly excited at the apprehension of responsibility, led him to perform himself, all and every part of the official duty; so that partly wishing to be lenient towards me, partly, and very properly, distrusting my capability, and partly, himself possessing a natural born intuitive love for the pen and the ruler, it followed that little sedentary occupation at all events fell to my lot on the way...'

1. *A Portuguese ox cart, by George Hunter.*

2. *Camp life, by William Pyne.*

Above left: **3.** *A Commissary circa 1812.*

Above right: **4.** *A Portuguese cacadore.*

5. *The retreat to Corunna.*

Above left: **6.** *General Sir John Moore.*

Above right: **7.** *Marshal Sir William Carr Beresford.*

Above left: **8.** *General Sir Rowland Hill.*

Above right: **9.** *General Sir John Gaspard Le Marchant*

10. *A view of Lisbon, by Landmann.*

11. *A view of Oporto, by Henry Smith.*

12. *Aqueduct of Segovia.*

13. *A view of Coimbra, by St Clair.*

14. *The Inquisition Building, Coimbra.*

Above left: **15.** *Don Julian Sanchez.*

Above right: **16.** *General Sir John Doyle.*

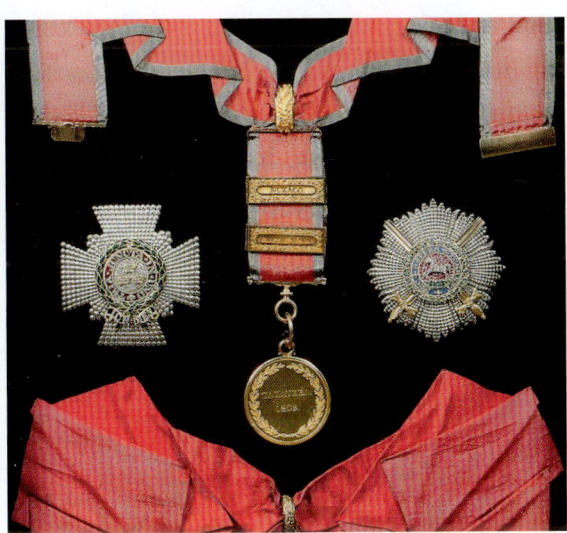

Above left: **17.** *General Howorth's Peninsular War medals.*

Above right: **18.** *Fort La Lippe.*

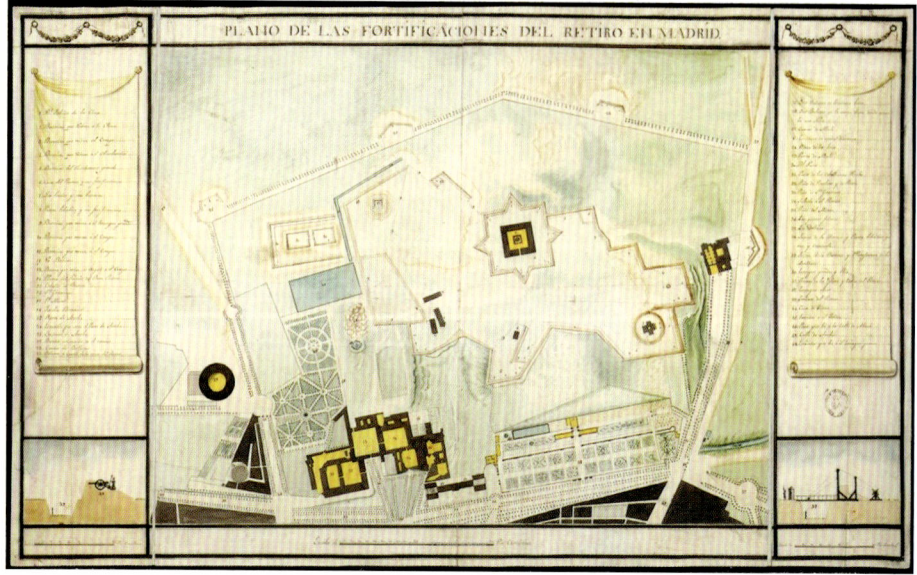

Above: **19.** *The Retiro fortifications – a contemporary map.*

Left: **20.** *Le Marchant's heavy dragoons charging at Salamanca.*

21. Marching the French Prisoners into Salamanca after the Battle 1812, *published by E. Orme.*

by making me his pupil, his means of living being much reduced by the war.

My duties were tolerably light during the first three weeks of my sojourn here, but I was fated not to eat the bread of idleness, for orders came from headquarters which I received on the 1 February for me (in addition to what I had then to do) to take charge of the depot of the place, an occupation which I had better explain from having had several others to attend to in the peninsula.

When an army moves from the place of disembarkation, which is intended to be the pivot of its future operations and advances into the interior of the country to defend it or in quest of the enemy, arrangements are made for its supply and maintenance by the establishment of magazines of provisions & forage &c, either in large towns or suitable places on the road at the distance of three or four day's march from each other (a common march being from 10 to 16 miles [16–26km per day]) which provisions &c are collected from the neighbouring country or brought up from the nearest sea port, by river or land transport. These depots serve to maintain the troops in front & the detachments going and coming from it, as well as reinforcements and to assist in the formation of others if necessary more in advance, so that a chain of them is usually kept up from the coast to where the army is operating or cantoned. And as it was principally stationed in the north of Portugal, Coimbra had become one of these large deposits & the great thoroughfare in the way, for it was on the high road to and from Lisbon and situated on a navigable river, the Mondego.

I had cavalry also to attend to, my work was therefore incessant from daylight to late at night & the great annoyance was that it could not be attended to with any degree of regularity from the usual want of assistance of clerks and other subordinates, which added greatly to the responsibility of the accounts, and occasioned constant anxiety.

I changed my residence to the High Street in the lower part of the town, to be nearer my office & new duties & which was in the midst of the occurring busy scene occasioned by the arrival & departure of numerous parties of troops &c consisting at times of single officers & men on their way to join their regiments to whom rations were required to be issued in detail, giving nearly as much trouble as whole regiments & this reminds me of a circumstance which happened in that branch of the service.

Mr Head to whom I have before alluded, had to examine the correctness of the ration returns of these small parties and issue checks [cheques] for the provisions &c. He sat in the same room with me and my attention was drawn towards an officer of the Guards (Aide de Camp to a General Officer) who had come to make up his return and sat himself down for the purpose opposite Mr Head. I perceived the former looking at the latter, who was holding down his head in the act of writing with more than usual attention, although Head himself had noticed him as he entered. A pause took place, the Aide de Camp then rose and said, 'Head, surely it is you,' extending his hand. 'My name is Head, Sir' was the reply, 'But times are altered and it is better that I should remain in obscurity.' They had known each other and been intimately acquainted in England. His friend however, persevered in renewing his acquaintance and all reserve then ceased. He was afterwards proposed to go and dine with the General who also knew him, but he positively declined. His character, which was a peculiar one, was most firm & determined & was exemplified under the following circumstances:

Being in London when the coronation of William the 4th [8 September 1831] was to take place, he was requested by a friend of his, the Knight Marshall,[4] (who was from ill health under the necessity of travelling abroad), to represent him at the ceremony and perform his duty and was accordingly furnished with a letter

---

4 The Knight Marshal was an office of the Royal Household, established in 1236. The Marshal and his men were responsible for maintaining order in the King's Court. Sir Charles Lamb, was the last Marshal, serving from 1824 to 1846, when the office was abolished.

authorising him to do so. When the time came, he took it to the Secretary of State's Office, to receive his instructions on which he was told the authority was considered insufficient for him to act and he perceived that there was an evident intention of putting him aside if possible and substitute someone in his place. The official folks had however, meddled with the wrong man in not knowing his determination of character. He declared to them that coute qui coute [whatever it took] he would attend: resolutely bent on doing so, he obtained the necessary information [on] how to proceed through some other channel, ordered his clothes and obtained from Astley's Amphitheatre[5] a well-trained horse on which to ride, and being well known to Lord Hill who as Commander in Chief[6] was to be present at the ceremony, he obtained his permission to go in his suite, by which he at once secured an entrance into the line of the procession, soon found his place and performed his duty. Some days after, having met Commissary General Sir Robert Kennedy to whom he recounted the particulars, he was asked if he had been knighted, to which he replied in the negative and being then told that he was entitled to it as a customary consequence & could not be refused, he applied for it at once and though some delays intervened he resolutely persevered and had the honor [sic] conferred on him. He has strange whims also, having perceived that the members of the municipality or corporation of the city (Coimbra in which we were then stationed) were in the habit of signing certificates of existing prices of provisions &c without paying any attention to their correctness, although on them individuals were paid for supplies furnished to the troops, at times to the prejudice of our government or public purse. He wrote out one to which he obtained the usual signatures purporting that the moon was made of green cheese & this he did to shew to those who examined his

---

5 The amphitheatre in Lambeth was the first modern circus ring,

6 General Rowland Hill became Commander-in-Chief in 1828.

accounts the little reliance which could be placed on such documents. He afterwards turned author and wrote several amusing works.[7]

The street in which I was dwelling, being the great thoroughfare through which all processions passed, my servant called my attention one day to a burial passing under my window. It was that of a young woman of a family in easy circumstances. They were carrying her to the church in which she was to be buried and she lay in an ornamental shell, dressed in gawdy apparel with her face uncovered. I had the curiosity to follow the procession and after the performance of the burial service, the body was stripped of its fine clothes, deposited in the grave, a proportion of quicklime thrown on it, the earth after & then the grave digger with his assistant jumped on it and trampled the whole, and thus ended the disgusting ceremony. The reason given for so heartless a proceeding being the inadequacy of the space & the necessity of having recourse to it as soon as possible for the accommodation of others. No wonder then that pestilential diseases broke out among the community frequenting those places of worship, and it was said that a priest had been poisoned in taking the Sacrament, the cause of which was accidentally discovered to have originated from this mode of interment, for some days after when the cup had been replenished with the sacred elements, a gleam of sunshine settled on a small streak floating on the air which on examination was found to consist of innumerable insects issuing from a chink of a grave and communicating with the cup which was supposed to have infected its contents.

At this period, the power and influence of the clergy over the community could hardly be conceived without being seen. It was next to idolatrous for when the bishop left his palace and appeared in the streets, all the people kneeled as he passed, receiving his blessing by making the sign of the cross with great dignity and effect. In a

---

[7] George Head wrote the *Memoirs of an Assistant Commissary-General, Forest Scenery and Incidents in the Wilds of North America* and *A Home Tour through the Manufacturing Districts of England in the Summer of 1835*, amongst many other books.

minor degree the influence of the lower clergy was exemplified in a similar manner.

My duty oftentimes required that I should go to the park of artillery on the other side of the river and on those occasions I visited everything remarkable within a short distance. I accordingly went to a quinta or country house called Quinta das Lacrimas [Lagrimas] (tears) which had belonged to the celebrated Ines de Castro & had been the scene of her courtship and misfortunes. One of the kings of Portugal when Prince Royal fell in love with her and married her clandestinely. His father would not countenance it and she was in consequence persecuted and at last poisoned.[8] The event is one of the most melancholy episodes in the history of that country. The house and grounds were hardly better than a common farm establishment but there was a fine orange grove, the fruit of which was most delicious. The Portuguese evince towards their women an opposite feeling to the Spaniards, the former showing great jealousy towards them & the latter giving them every liberty. Unless therefore, there was something attractive going on in the streets of Coimbra, few faces of the higher classes were uncovered and the windows being barricaded with jalousies,[9] bright black eyes were oftener seen through them than at any other time, being a remnant of their Moorish descent and customs, and yet it is inconceivable the liberty our officers enjoyed when curiosity led them to visit the nunneries.

---

8 Ines de Castro, the daughter of a Castilian noble, went to Portugal in 1340 as lady in waiting to Constance of Castile, wife of Peter, the Prince Regent of Portugal. When Constance died in 1345, King Afonso IV sought a new marriage for Peter, but he refused all candidates, declaring his undying love for Ines. Eventually Afonso ordered the murder of Ines, which was carried out by three men at the Convent of Santa Clara-a-Velha in Coimbra, who beheaded her. Peter became king in 1357 (Peter I) and sought revenge. In 1361 he captured two of the murderers and had them executed by having their hearts torn out. Peter claimed that he had secretly married Ines, but evidence shows that the Pope had refused permission for the marriage. The story of Peter having Ines disinterred and placed on the throne at his coronation for all the nobles to swear fealty to their queen is a myth.

9 Shutters with angled slats.

Among many of them, there was one outside the city in a village between one & two miles distance, by the front of which we occasionally passed in our rides.[10] When first we rode that way we enquired in fun from some old women lurking about the great gate, if there were any pretty nuns within. To which a ready answer was given by several being named and we were asked to go in, which we did without further ceremony, knocked at the gate and requested to see those whose names had been given us. The Abbess soon made her appearance with the young nuns mentioned by us and expressed great pleasure at our visit. They were tolerably good looking, but confinement made them pale and I may say uninteresting. The old lady retired, leaving us together until our departure and as I suppose we had made ourselves agreeable, they requested us to renew our call, which we did occasionally and as familiarity increased they shewed no backwardness in entering into little innocent amusements which they could do in perfect safety, for there was a double grating dividing the two rooms, and at such a distance that we could hardly reach each other's extended arms, but there was a small barrel half open in the wall turning on a pivot, by which we received sweetmeats &c and passed our coats and cocked hats for their inspection and they their hoods, they putting on our vestments and we theirs, a frolic of which no notice was taken, for if too long an interval occurred between our visits messages were received reminding us of our promises & when nearing the nunnery we had early indications that we were welcome by the waving of handkerchiefs from their latticed windows. There was either a great laxity of discipline at this time, or they wished to shew their gratitude to us in this way for defending the country.

At the distance of some miles there was another nunnery, most isolated in the mountains, exclusively inhabited by daughters of the nobility. It was of course richly endowed, the attendants being more numerous than the nuns and every visitor was entertained for three

---

10 Probably the Convento de Santa Maria de Semide.

days at the expense of the establishment. Some officers went there and were most warmly received and pressed to return, but it was too distant an undertaking to repeat the visit.

As the Commissariat duties on this line of road increased in importance, an officer of higher rank to me was sent to superintend them. Deputy Commissary General Lutyens[11] was appointed, and I of course served under him, which I was very glad of as there was a great deal too much for a young head like mine to regulate, connected as the service was with various lines of communication from Lisbon to the army, with several depots on the coast from which convoys of provisions were hourly received & forwarded on and an accumulating force in the town & neighbourhood. This officer was 15 years my senior, of German extraction and had served with the British and Austrian armies in Germany and being a very good looking man, a young and noble lady much his superior in rank took a fancy to him there. It was discovered by her friends & through the Duke of York who then commanded the army, everything was done by the family to prevent the intimacy going further, but in spite of every exertion on their part, he eventually succeeded in marrying her.[12] He had extraordinary peculiarities, one of which was an aversion to men that squinted or were otherwise deformed with whom he would if possible, have no official transactions, fancying that their dealings would be as crooked as themselves. We agreed very well together although he occasionally teased me for wearing mustachios.

Another strange character was placed under my orders as Principal Storekeeper to take charge of stores. An active, intelligent and plausible fellow, a sort of Portuguese but certainly not a legitimate one. He embezzled the public property for which I was responsible, giving me a great deal of anxiety and trouble, but as I was quite

---

11 Deputy Commissary General Charles Lutyens served in the Peninsula from September 1808 to February 1811 and later at Lisbon from February 1813 to April 1814.

12 Charles Lutyens married Frances Fludger on 6 May 1824. They were the parents of the artist Charles Lutyens and grandparents of Sir Edwin Landseer Lutyens.

ignorant and therefore innocent of his misdeeds, I was in time relieved of all difficulty. When detected he absconded and was supposed to be a French spy, and having been arrested afterwards, I was ordered to hold myself in readiness to answer a summons to attend at his trial, which either never took place, or that my services were more required with the army than in Lisbon where it was to take place. He remained in prison for many months and I last lost sight of him altogether.

To add to my difficulties at the time, a great inundation of the river occasioned by heavy rains took place on the 7 March, which flooded the lower part of the city and broke into the Commissariat stores under my charge and even covering the bridge of communication between both sides of the stream. Much [of the] provisions & forage corn, as well as private property was spoiled and it was necessary to remove the remainder in boats which were brought up to the doors of the upper tiers or stories [sic] of the buildings, a work of great exertion and anxiety.

At this time the city was crowded with military and for the first time the new[ly] organized Portuguese battalions in our pay, having three or four British officers attached to each of them, came up from the rear where they had been undergoing the necessary drill previous to their incorporation with our troops. They appeared in very good order, clothed from England in blue with other colours for facings, their cazadores [cacadores] or riflemen were in brown but resembled our own in style of dress and their grenadiers wore mustachios which, with their dark complexions, gave them an imposing look, and though Marshal Beresford's talents as a commander in the field will ever be doubted,[13] no one can question his abilities in organizing & disciplining an army.

The move of our troops towards Almeida in the beginning of May, corresponding with the concentration of the French in Castile,

---

13 Marshal William Carr Beresford lost his reputation as a field commander following the near-disastrous Battle of Albuera in 1811.

preparatory to active operations, were indications that the repose which had been enjoyed for some time was likely to cease, and as regarded myself I did not remain long in suspense, for an order soon arrived for the movement of the Reserve artillery to which I was still attached in the same direction. I was however, so entangled in the multiplicity of accounts & business connected with the additional duty imposed on me, that I could not proceed and therefore remained behind for a few days to give over to my successor everything relating to it and which I did with sincere pleasure, for I was heartily tired of the incessant toil and responsibility which I had been subject to for several months. And so trying had it been, that I earnestly solicited relief from duty altogether to make up my accounts, which had become very voluminous and intricate. I found it however useless, as no one could be spared for such a purpose under existing circumstances. I therefore bundled up my papers without delay and departed to join the troops alluded to and reached them at St Jago [Santiago near Seia], a small village, beautifully situated at the foot of the Estrela Mountains, the highest in Portugal, the summits of which were still covered with snow. Here I hoped to find leisure to wind up the affairs of my late duty, my present one being comparatively light.

The scenery in the mountains was quite alpine and the wolves were in considerable numbers, but I had no time to make distant excursions into the one or hunt the others in their fastnesses. I therefore set about the task I could not avoid and by getting up at 4 o'clock in the morning, immediately after break of day, and labouring all the day long with my two clerks, I succeeded by the end of June to wash my hands of all outstanding accounts which proved a great relief to me.

This calm did not however last long, for I had hardly reported the circumstance to the Commissary General, as it was my duty to do, when I received orders to take another abominable depot in my charge & which was established at a place called Pinhanços (the little dash under the letter c making it sound as an s) six miles from whence I was then stationed, to which I removed on the 6 July, finding I could no longer remain where I was although I had both duties to perform for some time afterwards, until relieved from the minor one.

By this time the army had been clustering in our front and round about Almeida to impede as far as was possible the French Army besieging Ciudad Rodrigo. I therefore got again into the thoroughfare of the army and up to my ears in business, with as usual most inadequate assistance and no remedy to fly to.

For some time all went tolerably quiet but when the French had taken that fortress with an overwhelming force which removed all doubt of their invading Portugal, excitement commenced & preparations were made for our retreat to the neighbourhood of Lisbon. The inhabitants were ordered by proclamation to make every preparation for abandoning their houses, destroy their crops, injure the machinery of their corn mills to prevent their being used and in short to put every difficulty in the way of an advancing enemy by rendering the country a desert. To add to the confusion and dismay of the time, unaccountable panics occurred in the neighbourhood of the army and spread to the rear all along the road to the distance of fifty miles, filling it with fugitives. The disorder reached the place I was in and extended much lower down, frightening everyone under a delusion that the enemy were already at their heels. Some detachments of troops coming up were stopped and others retrograded & the convoys of provisions, forage corn, wine &c conveyed on the carts & asses of the peasantry forcibly taken into the service, were in many cases either upset in the road or abandoned without anyone to take care of them, the drivers considering it an excellent opportunity to decamp with their cattle [mules], perhaps their only property to their homes, from whence they had been taken to convey their loads.

The French having halted to undertake the siege of Almeida, the alarms subsided and things went on as before, but orders were issued for every individual not immediately required with the army to proceed at once to the rear so as to keep the roads clear of obstacles for the expected retreat, and I received a confidential communication to burn or destroy in case of need, all supplies & stores in my charge which could not be carried away, on the enemy making his appearance. All soldiers' wives were accordingly included in the arrangement & they were collected and formed into brigades, or corps, each under the orders of an officer, were marched to the rear and rations supplied them during their absence.

The first and second day's march went on smoothly enough, but they soon became unruly and many deserted to return to their regiments and by the time they had reached my depot, they were in a state of insubordination and nearly drove their officers mad, for they abused them and would not submit either to order or regularity. One officer told me he had never had such a difficult and unpleasant duty to perform. The fact was, the provision allowed them was inadequate to their maintenance and few had money to procure them or to meet any other wants.

At this time all sorts of people were passing and repassing, among them a handsome French sergeant came in and presented his march Rout[e] for rations on his way to Lisbon. As he spoke English perfectly well my curiosity was awakened, and I questioned him. He informed me that he was an Englishman, and having been wounded at the Battle of Talavera was made prisoner with all those left behind, and whilst marching to France enlistment was offered him in the French Army as well as to many others and thinking to escape from captivity soon by it, he accepted it with the intention of deserting whenever the opportunity occurred and when the regiment he might be in came in the neighbourhood of our troops, he lost no time in availing himself of it. He was on his way to England to join a corps there, as it was not considered advisable that he should for the present serve in the peninsula. He was quite metamorphosed into a French soldier and it was only on his speaking to me that I made out who he really was.

My duty was incessant night and day, the only room I occupied served as an office, dining and bedroom. It was constantly thronged with people and to answer all calls with requisite alacrity at night

I thought it better to sleep on the bed in a small alcove partially dressed so that I might the more readily get up and attend to them, and this I did for several weeks without inconvenience from getting accustomed to it.

The siege of Almeida which the French had commenced was abruptly terminated by the blowing up of the principal magazine which rendered that fortress no longer tenable. The retreat soon commenced afterwards in earnest, but I did not put the order into execution which I had received to destroy any remaining stores in my possession, as I succeeded in getting them off by laying hold of or employing, every cart or other sort of transport going to the rear; what became of them however I never heard, and it was of no consequence so long as the enemy did not get them. By degrees the troops filed off in retreat, waiting until my turn arrived as I was only to quit with the last. I was of course ready to start at the very shortest notice for the enemy must be at hand when it took place. My perfect knowledge of [the] French language made me indifferent to being made a prisoner which led to my appearing bolder on occasions in which there was a chance of it than I really felt and this proved of use professionally and several times consequently.

On the 16th of September the rear-guard of our cavalry came into our village and as the room I occupied was in the most decent house, the Aide de Camp of the General who was expected to sleep there ordered me out at once. Remonstrance was I knew useless, although I protested against it by representing that the public papers in my profession would be safe nowhere else. I therefore moved everything to the only available place which was a chapel in which the stores had been deposited.[14] I was told to be on the alert as the enemy might press on from one hour to the other & the place would be evacuated. Myself and people, horses & mules, were huddled together in the building, the interior of which as customary was open and without

---

14 Almost certainly the Capelo de Santo Amaro.

pews, a few empty sacks were laid for me to lay upon on the wooden step at the foot of the altar, my people on some straw lower down with the animals near the large door & in that state, dressed as we were, we took some repose until the earliest break of day when we began our march, and departed before the cavalry on our way to the rear.

The immense concentration of force made by the French to invade Portugal occasioned [a] very great sensation with almost every officer in our army and led them to conceive the defence of the country to be impossible with the British force we could muster and the untried Portuguese army, even general officers wrote in a desponding way to their friends in England, giving it as their opinion that we must retreat, leave the country, and return home. Many of these letters were inserted in the newspapers of the day, and as Buonaparte obtained from that source much information on which it is supposed he put great reliance, the advance of his army was urged on and Massena their commander, hitherto the spoilt child of fortune, expected that we should quietly retire and embark.

Lord Wellington fulminated a very severe General Order[15] on the subject, conveying a severe admonition to those who had done so, in which he insinuated that he knew some of the individuals but that he withheld mentioning their names in hopes that the rebuke would put an end to so pernicious a habit.

The two months and a half I had been at Pinhanços was a period of great excitement in respect to passing events; to the responsibility of the accounts I had to render, and of transactions for which I was accountable, the documents were very voluminous and unavoidably in great disorder and confusion. The queries or questions by the Board of Audit consisted therefore of several quires of paper and were most troublesome to answer, especially from the lapse of time which had occurred and had I not most honourably performed my duty I might not have got over them easily. I annex a copy of the letter I wrote enclosing

---

15 General Order dated Celorico 10 August 1810.

my explanations which will give only a faint idea of the incidental duties a Commissariat Officer is saddled with at times in a campaign.

To the Comptroller of Army Accounts in Paris

Boulogne [-Billancourt] near Paris, 13 October 1815

Sir,

I have the honour to forward to you in conformity to the Commissary in Chief's directions, the explanations made by me to the Queries which have arisen on my Provision and Store Accounts for the service in the Peninsula from the 11 June to the 17 September 1810.

I beg leave to offer for your particular attention the following circumstances that occurred, still fresh in my memory, to enable you to form some conception of the difficulties I then laboured under in the execution of my duty & in keeping these accounts with that degree of accuracy necessary to render them without comment or observation.

When attached to Captain Lawson's Brigade of artillery and the Reserve at St Jago [Santiago], I was directed by Sir Robert Kennedy the 4th or 5th of July 1810 to take charge of the depot established at Pinhanços (a very inconsiderable and poor village) in the valley of the Mondego, with instructions to attend to both duties although at the distance of six miles from each other.

On receiving the magazine, the contents of which were considerable, from the late Deputy Assistant Commissary General Petkin,[16] I found the supplies contained in seven or eight small hovels, the tiles without cement or ceiling, and no guard for their protection; in which state they were

---

16 Deputy Assistant Commissary General William Henry Petkin who was dismissed the service on 9 March 1811.

unavoidably left and issued a considerable time afterwards, from the village not affording better accommodation.

The persons attached to me consisted of one clerk, Mr John Laidley (now a Deputy Assistant Commissary General[17]) a Portuguese of very inferior ability, without the least knowledge, did the duty of Storekeeper, in addition to a capataz or overseer of cattle, with some peasants as labourers and herdsmen; with this badly composed assistance at a time when inexperience cramped every arrangement, the theatre of war near, and the enemy expected to advance during the sieges of Almeida & Ciudad Rodrigo, the whole duty & responsibility fell on me of attending to the detailed supply of numerous detachments of the army passing to and fro, and no commandant in the village to refer to in cases of doubt or difficulty, issuing with unavoidable difficulty from the same store to the numerous demands of the Commissariat Accountants & receiving the continual & extensive convoys of provisions and Quarter Master General Stores, generally loaded on small bullock carts & asses, arriving from the rear in the greatest confusion, some of the carts broken down in the rugged and bad roads & others deserted and left by the drivers to be pillaged by the peasantry which afforded no small share of anxiety & exertion to get the supplies collected & brought up to their destination, and in addition to this, no considerable employment, I had to attend to the pasture and keep of 5 or six hundred head of cattle in my charge.

To look into and complete these voluminous accounts which also included cask transactions, no time whatever was afforded me, having been immediately after the

---

17 John Laidley became a Deputy Assistant Commissary General on 11 January 1812, and was attached to the Royal Waggon Train.

evacuation of Pinhanços, detached in forming another depot at Espinhal, more in the rear, and subsequently employed to this present time on most active duty in the peninsula and in this country. I have therefore entirely depended on my memory in the solution of the queries in question. I have the honour to be &c &c Tupper Carey

In proceeding to the rear I got an order to go and form another depot at Espinhal for the supply of Lord Hill's corps which had come from the south of Portugal to join Lord Wellington. I arrived there on the 20 September; the order to the inhabitants to abandon their dwellings and flee away on the approach of the enemy was sadly evidenced all along the road we had been passing and it was most melancholy and heart-rending to pass through deserted towns & villages with a few stragglers only lingering to the last moment before tearing themselves from their hearths and homes, from which the greatest number had never before been absent and no one but an eye observer can form an idea of such a scene. The desolation was complete, for many of the crops were still on the ground & on the vines and only a proportion carried away by the people to the nearest mountains where they had taken refuge, or across the River Tagus where the more wealthy were enabled to retire from having conveyances at their disposal.[18] Without loss of time I set about collecting supplies and receiving them from the rear, that is from depots nearer Lisbon and here I waited the march of events.

Our troops continued to retire before the overwhelming masses of the enemy by a road nearer the seacoast than the one on which I was stationed and they halted on the northern side of the city of Coimbra to protect it, on the heights of Busaco, a very strong position and where a battle was fought on the 27 September. The movements of

---

18 This shows clearly that the 'scorched earth' policy ordered by Wellington had only been partially carried out, leaving much for the French to find.

all concerned, both with the army and in isolated situations depended on the result of the action and for three or four days we were in great anxiety and suspense from the various rumours in circulation, some favourable and others to the contrary, for not being on the direct line of retreat of the troops towards Lisbon we might have been overlooked.

On the 2 October however, orders for a retrograde movement arrived and [were] to be effected without delay for although the enemy had been repulsed he had since succeeded by superior numbers to turn our left flank and I was directed to destroy the supplies which could not be removed. No infantry took the road on which Espinhal is situated, a brigade of cavalry only passing that way to cover the right flank of the army and having no transport to carry anything away, I threw open the doors of the magazine and with the concurrence of the General commanding, invited the soldiers as they passed through the town to take away what they could. In an hour or two 20,000 pounds [9.1 tonnes] of biscuit, 28,000 pounds [12.7 tonnes] of oats, and 40,000 pounds [18.1 tonnes] of Indian corn were carried off by the 13th Light Dragoons and Portuguese cavalry and as the straw (60,000 pounds [27.2 tonnes]) which had been collected was not portable at such a moment, it was thrown in the streets and trampled under the horses feet to render it useless to the enemy. It was a lamentable scene of war & in character with the desolate appearance of the town; I had at first contemplated setting fire to it but as it would have endangered the safety of the contiguous buildings, I had recourse to the first alternative.

I quitted the place immediately afterwards & continued with the people under me on my way towards Lisbon, stopping for a night in the large town of Thomar [Tomar] where the same scenes of distress and evacuation on a larger scale were going on as I have before described, for the inmates of numerous convents and nunneries added to the throng dispersing in all directions.

While pursuing my Route, I was not allowed to be idle, for I assisted in emptying the depots on the road and on arriving at

Golegao [Golega], a short distance from the Tagus where there was an extensive one, I was directed to embark if possible the Quarter Master General stores, such as bales of blankets, shoes and many other etcetera.

I had no transport to convey them to the riverside and as I could not obtain any in the midst of the confusion, a company of Portuguese infantry was ordered to assist me; parties were sent out about the country and after much trouble we succeeded in collecting some carts to the despair of the poor drivers who were conveying their property away. But there was no help for it and as we promised to discharge them as soon as the work was done, we got the stores conveyed to the river in a very short time and they started back at once. How to get them removed by water was found to be the greatest difficulty; no boat could be procured, every person had disappeared and we could obtain no information for our guidance. At nightfall a few boats were seen creeping down along the opposite bank, evidently avoiding the one on which we were as that on which the enemy would first make his appearance. There appeared to be no alternative for our party but that of remaining on the spot for the night and the stores were heaped up so as to enable us to make some sort of defence in case of need, we opened some of the bales of blankets for those who might require them for we were on a low bleak shore without shelter or covering of any description, exposed to a cold and misty exhalation arising from the river. Sentries were placed and a sharp look out kept up, several horsemen were perceived at different times through the haze, hovering about but a shot having at last been fired at one we saw no more. They were supposed to be peasantry but might have been an advance of the enemy for we were completely isolated from the army. At day dawn the captain of the company got uneasy and told me that as he was responsible for the safety of his men, he could no longer remain in so exposed a situation. I begged him to have a little patience and named an hour when he might depart. We had hardly however settled this important point when several large boats were perceived coming down as before on the other side, but matters being now urgent, it was resolved to bring them to if possible. Two shots were accordingly fired at them or over them and the soldiers shouting to them that we were friends they at last came over, the stores were huddled into them in the greatest hurry, the captain and his men embarking evidently quite delighted, but as I had my horse with me and could not easily put him on board, they wished me good morning and left me alone to find my way by land as best I could.

I put spurs to the animal and speedily got back to Golegao [Golega] keeping however a sharp and anxious lookout on the road, for I did not know who I should meet with, friend or foe; fortunately it was the former in the shape of the rear-guard of the army and I felt quite happy at having so successfully performed the duty entrusted to me.

The scenes of distress on the road seemed to increase as we neared our destination for as the distance lessened to a place of safety in the neighbourhood, the young and old, lame and bedridden were flying to it and concentrating from all parts, filling the road with all sorts of conveyances, mostly uncovered bullock carts, exposed to all weathers without the certainty of shelter for the night and the poor creatures evidently suffering every anguish to which such a trial subjected them. It was therefore a great relief when we turned to the right into a more unfrequented road with instructions to join Sir William Erskine's Brigade[19] of infantry preparatory to its entering into the famous lines which protected Lisbon, the extent and importance of which comparatively few in the army had any conception until they were within them, the general conviction being that we should all be in England before a month could elapse. Our surprise was therefore great and I may say not over agreeable, and from the privations which had been experienced in the retreat, many were greatly disappointed when they found the likelihood of our still remaining in the country.

---

19 General Orders of 9 October 1810 appointed Carey to Major General Sir William Erskine's 1st Division.

FEEDING WELLINGTON'S ARMY IN THE PENINSULA

I joined the brigade consisting of the 50th (or dirty half hundred as they were nicknamed from their black facings), 71st and 92nd Regiments on the 10 October at Sobral [de Monte Agraco], situated at the foot of the lines nearly in their centre, and when about entering them; there was evidently an object in our manoeuvring not to take that step until forced to it, or until the enemy had made serious demonstrations for the necessity of our doing so. They were hourly expected and our troops were prepared to give ground, but only when imposing forces shewed themselves in our front. The night was therefore spent in great uncertainty in the rear of the brigade with no place indicated for a lodging, the weather was stormy and wet and two Commissariat officers similarly situated as myself having accidentally met, we consulted together and determined to put up wherever we could meet with shelter; having in our search fallen in with an isolated cowhouse which had much of the roof uninjured. We at once turned into it with our attendants and horses, most thankful even for the miserable accommodation. Food we had none excepting some biscuits and spirits and for the horses, straw taken off from the thatch of the roof, and as we were drenched with wet & were cold, a fire was the first thing thought of. The place had been before occupied and a corner of the roof removed for the smoke to escape, the fire was soon kindled, around which we sat (not on chairs for cattle do not require such things) but on the ground, munching our biscuit, the rain coming in partially all the while through the smoke, fatigue forced us at last to take some rest if possible. The floor was a consolidated mass of manure with of course bare walls as the only furniture and we laid down as we sat near the fire with our cocked hats in lieu of night caps. Sleep soon came on, but towards morning we were greatly alarmed by a shriek from one of the party whom we found in a fright on his legs, rubbing his face; and the cause was soon ascertained. The fire during the night had progressively dried and burned the floor of manure and spread underneath until it had reached him. Part of his cocked hat was burned, his cheek had also suffered and had it not been for the pain which awoke him, it might have been of serious consequence to his eyesight. On getting up we found we should ere long have been put to the same ordeal. At the moment, the aspect of the scene blended the comic with the serious, for in the midst of comparative darkness, the embers of the fire being the only light, everyone of course were on the alert and until the true cause was ascertained we fancied it to be an alarm of the enemy.

The sensation I felt on getting up I shall never forget, for the side on which I had laid had been warmed by the underground heat and the other was cold by the partial wet which had descended through the aperture in the roof, keeping as we did near the fire; and it was only after a violent exertion and taking a glass of spirits that I succeeded in restoring the equilibrium of sensation and temperature of the body. The buoyancy of youth made us soon forget this inconvenience, accustomed as we were to such occurrences, this one being mentioned as a sample of the life we were leading.

The dawn of day saw us out of this uninviting accommodation and we joined our troops, who were still awaiting to see what the enemy intended or was about. The day did not pass without the expected stir, for an attack occurred in the afternoon and our troops gradually retreated within the lines. In my way to the rear while the skirmish was going on, I met Lord Wellington coming up with some of his Staff and he asked me in his usual sharp and hurried manner what was the matter. I answered that it was nothing serious, on which he rode on expressing 'Ha ha', this was the only time I had the honour of being spoken to by him, although I may say I saw him daily and almost constantly for several years. Although in a place of security the troops could not immediately occupy their permanent quarters, they were therefore put [up] for the night as conveniently as possible and I recollect the whole of the 50th Regiment, upwards of 600 officers & men being huddled up in one house and so packed up as almost to lay on each other, to which they could have no objection from being at least under cover with very bad and stormy weather outside.

My accommodation was somewhat better and infinitely superior to the previous night, for I had my baggage and servants with me.

Next day the troops were put in the houses they were to occupy for some time and the routine or business of a month commenced. The ground allotted to the brigade I was attached to in the defence of the lines, was on a height immediately overlooking a ravine which separated us from the enemy, who occupied one opposite, but much lower, right immediately in our front and our respective sentries could not be more than 100 yards if so much asunder. On our left was a gorge or ravine leading into the lines and which being considered one if not the most vulnerable part of them was occupied by the 1st Division of infantry, but so situated as to be out of the sight of the enemy. On our right lay the high mountain of Sobral or Agracia [Monte Agraco], the centre and key of the defence, on which there was a telegraph communicating with headquarters where Lord Wellington resided,[20] Lisbon & other points, from the top of which, which was strongly fortified nearly the whole of the enemy's positions and cantonments could be seen as well as their movements.

The village of Zibreira [da Fe] occupied by us, was on the flat of the hill forming our position and my house, or hovel I should say, overlooked the ravine from whence I could have slung a stone and reached the French sentries or videttes. On the slope leading down to the bottom, a succession of zig-zag breast works were constructed under the superintendence of our general to strengthen the defences and as employment to the men. The town of Sobral [Monte Agraco] lay down in the plain and the vine being the principal object of cultivation almost every house had huge vats or casks for storing the wine after the vintage.

The French finding it necessary to have an advanced post in front of the town for which there was no shelter, had recourse to a curious expedient which they adopted under our eyes, by rolling these casks

---

20 Wellington's headquarters were based at Pero Negro.

to the spot and making a street of them. They secured them of course from rolling, built chimney places and opened windows and when we afterwards visited them after their retreat, they were found as comfortable as ingenuity could make them. The appearance of this village was singular and showed that our enemy was most clever in making the best of a difficulty. They had had long experience and had recourse to means which we as allies would not have dared to employ in a friendly country; they neither respected the persons or property of the inhabitants, for they laid hold of everything within their reach and turned it to their use. They were in fact an organized army of ruffians, who set every law or order at defiance and their chiefs were hardly better; so at least it appeared by their conduct in Portugal.

We had not been long in our present situation before Marshal Massena[21] commenced a series of reconnaissance's to ascertain where an attack might best be made on our lines, the place we occupied being considered by those who knew the country (for he had several Portuguese noblemen, gentlemen & officers with him) as the most assailable. We were often favoured with his presence accompanied by his numerous and brilliant Staff, every one of whom could be distinctly seen from our elevated situation, and it was so frequently repeated that the commanding officer of artillery who had six guns in battery, at last requested leave to try the range of his guns by firing at him, but it was positively forbidden, first because the guns were masked and surrounded by abatis, unknown to the enemy, which would have proved of essential use in case of an attack, and secondly because it was positively enjoined that no gun or musket was to be fired without urgent necessity and should that occur an immediate report was required to be made to Lord Wellington; so anxious was he to know of the slightest occurrence in this part of the defences considered the weakest.

---

21 Marshal André Massena, Prince of Essling, commanded the Army of Portugal in 1810.

In the gorge or ravine alluded to there could not be less than 10,000 men mostly concealed from the enemy who most decidedly would have been roughly handled had they made an attack. It was nevertheless expected hourly, particularly about the dawn of day. Accordingly, all the troops every morning got under arms at their respective alarm posts an hour before daybreak,[22] baggage packed, loaded & ready to start. The Commissariat were of course included in the arrangement and as soon as daylight enabled the generals to ascertain that the enemy were in a state of quiescence, the troops were dismissed. This was an everyday occurrence of which some individuals who were not immediately under the eye of military control or discipline, overlooked occasionally and I must say I was one of those who committed that great imprudence and had an attack taken place I must have been in the midst of it most probably in a state of nudity as I undressed every night.

After some time, the French began to be in want of provisions and the Commissariat stores under my charge being visible to them, it must have been a most tantalising sight to perceive the convoys of biscuit &c arrive and be distributed to the troops. Their capture would have been an object of preference no doubt, but they would have been disappointed by the arrangement before described. Under such circumstances we could hardly be absent from our posts for any length of time, and the only excuse for being away at any time was in quest of provisions which were regularly drawn from the magazines in the rear, of course nearer Lisbon, within a second line of defence prepared to receive us in the event of our being driven from the one we occupied; there being still in addition another as a *dernier resort*, [last resort] which encircled St Julian's [Sao Juliao] fort at the mouth of the Tagus commanding the entrance of that river and separated from Lisbon, into which the British troops would have retired and embarked without molestation, protected by the Navy,

---

22 Sunrise in Portugal in October is around 7 am.

leaving the Portuguese authorities to make the best terms they could for themselves with the French.

These lines were a magnificent and as they proved, a most successful undertaking and may be said to have led to the first great check to Bonaparte's victorious career.[23]

To Lisbon we dared not go and [Cabeco de] Montachique the depot alluded to, was the extent of my rides, to the Commissary of which I paid occasional visits on duty and I there remarked the strange expedients at times resorted to, to bring up the supplies to the army from Lisbon, in forcing the hackney coaches and gentleman's carriages to carry sacks of biscuits &c, long files of which odd conveyances were seen covering the roads & hurrying to their destination, to get rid of their troublesome burdens so as to be out of the way of any occurring or untoward event which might have compromised their safety. This was to them an irksome task, but it could not be avoided as other transport better adapted to the purpose to the extent required could not be procured in the cooped-up corner of Portugal then occupied by us on the northern side of the River Tagus.

Day after day passed in suspense awaiting the enemy's attack; there they were constantly before us and near us, and from the heights we occupied we could have observed every movement they made during the day, but all was constantly quiet and for the whole time we were thus situated not a shot was fired to disturb the good understanding between the opposite sentries, or the repose of the masses of troops ready for contest and watching with intense interest and attention any symptom from which to infer that something would soon take place. This state of watchfulness had something imposing in it in the constant stillness it occasioned.

Matters were not however carried on so quietly on the right of our lines on the Tagus, for our Navy having brought up some gunboats,

---

23 He forgets the Austrian victory of Aspern-Essling in 1809.

our tars gave the enemy constant annoyance and killed one of their most promising generals (St Croix[24]).

The French having exhausted the stores of provisions collected from the country as reported by deserters, rumours got in circulation that finding the lines impregnable they must take some great offensive measure, or retreat. Orders were accordingly given to be vigilant at night but on no account to occasion any disturbance to ascertain what might be doing as it might be a feint to draw us out of our stronghold.

Before break of day on the 15 November, our sentries on being relieved, reported that as far as they could discern the French sentries continued at their respective posts but had remained immoveable for some hours which was not usually the case, but being forbidden to ascertain the cause of this peculiarity, the report was simply conveyed to the officers in command on the spot & by them to Lord Wellington and the solution of the mystery only took place at day dawn [sic], when it was discovered that the retreat had actually commenced and that the sentries had been replaced by men of straw with a cap and shouldering a stick in lieu of a musket, a good imitation during the night and by which the enemy's army got a start of several hours. They were not however immediately followed except by patrols, under a suspicion that it might be a trick or ruse to get us in the plain and meet us on more equal terms. When it was ascertained to a certainty that such was not the case, we issued from our eminences and followed them and in our first day's march perceived the ingenious contrivance adopted by them not to lose their way during the night over a moor they had to pass, by placing at short intervals high poles with large bundles of brushwood at the top, by following which they got into the regular road.

We passed a place where a French picket consisting of a few men defended by an abatis had been surprised and gallantly captured by

---

24 Brigadier General Charles, Comte d'Escorches de Sainte Croix was killed by a cannonball on 11 October 1810 at Vila Franca de Xira.

our dragoons[25] and immediately in the rear of it there was a farmhouse which had been occupied by a post. In going into it, proofs of the scarcity experienced by the French troops were visible, for there were quarters of a young ass hanging in a sort of pantry evidently prepared for cooking.

Our resting place for the night was to have been in a small town, but it proved anything but agreeable quarters, for our foes were determined to annoy us in every way. They had not had time to destroy it, or did not that we might not imagine that their retreat was to continue, but in going into the houses they were found in so filthy and indecent a state and purposely done, that we preferred occupying barns and sheds for the few hours of night. They thought it I daresay a good practical (though it was a most dirty) joke.

As we advanced we found the country a desert and the solitude it occasioned was quite distressing, with not a vestige of an inhabitant alive to welcome us, everything had the appearance of desolation, the poor wretches who had trusted in them, or whom they caught in their forages, were found hanging on trees, and some were discovered disposed of in a different way, for they had thrown them into the large wine vats with wine in them, which rather than destroy they thus rendered useless to tantalise us. If discovered in time the contents were not of course consumed, but it was not the case in every instance, for in coming into settled quarters before this disgusting trick came to our knowledge, many vats were drank before the unwholesome dreg was discovered in the bottom and it happened I recollect to a regiment of cavalry, the officers of which boasted of the goodness of their wine, and it was for some time a standing joke against that corps.

The atrocities, horrors, mischief and tricks committed by the French throughout their retreat from Portugal would fill volumes. On one occasion being quartered for the night near a nunnery on

---

25 On 16 November. The 16th Light Dragoons captured two officers and seventy-eight men.

our present march, and not having as yet seen the inside of one I went in out of curiosity. It was still daylight, as a matter of course it had been pillaged and ransacked, the books, papers and furniture were broken and strewed about and as an amusement the plunderers had taken down the various saints from their niches in the church and taken them to the refectory or eating room and arranged them in groups after having dressed some of them in various habiliments to make a variety. It was a sort of masquerade; some were embracing, others were kneeling in attitudes of prayer to those whose dress was unchanged: ridicule of religion was their object as I believe there was not a shadow of it in the French army. The building itself was on a small scale & had nothing interesting about it.

In their retreat from Santarem to the frontier [in March 1811] the same scenes of devastation and destruction were renewed. In Golegao [Golega] a small neat town, a report having reached the French who were then occupying it, that church plate had been secreted by the priests, they set about seeking for it and it being the custom to bury it, their search must have been of the most revolting kind, for when we passed through, the scene that presented itself could hardly be described. The whole floor had been as it were rooted up, from one end to the other, with great labour and the bodies in various degrees of decomposition and decay were either heaped up or strewed about just as they had left them, and yet after all, they were disappointed of their object as they did not find it.[26]

The pursuit of the enemy lasted a few days only, for when they reached Santarem and country adjacent, they took a strong position there in which they remained for nearly four months until they had exhausted every means of subsistence and made another desert. When found there after our last day's march, it was supposed their stay would only be temporary and to hurry them on an attack was

---

26 This must refer to the Igreja Matriz de Golega, otherwise known as the Igreja de Nossa Senhora da Conceicao built in the early sixteenth century.

ordered but countermanded immediately, for it was ascertained in time that they were strongly entrenched.

While the attack was pending and the troops *en echelon*, on and off the road were waiting in masses, I went to the extreme point of our advanced sentries and perceived the town of Santarem at a short distance on the brow of a hill and only approachable by a causeway across a swamp, the hill being evidently covered with abatis (consisting of felled trees with their branches pointing towards or from whence an enemy was expected), among which guns no doubt were masked and supported by other fortifications intended for a defence of some duration. There is something peculiar, and I may say awful, in the stillness which prevails between the advanced posts of two hostile armies when both are in a momentary state of quiescence previous to an expected contest. Silence occurs without bustle and yet both sides are watching with intensity each other's intentions and proceedings. A wanton act of mischief was committed by the French in making the abatis alluded to, in cutting down the olive trees for the purpose, by which they destroyed the produce of the land for several years and thereby deprived the inhabitants of their usual supply of oil forming one of their most important articles of food and light.

We on the contrary were positively enjoined not to injure trees of this description even when none other were to be had for cooking, which at times forced us to strange expedients as substitutes and it was a great act of forbearance on our part to spare these trees as they were known by every old soldier that they burnt best, even when green.

It having been determined by our chief that we should not act on the offensive, the troops were ordered in various cantonments and the brigade I was attached to proceeded to Alcoentrinho,[27] a small town or I should say village to which a few miserable inhabitants had returned in hopes of picking up a subsistence by our presence. It was situated a few miles from Cartaxo, Lord Wellington's headquarters.

---

27 This would appear to have been in the vicinity of modern-day Povoa do Manique.

The former was a most secluded spot in which nothing material occurred to break an everyday monotony during which we glided through the remainder of the year 1810 and entered 1811.

On our arrival there and taking up our quarters for the night, my servants could find no wood in the cottage we occupied, but as there was a large quantity of broken oil jars in an outhouse, pieces of them were heaped up on the scanty fire which had been kindled and as they were well saturated with oil we succeeded in having our victuals dressed and warming ourselves.

As we expected to remain in this place for some time until we drove the enemy away by force or starvation, or that they did it to us when reinforcements arrived which they were expecting, I set about my usual drudge work of making up the voluminous accounts of Pinhanços, and those of Espinhal which occupied all my leisure time and well it was so. For there was nothing to occupy anyone unless it was with the various reports in circulation, most of them without foundation respecting our movements, or those of the enemy, who it was expected might endeavour to cross the River Tagus, make an eruption into the Alentejo and another attempt on Lisbon by that side, which had not been equally fortified, for they were hemmed in on all sides by ourselves in their front, and on their flanks and rear by the Portuguese militia and Ordenanza, a species of *levee en masse* who allowed no foraging parties to move but such as were too strong for them to wander in search of provisions &c, so that a cordon of desolation surrounded the French army as it were round a wild beast, occupied by no-one and only traversed by patrols and forage parties on their respective duties. It was therefore a work of time and famine to decide this state of things, for as far as regarded ourselves we had ample provisions brought up the river from Lisbon and other places including the United States and England.

How our officers amused themselves in this remote situation was a riddle to me, for they had nothing to do, no books to read, no easy chairs to lounge on or show places to visit, or any other resource to occupy the mind & they could not be long absent from their regiments. Parades, drills and guards being the only duties they had to attend to.

The Honourable Colonel Cadogan,[28] Lord Wellington's brother-in-law[29] commanded one of our regiments, the 71st Light Infantry, and in consequence we were occasionally enlivened with his lordship's presence on a visit to him. He was a most gentlemanly, kind man but was subsequently cut off in this prime of life at the Battle of Vitoria at the head of his corps.

Another colonel of the name of Stewart commanded the 50th Regiment.[30] He was a singular man and adopted very whimsical modes of punishing his men. I happened accidentally to be present at a punishment parade where something of the sort was to take place. The culprits were brought forward for the purpose and after being stripped, he addressed them & told them that he intended to commute their punishment in his own way. They were entitled to their rations of spirits of which they could not be deprived, but he was determined they should have them as he thought would suit them best. The drummers were accordingly ordered to rub the men's backs with the liquor until it was evaporated & at times it was done on their stomachs, much to the amusement of the witnesses but to the disappointment of those concerned and it was found to have a salutary effect in repressing crime, spirits being extremely scarce and not always to be obtained from the sutlers.

A pioneer from one of the regiments was employed in issuing that article from the Quarter Master's stores to his corps and having a larger thumb than usual, managed to break the handle of the measure

---

28 Lieutenant Colonel the Honourable Henry Cadogan, 71st Foot, was killed at Vitoria in 1813.

29 Henry Cadogan's sister Charlotte was originally married to Wellington's brother Henry Wellesley, until she had an adulterous affair with Henry Lord Paget. Cadogan challenged Paget to a duel. They met but Paget did not aim at Cadogan and neither were hit. The duel was then abandoned, honour being satisfied.

30 Lieutenant Colonel Charles Stewart, 50th Foot, died 11 December 1812.

used for the purpose and in bailing it from the cask, the head of which had been removed, the thumb was constantly in the measure by which, in having to deliver a certain number of measures, he found himself at the end of the issue in possession of a considerable surplus which he of course appropriated to his use and got merry on it. He was however soon detected and the soldiers would not rest until the fraud was put an end to and the measure repaired. Before it was done many a hearty curse had been bestowed on the offending member.

1811

I rode occasionally to Cartaxo on duty and for news, but all was surmise and few knew what was really going on & those few kept it to themselves. The general opinion however was that when the reinforcements expected by the French arrived they would attack us, or famine must speedily force them to a retreat.

In one of these rides I was present at the funeral of the Marquis de la Romana,[31] one of the few good Spaniards; he had come to join us with a few troops of his nation, his death was considered a public loss to the cause of Spain and he died of a broken heart in deploring the misrule and misfortunes of his country. The funeral pageant was a military one of course, the apparent difference in it being by the admixture of British and Spanish officers, he being highly respected by both.

Evident symptoms of the movement alluded to occurred in the latter end of February and we were ordered to keep in readiness for whatever event might happen. To my great regret however, illness came upon me and though I hoped to overcome it without laying up, it gained ground so rapidly that when the French commenced their

---

31 Lieutenant General Caro y Sureda, Marquis of Romana, commanded a division of Spanish troops which had been repatriated by the Royal Navy from Denmark. He died of a breathing problem on 23 January 1811.

retreat to the frontier of Portugal and into Spain in the beginning of the month of March, after one day's march I was driven to the necessity of taking the advice of the surgeon & go to Lisbon where it was customary to send officers and men for the recovery of their health. I accordingly departed sorrowfully for that destination, through a country bearing the same calamitous evidences as before described of the infamous conduct of the French army in the destruction of everything for which they had no use, and it was only after re-entering the Lines of Torres Vedras by Vila Franca [Vila Franca de Xira] that accommodation & lodgings having a slight degree of comfort could be obtained.

I arrived in Lisbon in four days in a state of great exhaustion & having no place to go to, I threw myself on the kindness of a lady, a Mrs Morrough from whom I had already received much attention. She took me in at once & pressed me to remain, but as I required medical treatment I obtained military quarters in three days and went to reside in Rua do Pau da Bandeira, in the district called Buenos Ayres [Buenos Aries], the most salubrious suburb of the city, from which there is one of the most beautiful views in Europe, it overlooking on the right, the entrance and opposite side of the river; in the centre the river itself teeming with a magnificent squadron of men of war and an innumerable fleet of transports awaiting in case of need to carry us off, and on the left of the landscape was a great part of the city itself, beautifully situated on seven hills with a good deal of mercantile shipping and both banks of the river extending as far as the eye could reach.

A comfortable bed such as I had not been accustomed to for months, repose and good diet, to which I had equally been a stranger, performed wonders in bringing me to a state of convalescence. But it took months to get up my strength and render me again efficient to rough active duty in the field, although I soon got rid of my doctor who was a Naval medical officer whose acquaintance I had made and as I could not remunerate him by the offer of a sum of money which might have hurt his pride, he succeeded in paying himself as he thought best, for he got me to cash a bill of his for £15 on his Agent in London, which was dishonoured and I never heard of him more, or the money.

I was not allowed to eat the bread of idleness in my convalescence for when able to walk and work, I was attached to the office of Deputy Commissary General Vaux[32] in which all the accounts of the department were received and there from 8 o'clock in the morning to 4 o'clock in the afternoon, I was with several others occupied in pouring over uninteresting papers and making calculations without end. Our chief took it more leisurely, he was fond of gaiety, a good singer and I suspect not idle in the dissipations of the place, which in the end led to his ruin, for he was at last dismissed the service.

He was most gentlemanly and kind to us all but too fond of amusement to perform satisfactorily the very important duty confided to him. He took lessons in singing and his private apartments being next to the office, the first intimation of his being up was usually announced by a symphony which rather disturbed our serious occupation and was only concluded by making his appearance about 11 o'clock to assist in our labours. With such an example before us it could not be expected that we would profit by it; it was a source of disgust to me, and I was not therefore anxious to become permanently fixed there, as such a sedentary life did not suit me and I soon got tired of it.

In coming to Lisbon a second time (having been there last year on my first arrival in Portugal from England) my acquaintance as you will have perceived, was renewed with that excellent old lady, Mrs Morrough in her having so kindly received me in her house when unwell which I never can forget; and as I was always welcome at her house it proved a great resource to me and made my sojourn to Lisbon much more pleasurable than I could have expected.

---

32 Deputy Commissary General John Vaux served at Lisbon from February 1811 to April 1814. It would appear that he was declared bankrupt in 1828 having retired from the Commissariat Department.

3RD CAMPAIGN

To my old friends Messieurs Sandeman, Gooden and Forster of London[33] (the nephew of the former subsequently married the daughter of the latter, who was my brother in law[34]) I was indebted for an introduction to her as well as to a Mr Sealy, an influential merchant who was also very kind to me. Mrs M[orrough], was of Irish extraction and a Roman Catholic but not apparently a bigoted one. I accompanied the family, consisting of herself, their principal clerk, a daughter betrothed to him and another lady occasionally to Mass and if accidentally nearer than them to the basin of holy water, I dipped my fingers in it, which they touched and crossed themselves and yet they knew I was a Protestant. I visited them frequently at their country house, called a quinta, beautifully situated on the banks of the river. The house was large and the hall and staircases were curiously ornamented all round with Dutch glazed tiles to the height of five or six feet from the floor, representing religious or other subjects, which mode of decorations resembled in some measure fresco paintings and kept that part of the building cool by the glazing of the tiles, being a repellent of heat. The gardens were extensive and the luxuriance of a warm climate was strikingly exemplified in the size and beauty of the fruits and vegetables, which were constantly irrigated from the river by means of Persian wheels, and other contrivances; there was also a profusion of flowering shrubs but no attempt at an ornamental display such as would embellish an English parterre or lawn, clipping and keeping the branches within bounds being the extent of Portuguese taste and gardening.

Being allowed an occasional Holy day from office work, I accompanied this family one day to see a celebrated object of Roman Catholic superstition a short distance from their house. It had been brought to Lisbon from one of the principal towns in the interior on

---

33 George Sandeman was the senior partner, the other partners being two nephews.

34 His sister Elizabeth Carey married Albert Forster, making him his brother-in-law. Their only daughter (also Elizabeth) married George Sandeman.

the recent invasion of the French and was deposited in the church of a convent, its escort on its way down occasionally consisted of our own Protestant troops who were little aware of the absurdity they were employed in protecting with so much care. Its history is ridiculous but was nevertheless conscientiously believed by all who visited it devotionally.

In Portugal as well as in Spain there are many descendants of the Moors originally Mahommedans who from necessity, profess apparently Christianity and are called *Christans Novos* or New Christians. One of these new converts, but a follower of the prophetic church, doubting the real presence when in the act of receiving the Sacrament, instead of swallowing the consecrated wafer, slily spit from his mouth into his pocket handkerchief, and carried it home, having satisfied his curiosity he put it away as it was, in a cupboard or closet and thought nothing more of it for the moment; in the middle of the night however he was awoke by a strain of music, the meaning of which he could not understand, nor from whom or whence it came. It was repeated nightly and became from day to day more intense and at last was heard by his neighbours who wondered at, but could not explain how it happened. Public curiosity was excited at the occurrence and in the end attracted the notice of the clergy, who supposed the house to be haunted. Preparations were therefore made to exorcise the evil spirit, a procession was soon on the way to quiet it and as it entered the dwelling the music recommenced, the procession proceeded from whence it appeared to come and on entering the room a ray of light appeared to hover around the cupboard, and on opening it the host was found deluged in blood laying on the handkerchief. The supposed convert got frightened, confessed his crime and expiated his sin in an *auto da fe*,[35] the circumstance was considered miraculous and the handkerchief & its contents became the greatest acquisition the city could possibly possess. When we approached the place of pilgrimage, hundreds of persons were already at the

---

35 The pronunciation of the judgement of the Inquisition.

doors waiting their turn to go in. We followed the living stream and at last entered the church where this extraordinary curiosity was to be seen. It was placed on a large table contained in a superb and highly ornamented glass case; everyone immediately about it were on their knees praying, smiting their breasts, or crossing themselves, while others were looking at it in silent adoration and as they arose to depart each left an offering on the table which already groaned with heaps of money laying on it. The scene I must confess was full of interest from the genuine feeling evinced by the multitude. The only regret being that it could be so sincerely expressed & wasted in the belief of such a delusion. Having undertaken to be a good Catholic on the occasion, I did all that was prescribed to me in genuflections &c but determined to examine this singular idol, for I can give it no other name, when I got close. I did so and it appeared to me to consist of a fine white handkerchief rumpled up and on it lay the wafer partly decomposed with a few particles of matter resembling discoloured blood and flesh, very cleverly arranged to lead one to the conclusion that transubstantiation had taken place. When my party had paid their devotions and gratified their religious feelings, we departed following those who had equally performed the same duties. Objects of this description abounded everywhere in these countries to help keep up superstition and ignorance.

While in Lisbon I was present at another ceremony which though different, showed in some of its arrangements, an equal degree of absurdity, which after ages would hardly believe & this was in celebrating St George's day. The titular saint and protector of the city, his statue or effigy was kept in the castle and so contrived that it could be placed on horseback. On the previous evening it was informed in form that he would be required to command the garrison on the following day and was to give the watchword of the night and honour the procession by his presence. A return or state of the garrison was presented to him and he in reply as a matter of course was made to say that they might reckon on his company; in the meantime measures were taken to deck him out appropriately, jewellery to an enormous amount was borrowed from the nobility & others for the purpose, a horse superbly caparisoned was also provided and when both were joined together a more brilliant and valuable display could hardly be conceived.

Early on the 23 April, the garrison which had been increased for the occasion, turned out in full dress and lined the streets through which the procession was to pass, extending from the castle through certain parts of the city. All these streets had been laid down with fine sand and the houses from top to bottom with silk and satin draperies of every colour according to the fancy of the owner. I occupied through a friend's kindness, part of a balcony in Golden Street [Rua do Aurea] nearly in the centre, which being straight and tolerably broad embraced nearly the whole length of the pageant in looking to my right and left. It began by a most brilliant Staff going up to the castle and bringing back the saint as their chief in their midst; the members of the government, the nobility of every grade, the clergy including all religious fraternities, the military and every public functionary as well as every respectable private individual in their best attire and a more gorgeous scene or *coup d'oeil* I never witnessed or could be seen. I do not venture into details of the order of procession but the most conspicuous objects which attracted my attention, after the living part, were the crosses of the different convents, their size was enormous, requiring many men each to carry them & they had to put them down at short distances. They were gilt, massive and diversified in their make, and gave great effect to the ceremony considered the first without exception in the kingdom, and it was said the king and Royal family attended it when in the country, which must have greatly added to its magnificence, particularly when in peaceable times.

The circumstance of the effigy of St George taking the command of the garrison on this day and having a state, or return of it presented to it was not singular in those times, for many other saints were appointed colonels of regiments and were supposed to lead armies. Religion, or I should say its outward ceremonies, were engrafted on the habits of every individual in Portugal as well as Spain; no man's mind could be said to be his own, it being under the guidance of his confessor, church and state in close combination, ruled over the community with unbridled despotism and to keep it amused and in good humour or abject dependence, ceremonies of the description alluded to were of frequent occurrence. Saints of all sizes were placed in niches or glass cases at the corners of the streets, none of which were passed without bending the knee, making a sign of the cross, or a short prayer so that the mind, such as it was, was on the perpetual stretch to fulfil what was explicitly enjoined. Yet all this constant round of religious duties did not appear to have the slightest moral effect on the characters of those with whom we came in contact, or had dealings with, all were almost universally dishonest and consequently our intercourse with the natives was very limited and confined to business. Ignorance of their language was certainly a great obstacle to familiar intercourse, but their distrust of [us] socially was such that few English officers were ever admitted in the domestic circle, the jealous disposition of the men obliged the women to be cautious in giving us open encouragement towards an acquaintance and it was only on going to church or coming from it, or occasionally on promenades that they could be seen or admired. They were not the less disposed in our favour and had recourse in shewing it to many ingenious devices, a rose brought by an old woman round the stem of which a thin note covered with a green silk ribbon and hardly increasing the bulk of it, was one of the many expedients of communication which were multiplied without end according to circumstances and in general so well contrived as to baffle detection and it occasioned much demoralisation [turning aside morals] notwithstanding the danger of assassination by the stiletto.

Putting aside the feeling of the men on this particular point, their manners towards us were almost friendly and at times ridiculously so in our eyes and from being the most courteous people their attentions appeared superfluously overdone. 'Illustrious Sir' was the common mode of address in a letter and in personal intercourse out of doors the head was always uncovered. Two beggars covered with rags on meeting, bowed and took off the hat to each other and using the most fulsome compliments as to their health &c, in short, the extent of courtesy among all ranks was carried to an excess hardly to be conceived and never since witnessed by me, not even in France. Meeting a beggar and telling him you had no coppers by you, he readily offered to give you change for silver, or smaller copper for the larger you might possess, so that you were under the necessity of giving him a downright refusal to avoid his importunities.

Previous to the invasion of Portugal by the French, Lisbon was the most dirty city perhaps in the world, every sort of filth was thrown into the middle of the street and the accumulations were such that people on one side could hardly see others on the other side. By the exercise of arbitrary power this was soon corrected, but when they were expelled the nuisance was renewed though not to the full extent as formerly, for it was not considered prudent for us to enter into municipal arrangements which might prove distasteful to the inhabitants. The removal of the nuisance was therefore left as heretofore to the occasional heavy falls of rain which from the steepness of the streets swept all before them into the river until another accumulation required the same process. The only scavengers were packs of half-starved curs and innumerable rats which, strange to say, never interfered with each other and were almost insupportable to persons having to go out at night. With such impurities I cannot understand how the plague and other diseases were not occasional visitors, the stench being bad indeed.

I occasionally went to the Salitre Theatre[36] from which I had to cross the city to reach home. There were no lamps in the streets except the few before the saints [effigies] and I may say it was an affair of danger to go that distance: the dogs snarled and the rats crossed your path nearly tripping you and as the houses had no cesspools or sewers, all was

---

36 The Teatro de Salitre was one of the first theatres opened in Lisbon in 1782 and continued in operation until 1879 when it was demolished.

consigned to the street at that hour of night with the simple notification from the window required by law viz 'aqua vi' (here goes water) and a perilous shower it was at times coming as it did from every story [*sic*] and it could hardly be avoided, for in making a dart sideways the chance was that you might find yourself knee deep in a mass of accumulated liquid manure in the middle of the street, worse perhaps than what you were endeavouring to avoid, and as you went along you heard these avalanches in various directions; besides which street robberies were not unfrequent. It was therefore running amuck of the worst description and many an officer had his clothes completely spoilt. This is no exaggeration and it was so great a nuisance that many were deterred from going out at those hours unless it happened to be moonlight.

Of the sights in Lisbon such as museums &c I was not aware that any existed and if they did they were most probably closed in the then unsettled state of the country. Of externals, the churches were the most striking objects and though there were none conspicuously superior to the others, the chiselling of the exterior decorations in very hard stone was very beautiful. In the interior, gaudiness of ornament in respect to decorations of the building and [the] showy tinsel dress of the saints, prevailed as usual to attract and gratify the senses. In one church however, there was an object of attraction different from any others in one of the chapels, being entirely cased in mosaic; representing saints and other devices to the exclusion of any other ornament excepting the altar in imitation of those in St Peter's at Rome. It was the first work of art of that description I had seen and I thought it at first to be paintings on the wall.

In the old city, vestiges of the great earthquake in 1755[37] were still visible in some walls of churches still standing in ruins, which though of the most solid construction were rent from top to bottom.

---

37 At 09:40 on 1 November 1755, Lisbon was struck by an earthquake estimated by seismologists to have measured 7.7 on the Richter scale. The earthquake was followed by a tsunami which engulfed much of the lower city and fires also raged destroying much of what remained. Estimates of deaths vary wildly from 12,000 to 50,000.

It must indeed have been a most awful event and is still alluded to with dismay and no wonder, for occasionally visitations in a milder form occur to create uneasiness. When there, one occurred; several of us were at dinner when a noise resembling the rumbling of carriages was heard as if under our feet, but yet so strange as to appear unearthly. Immediately after, the glasses on the table began to totter & the apartment to vibrate and slightly rock. We stared at each other, but it struck none of us at the moment that it was an earthquake. We were however instantly undeceived by the alarmed people, the most dreadful screams were heard and it was frightful to see the people rush in the greatest consternation from the houses into the streets, where they thought they would be in greater safety. A calm succeeded and we learnt that it was not at the shock which had passed that they had got frightened as it was not a violent one, but in expectation of a worse one which often followed its milder precursor. It however did not fortunately follow on this instance, for we had quite enough of what had already taken place and were glad to escape with the apprehension it occasioned, for after witnessing such a scene at which the stoutest hearts must be appalled, the dread it usually occasions in the community can easily be imagined.

Putting aside the miseries which the great catastrophe alluded to occasioned, it proved like the great fire of London of great advantage to posterity, in the rebuilding of the city on an improved plan, the principal features of which was Black Horse Square (there being an equestrian bronze statue of one of their Kings in it[38]) another [square[39]], and two large streets called Gold and Silver Streets[40] which, according to ancient custom of keeping trades separate, were

---

38 The Praca do Comercio, better known to many soldiers as Black Horse Square, is a large plaza fronting onto the River Tagus and housed most of the Portuguese ministry buildings. The statue at its centre depicts King Jose I on horseback.

39 King Pedro IV Square is better known as Rossio Square.

40 The Rua Aurea and Rua da Prata still exist.

occupied, the former by goldsmiths and the latter by silversmiths, but their shops compared with the external display in those of London were mean & paltry, arising probably from the apprehensions of robbers and from a habitual dread that too great a show might render them liable to extortion from arbitrary authority.

In one of my occasional rides I visited the great aqueduct which supplies the city with water;[41] it is regarded by the natives as the eighth wonder of the world and it is certainly a stupendous work, connecting by a row of arches two hills across a deep valley; from whatever point it is seen its grandeur is striking, more especially when it is viewed from the foot of the centre or great arch, so broad and high in its span as to admit, was there water [beneath], a line of battleships to sail through with all its sails set. Had however, the principal of hydraulics been understood when erected of water rising to its own level, pipes might have been substituted in its stead, although it is now asserted that they could not have answered, as the water is calcareous & leaves such a sediment or encrustation in its course which if not removed occasionally would block up the passages.

I lived in the neighbourhood of the residence of one of the richest individuals in Portugal, Bandeira by name. His palace is in a row of a street but had fine gardens in the back.[42] He had been it was said, reduced to poverty by the extortions of the French generals who were quartered on him and who obliged him to keep open table for them, their Staff and anyone they chose to invite, receiving at the same time and putting in their pockets the allowance granted them for the purpose by the authorities of the city, a mode of proceeding adopted by Junot the commander in chief and which was followed with alacrity by those under his command who could with impunity take it on themselves thus to pillage the inhabitants of a country which they declared they were entering as friends and protectors.

---

41 The Aqueduto das Aguas Livres built between 1731 and 1799.

42 Jacinto Fernandes da Costa Bandeira (1777–1818), a very wealthy merchant.

At the time I first arrived in Lisbon the city was still crowded with fugitives from the country which had been occupied by the enemy and it also swarmed with our soldiers & sailors from the large fleet & fresh arrivals from England, which gave it an air of bustle which gradually disappeared when it became evident from the retreat of the French that they could not return at least for a season. Most of the transports and part of the fleet were therefore sent home and no one could regret it, for it was melancholy to hear of the numbers of our sailors who were daily & nightly assassinated in drunken broils with the lowest grade of inhabitants who scrupled not in a state of irritation to use their murderous knives in avenging themselves; absolution being easily obtained in the belief that Protestants had no souls and might be destroyed like dogs, and though our admirals interfered, witnesses could not be found to convict the perpetrators and the murders continued.

Lisbon being the greatest port and the only one in which large ships could enter in Portugal, continued throughout the war the pivot of operations to our army. It was therefore the centre of great activity and bustle and was besides the headquarters of the Navy. Reinforcements of troops arrived there from England & were equipped for the interior; in it the General Hospital was established and it also contained the Grand Magazines of provisions, forage, ammunition and every description of stores connected with the material of our army, nearly all the money required for the public service was obtained there by negotiation. In short, everything necessary to carry on the war emanated from thence and it of course collected many speculators and money making men. In a small contractor with whom I had transacted business in 1809 on a very small scale, I recognised the future Portuguese Rothschild, of the name of Sampayo.[43] He had already risen to importance and it was him who fixed the rate of exchange when he appeared on change & he at last monopolised the

---

[43] Henrique Teixeira de Sampaio, 1st Conde de Povoa and Barao de Teixeira (1774–1833).

negotiations of the Treasury bills, so that everyone requiring to make a remittance had to apply to him for a bill. Fortune spoilt him and [he] was so lavish of her favours that he became almost indifferent to them; he was in the habit of carrying in his pockets bills to a large amount, so long at times, that when found they were hardly legible and could not be made use of. Of the extent of his money transactions with the British Commissariat no one concerned in mere private affairs could form an idea. They were enormous and embraced the principal part of the expenditure of our government in Portugal, amounting annually to millions of pounds sterling and no one can conceive the waste it occasioned; one item out of very many may be cited, from the scarcity of coin, the premium on it in exchange for bills payable at the Treasury in England amounted at last to a loss of 25 per cent, the soldiers being paid in dollars at 4/6d. each and the government buying them at 6/- in their negotiations.

Time wore on and being perfectly recovered, I was in daily expectation of being called up to the army, but the storekeeper who had plundered the public stores in my charge at Coimbra to whom I have before alluded, having been arrested, I was detained some time longer in case his trial came on. It did not however take place and in July I received orders to hold myself in readiness for active service after a residence in Lisbon of four months and a half, and I was not sorry for the move as the place was very dear and temptations to expense without end. Before I left I met a Guernseyman of the name of Dobree[44] one day in the streets just arrived from the island who gave me a deal of gossip which made me long to go back again, besides which I occasionally had other souvenirs from home in the shape of butter, packets & clothes sent me by the kind attention of my dear mother.

---

44 As he does not mention him being a Commissary he almost certainly refers to a cousin of Deputy Assistant Commissary General John Dobree, who served in the Peninsula from November 1808 to January 1809 and then from May 1810 to April 1814, his siblings being too young.

During my stay in Lisbon the French had been ejected from Portugal but had got hold of the important Spanish fortress of Badajoz after a short siege, through the treachery of the governor only a few days before it might have been relieved.[45] A great deal of hard fighting also occurred on the frontier round Almeida, the French garrison of which eluded the blockade of our troops by a ruse and got away during the night although completely surrounded by them, much to the mortification of Lord Wellington.[46] It was in fact so bold and hazardous an undertaking that no one imagined that it could ever be attempted; endeavours were also made to recover Badajoz and in attempting to besiege it & cover the operation, the sanguinary Battle of Albuera was fought which did not redound to the military credit of Lord Beresford as a tactician.[47] No one ever doubted however his capacity for organising an army but from that day his abilities to manoeuvre were questioned and not much relied on.

Many rumours were afloat regarding some of the regiments which fought there especially in respect of the 3rd or Buffs who were reported as having been annihilated excepting about 50 officers and men still remaining; and that being the case this little band were ordered to the rear preparatory to be sent to England for regimental [re-]organisation, when lo and behold at a parade held before their

---

45 Badajoz was besieged by the army of Marshal Soult from 27 January until 10 March 1811. The Spanish defenders under General Menacho put up a spirited defence, but on his death on 3 March, his less able successor General Imaz capitulated despite knowing that a relief force was on its way.

46 When the French were forced out of Portugal in March 1811, they left a force of 1,400 men in the fortress of Almeida under the command of General Brenier. Following the defeat of a relieving force at the Battle of Fuentes d'Onoro, Brenier abandoned the fortress in the night of 10 May, blowing up its defences and successfully crossing the bridge at Barba del Puerco into French territory, losing less than a quarter of his troops. The Duke of Wellington was apoplectic with rage when he heard of the escape.

47 Fought on 16 May 1811, Albuera was an extremely bloody and indecisive battle with both sides losing over 7,000 killed, wounded and prisoners. Marshal Soult retiring afterwards allowed Beresford to claim a victory, but to the soldiers who fought in it, it was a bloodbath for which they blamed Beresford.

departure for Lisbon 600 men made their appearance and reported that they had been made prisoners & got off during the night in the confusion which occurred in the enemy's camp after their defeat, in consequence of which the regiment went for a length of time under the nickname of the 'Resurrection Boys'.[48]

I left Lisbon on the 18 July 1811 accompanied by a Portuguese of the name of Ferriera who had been a clerk in the department and hoped through my means to be again employed, and a Mr Beckett,[49] a great woollen manufacturer of Leeds, whose acquaintance I had made at the house of my very kind friend Mrs Morrough. He had come to enquire into the nature of Merino wool & wished to ascertain by personal enquiry and examination the particular species of sheep which produced it and every particular connected with their pasture, treatment &c by going on the spot; he wished also to see something of campaigning, having many friends in the army and as I found him an intelligent and gentlemanly man rather my senior in age, I was glad of his company.

Decent accommodation for sleeping ceased after we had passed the lines of defence within which no enemy had entered, for few only of the inhabitants had as yet returned home or put their houses in any order. Indeed from Villa Franca [Vila Franca de Xira] to Abrantes the destruction of buildings &c was to an extent without parallel (unless a comparison is made with the Palatinate[50] in the time of Louis the

---

48 The battalion numbered 909 other ranks of which 695 were with the battalion in April 1811 (others sick and on command). The May figure is reduced to 537 in total with only 102 with the battalion (with 214 listed as dead and the rest sick/wounded and on command), by August it is up to 676 other ranks with 405 with the battalion and by September they were up to 934 other ranks with 536 with the battalion. However, this includes 300 men having arrived in August from the second battalion, therefore claims that large numbers of prisoners escaped from the French cannot be borne out by the figures.

49 Mr John Beckett was a partner in the bank of Beckett, Calverley & Co. and he also had merchant interests, importing and exporting to Portugal. He was from a family of wool merchants. He owned Somerby Park in Lincolnshire.

50 The Palatinate is the area of South-West Germany.

XIV of France) and done in wantonness by men having more the semblance of a banditti than a disciplined army.

The towns of Golegao [Golega] and Santarem suffered most ill-treatment and among the heaps of rubbish accumulated in various parts of the latter town, during the time of its occupation by the French, the bodies of children were found which had died from want & misery and had no one to bury them. Half of the inhabitants were supposed to have perished from hardship, famine and disease in this wretched warfare and never saw the day of again taking peaceful possession of their homes [which were] mostly in ruins. My friend was astounded at the desolation thus exhibited on our journey and soon repented of having left Lisbon and its comforts. It was intensely hot and though a fine healthy & athletic man, the change of food & intense heat of weather brought on him dysentery which was then prevalent and as the symptoms became violent & pulled him down, I soon had to nurse him.

I had brought with me a Brazilian cot similar to a sailor's hammock entirely made of white cotton netting, which could be hung up in a room by driving a couple of nails in the walls or between two trees if in camp, its greatest comfort being when thus suspended to defy the approaches of vermin which swarmed everywhere, particularly in the filthy houses we were likely to be lodged in, to such an extent was this annoyance that it was at times impossible to remain in them; the fleas were in such multitudes as really to blacken in appearance the blankets & the bugs issued from every crack and corner in numbers hardly credible, but by those who suffered from their persecutions, beds or bedsteads were a scarce article at this time and unless your own mattress, with which you travelled, could be placed on the large boxes in which the inhabitants kept their valuables or corn should such have been spared, or cot suspended, the only resource against the molestation was to bolt and seek repose wrapped up in your cloak in the garden or street, leaving the blankets &c in the possession of your enemy until morning when a very summary process ejected him and that was by putting the bed clothes in the sun, the heat of which made these insects hop off as so many parched peas and disappear summarily. This cot I resigned to my friend until I could get him to a place where he might be attended to by a doctor, whom we found at Abrantes on the River Tagus.

During the eruption of the French in Portugal this place was of great service to us, for being an old Moorish fortress intended to cover the communication between both sides of the river by a bridge of boats, it had been fortified and retained by us and it had since become the great thoroughfare from Lisbon to the army now principally stationed near Elvas, as well as the head of terminus of the water channel for the conveyance of provisions &c.

Being partly situated on a hill & down the slope of it, the view was most extensive & beautiful & the ancient battlements of the castle having in many places remained without alteration with the old stairs leading up to the walls and the standing room on them for the archers to shoot from, protected by a small parapet still perfect, took me back to days of yore when the Muslim had the dominion.

This place was a thorn in the side, or more properly speaking, in the back of the French army, for it was in their rear while in front of the Lines and was the only practicable way for attacking Lisbon on the southern side of the river. The place having therefore escaped from being plundered, we again met with some comforts and I was enabled to leave my suffering friend under the care of a brother Commissary who most kindly and effectually attended him, for I learnt that he had speedily become convalescent and was gone back to Lisbon quite cured of the little specimen he had had of campaigning and of taking journeys after Merino sheep.

I lost no time in resuming my journey and arrived at Portalegre on the 25 July; situated in the province of the Alentejo a part of the country which the French had not visited & our travelling was therefore comparatively free from inconveniences. Lord Wellington's headquarters had just arrived when I reported myself and I was set to work in the office of the Commissary General (expected from Lisbon) by Assistant Commissary General Dumaresq,[51] a Jerseyman who had the general superintendence for the moment.

The duty was excessive, being from 6 in [the] morning until 9 at night with only time allowed for meals; a sharp drill for a commencement and might have continued, in expectation that we should remain where we were for the remainder of the summer, which notwithstanding those official exertions, was much desired by many from the accommodations and means of subsistence being the best in Portugal. This dream of quiescence and luxury was however soon disturbed, for the army was suddenly ordered to march to the north by the picturesque ford & ferry of Villa [Vila] Velha on the Tagus (over which a flying bridge was subsequently constructed for greater celerity of movement) and occupy a poor and wasted country near the fortress of Almeida.

I reached Castello [Castelo] Branco about halfway & was directed to remain there for the moment to hurry on the convoys of provisions &c after the troops, who were going to prevent if possible the introduction of supplies into Ciudad Rodrigo then occupied by a French garrison and blockaded by the Spaniards & our troops and as the operation continued longer than was expected and headquarters had proceeded on, I was not called up to resume my situation in the Commissary General['s] office, but was directed to remain where I was & continue the duty entrusted to me until ordered once again to take the depot of provisions under my immediate charge.

Castello [Castelo] Branco had become the great thoroughfare to the army and a General Hospital station, so that I found myself in

---

51 Assistant Commissary General Thomas Dumaresq who served in the Peninsula from October 1810 to September 1813. The Army Lists show that Carey is correct and that the Challis List is incorrect in showing him as a Deputy Commissary General. Captain Lionel Challis between the wars painstakingly produced a card index of the services of every British officer that served in the Peninsular War or 'Peninsula Roll Call'. The cards now reside in the library at RUSI, but a digitised version is available online at www.napoleon-series.org.

the exercise of another troublesome occupation which under existing circumstances could not be carried on to the satisfaction of all parties. Provisions and forage corn were scanty, all who applied to me expected to get what they would have been entitled to had abundance prevailed, but it could not of course be done. I was therefore beset by applicants describing themselves as starving, among whom was the whole medical staff of the station, with the chief at their head, who not only loudly importuned for themselves but for the sick and it not being in my power at all times to act up to their wishes, innumerable complaints were forwarded up to headquarters and when the difficulties had been obviated on the spot, I received, to add to my embarrassment, violent *Philipperis* [admonishments] from the Commissary General for not doing what was impossible. It was not the age of enquiry, first to ascertain the cause of the difficulty & lay the blame on the right person, as that would have been too slow a process, but the blow was given and whether right or wrong it was supposed at any rate to stimulate exertion in overcoming future impossibilities.

As my occupations were incessant I had hardly time to escape from them out of the town. An occasional hour's ride being as much as I could well afford, but during that time I saw enough of the country to satisfy my curiosity. The city as it is called had the appearance of a poor country town with a few good houses in it, surrounded by an old wall and is situated at the foot of a high conical hill on which there is an old castle from which it derives its name. From the top of it is a most extensive view of mountain, hill and dale and having been a border fortress was in those times from its height, a conspicuous object from whence to convey to the surrounding villages the alarm of an approaching enemy. The country was poor and barren, uninteresting and scantily cultivated with large patches of gum cistus, the haunt of wolves, who abounded in every direction and could be seen at the dawn of day returning to the mountains after a nightly prowl in search of food; they were most destructive to sheep which could only be preserved by dogs of formidable size. I never saw more beautiful and powerful animals, they carried a huge collar bristling with spikes and their sagacity equalled their appearance for unless they remained within the fold at night on the defensive with the shepherd to back them with his long pole which he knew how to use most effectively, they were sure to fall a sacrifice to the cunning of their adversary whose ruse was to decoy them singly from the fold as if taking flight and then with the assistance of others lying in wait for the purpose, dispatch them, a dog being hardly more than a match for a wolf even with his collar, but when in contest both being occupied in the strife, on the shepherd coming up he could deal his blows as he liked and so effectively that the poor wolf had little chance against two antagonists.

There was no difficulty in seeing a wolf early in the morning and he could be easily approached at the distance of 1 or 2 hundred yards, his appearance being that of a large ugly, shaggy, dark brown dog and when attempted to be approached nearer, sneaking away as if reluctantly, and occasionally looking back to see if he was pursued. The times were to them those of abundance and surfeit, for the roads on which the army moved were sprinkled generally with dead mules, oxen & asses which were soon picked to the bone and in these banquets they were usually assisted by vultures numerous as themselves. They seldom quarrelled and if perchance a sudden turn of the road brought you suddenly on one of these meetings, the wolves were taking the first course and the birds were waiting at a short distance like patience on a monument for their turn. If however there was room for all the guests, they might be seen partaking of the food at the same time.

I took a fancy to one of these sheep dogs in the shape of a puppy, intending to rear him and bring him home, but I failed in domesticating him for he took every opportunity of escaping from my lodgings and was always found in the fold among the sheep, and after many trials I found his instinct was greater than my perseverance. My clerk,

3RD CAMPAIGN

afterwards Sir George Head, undertook a more difficult task, that of rearing a young wolf and for a time the attempt succeeded and all went on peaceably, until fits of his savage nature occasionally broke out by his snapping at strangers when loose, which became more frequent as he grew older, and it was found at last necessary to destroy him as no one was safe who came into the yard in which he was kept.

Among the reinforcements which had lately arrived from England there was a Heavy brigade of cavalry consisting of the 3rd Dragoons & 4th and 5th Dragoon Guards[52] to the command of which my countryman and kinsman, Major General Le Marchant[53] was appointed[54] and on his way to headquarters, I called on him and was very kindly received. He asked me if I felt inclined to be under his orders, for if I did he would apply to the Commissary General for that object. I readily accepted his offer for various reasons, the principal of which was my anxiety to go again into the field with troops, to be in the midst of occurring events and avoid the troublesome and thankless office of sticking into a depot in the rear, in which neither credit [n]or advancement could be obtained, and having as I conceived incurred the displeasure of my chief unjustly, some exertion in a different line of duty was necessary to relieve me from that odium; and feeling as I did a consciousness of having always done what was required of me, I knew that time and opportunity alone would remove any existing impression of that nature that could exist.

I had heard of an intended promotion in the department and from what I have just written was not over sanguine as it regarded myself. A short time after however, when least expected, I was agreeably surprised and gratified to find that I had not been overlooked. I knew that a new Commissary General was coming up from Lisbon and

---

52 3rd and 4th Dragoons. The 5th Dragoon Guards did not arrive until October, the other two regiments having arrived in August.

53 Major General John Gaspard Le Marchant. He was killed at the Battle of Salamanca.

54 The General Order announcing the formation of the brigade is dated 29 January 1812.

[was] to pass through my station. He came and I went of course to pay him my respects and would have invited him to dinner had my establishment warranted it, but it was on too humble a scale to make the attempt. He told me in conversation that he had the list of promotions among his papers but had not it about him, neither did he recollect names. Seeing my anxiety however, he was so good as to go in another room and look for it and having found and perused it, he announced to me the gratifying information that I was promoted, and among the fortunate ones, to the rank of Assistant Commissary General, commission bearing date 10 August 1811, a step of the greatest importance to me as by it I was eligible to higher employments.[55]

At times the Spanish guerrillas distinguished themselves in surprises, and during the month of October a very cunning ambuscade occurred in which the French governor of Ciudad Rodrigo[56] fell into the hands of Don Julian Sanchez, the famous guerrilla chief. The cattle of the garrison went out occasionally grazing and being on the watch for them in case they exceeded the bounds within which they could be protected, he pounced on them in the act with the governor, who in his ride had equally gone too far, trusting no doubt to the fleetness of his horse. In his way down to Lisbon as a prisoner I dined with him at our commandant's, and from knowing French I found him very entertaining in many ways. He was very talkative and cheerful considering his situation and circumstances and finding the table not very well lighted he begged that more lights might be put on as he could not enjoy his dinner in comparative darkness. There was much cunning in his countenance and he was very naturally much incensed against the guerrillas whom he called a set of brigands for having played him such a trick and for the petty annoyance they were to the French armies. His opinion was that the affairs in Spain were going *à*

---

55 Published in General Orders of 20 November 1811.

56 Brigadier General Reynaud was captured by Don Julian Sanchez.

merveille [perfectly] for the French, although he acknowledged that the war was the most cruel and harassing to them which they had ever undertaken.

A week however had hardly passed since his departure when a most dashing affair as a surprise, took place at Arroyo de los Molinos [Arroyomolinos][57] to falsify his assertions of the prosperity of his nation, for a whole brigade were almost all taken prisoners by Lord Hill in which the good feeling of the Spaniards was exemplified in a most patriotic way, for owing to circumstances our troops were unavoidably obliged to encamp all night very near the place, and though it was known to many of the inhabitants, not one divulged the fact, and the French slept unconcernedly and were next morning pounced upon before they were prepared for resistance.

My avocations continued for some time longer much as usual without any occurrence worth relating. I was quartered on a padre (a parish priest) a man of superior intelligence who had travelled and was more communicative than most of his cloth and that was because he spoke a little French. He was beyond the mark of intellect of his nation. The olive oil in common consumption & one of the indispensable ingredients in Portuguese cookery, had a most nauseous taste to anyone but natives and having seen in France & Italy the mode of making it, he thought he might introduce in his country the improved method. He tried it on his own property but it would not answer, for no one would purchase such a tasteless article and such was the force of habit that he was under the necessity of retrograding from his intentions and perpetuate this disgusting relish which made people hardly approachable after they had taken their meals, in which this oil & garlic were the principal ingredients.

He used occasionally to amuse me with professional anecdotes but more especially in respect to confession which to him at times

---

57 This action occurred on 28 October 1811, General Hill's corps surprising General Girard's force and killing up to 500 and capturing around 1,500.

was most wearysome [*sic*], when he had old women to hearken to, for he said their long stories of imaginary sins, wicked thoughts and other most stupid matter provoked him at times almost beyond endurance when he had something else to attend to and yet he was obliged to listen to them without curtailing their ideas. I am sorry to say his morals were not apparently in accordance with his enlightened mind, for he followed the custom of having a *niece* at the head of his establishment who quietly regulated it, and it being habitual among the clergy it created neither scandal or surprise.

I had no town acquaintance with the exception of meeting a priest or other person at the Post Master's house, the usual place of assembly for gossips to hear the news and I knew the Post Master from having business to transact with him, for he was one of the contractors for the supply of the troops. I found him an intelligent person & one of the very few who knew anything beyond the neighbourhood; when Marshal Junot[58] first invaded Portugal in 1808, and passed through Castello [Castelo] Branco, my acquaintance was then Post Master and was, so he said, called in to concoct the proclamation to be addressed to the Portuguese nation, the rough draft of which he had in his possession and as a great favour he gave it to me and it is now among my papers.[59] It promised protection, peace and freedom, and the result was 'such protection as vultures give to lambs, eating and devouring them'.

I having waited with some impatience the result of General Le Marchant's application to change my duty, I was put out of all further suspense in the beginning of November by the receipt of an order to join the 3rd Dragoons under the command of Major Clowes[60] which were arriving from Abrantes &c and it was notified to me at the same time that a successor to my present charge would soon be sent, at

---

58 Junot was a General de Division. He was promised a Marshal's baton for capturing Lisbon, but it was not forthcoming.

59 Unfortunately no longer extant.

60 Major William Clowes, 3rd Dragoons. He resigned from the army on 10 December 1812.

which I was much delighted; he did come and when on the point of transferring to him everything concerning it, as bad luck would have it, he fell sick of an ague from the place being unhealthy and was obliged to proceed at once towards Lisbon leaving me for the present saddled with two duties, but as there was fortunately no chance of the troops moving, I did not mind it much.

The regiment having come up, I was introduced to all the officers, who were a most gentlemanly set of men & with them I served for a whole year, in the subsequent most brilliant campaign. Having just arrived in the country they were without experience and I could perceive they were not much in raptures at the little roughing they had experienced after the comforts of home. They now prepared to take the field in completing their equipments and baggage animals, and for the latter object a dealer in mules came with a number to dispose of and many were accordingly purchased. Among the number for sale was a very fine grey one upon which every eye was fixed in its favour, but he kept it back apparently unwilling to recommend it; he however at last offered it for a trifle to the commanding officer, if in three days it could be rendered serviceable, declaring at the same time that it was most vicious. The offer was accepted and the rough rider of the corps[61] bestrode it immediately, and the moment he was mounted & had given it the rein, it rushed to a wall and scraped itself along it in such a way as to injure his knee severely. It was then taken to the open fields where it kicked and reared until quite exhausted. Next day and the day after a similar scene took place with the same result and when every man had had his turn of riding who chose it, the endeavour was given up as hopeless as to the astonishment of our dragoons who had never before had such an obstinate animal to deal with, the dealer declaring that everything had before been done to tame it without success and the only use he could put to it was to carry heavy burdens when its uncertain temper would allow it.

---

61 British cavalry regiments appointed a 'rough rider' (a private or NCO) to train new horses and to teach equitation under the supervision of the Riding Master.

It was customary to sell cast horses of the artillery and cavalry as were rendered unserviceable or required rest and treatment to recover them and they were usually sold for a mere trifle, oftentimes not realising more than a dollar (4s/6d) or two, and one of these periodical sales took place while I was in Castello [Castelo] Branco. In the midst of it, my Portuguese groom came to tell me that there was an artillery horse with a supposed incurable quittor[62] on one of his feet which he thought he could cure. I gave him leave to buy it in consequence, which he did for one dollar and by care and quiet it became perfectly sound and I afterwards sold it for 100 dollars, the only advantageous transaction I recollect ever to have made in horseflesh.

General Le Marchant came to reside at Castello [Castelo] Branco and was quartered in the Bishop's palace outside the walls of the town, which palace would have been considered a fine building anywhere.[63] It had a parterre garden very well laid out and orangeries, which almost made it a show place, compared with any other place in the neighbourhood. I occasionally dined with him and our conversation often turned on Guernsey, but having lately lost his wife he was in bad spirits.[64] Fortunately for him the duties of his brigade gave him full occupation; it was the finest and strongest in the peninsula mustering above 1,400 horses or I should say sabres, they looked very well with the exception of still wearing the old fashioned cocked hat which looked antiquated and tasteless and must have been most uncomfortable to the men in rainy weather, for when saturated with water the cocks of it hung down like the ears of a spaniel. As a whole however they made a most formidable appearance mounted on

---

62 An old term for a condition that involves the death (necrosis) of collateral cartilage in the foot following an infection. This often causes occasional lameness and in extreme cases can cause permanent deformity.

63 The incumbent was Bishop Vicente Ferreira da Rocha who was bishop from December 1782 to 25 August 1814 when he died.

64 His wife Mary (née Carey) died in 1811 during childbirth.

magnificent plump horses fresh from England, yet it was anything but encouraging to bring forward men as they were, without the slightest experience in war to contend with an enemy inured to it for many years.

Christmas day passed without a move and we were consequently left to enjoy it as best we could and as I thought I should do more than usual on the occasion of my recent promotion, by keeping it merrily with the members of the department within reach, I invited them to dinner and my servant was ordered to exert himself in procuring the best victuals that could be procured in the place and neighbourhood. We did not muster more than six including a young Guernsey man on his way to headquarters who had recently arrived from the island and just entered the department;[65] the first course consisted of soup & bouille, the second of a fine round of corned beef,[66] roast turkey and half a ham and the third of a rice pudding & cheese followed by fruit and a plentiful supply of good Douro wine to which we did full credit by toasting our absent friends &c. It was a very unusual meal in the very poor country we occupied and must have cost much ingenuity & labour to my servant as the expense did to me in getting it; two important requisites we could not however obtain in the way of knives & plates, forks &c, the supply of which was very scanty, but the deficiency was made up by good appetites and buoyant hearts which enabled us to enjoy ourselves most happily and more so by me than I had done for the past two years.

Being obliged at times to ride out on duty in superintending the collection of forage, I often went in villages remotely situated and where troops were never seen, being quite out of the line of movement.

---

65 This would appear to be Mr Joseph Gillespie who was appointed a Deputy Assistant Commissary General on 24 January 1812, having arrived in the Peninsula in November 1811. See General Order of 18 March 1812.

66 Corned beef from Ireland had been used by the Royal Navy since the seventeenth century. At this time it came in three qualities, 'small beef', 'cargo beef' and 'best mess beef'.

The inhabitants were half wild and in a state of ignorance hardly to be imagined, priestcraft walked triumphant and the poor creatures were made to believe everything that was told them by their pastors, some of the saints in the churches had moveable eyes and arms and when a sermon was preached and the saints invoked, they were made to raise the one & appear to shed tears from the other when required, as a sign of approval or recognition of the appeal made, machinery was of course resorted to and as it was only practised where it could be done [in] safety. The more knowing Catholics treated it with contempt and having been accompanied in one of these excursions by my Portuguese clerk, Signor Alves Ferreira, he told me in ridicule of the absurdity, that on a recent occasion when the image was called upon to show the usual signs of vitality, the clown whose business it was to pull the wires and [who] was concealed in a hidden place, impatiently called out that the saint was dull and would not stir, which occasioned much dismay to the officiating priest & surprise to the poor ignorant auditory.

On another occasion having found a capital trout stream, I prevailed on an officer who had a fly fishing apparatus to accompany me; we descended from the village to a mill situated over a good run of water and asked the miller where the fish were in the greatest abundance; he pointed out the spot but said it was useless to attempt catching them as he had never succeeded and we should do the same. Hook and line had been his tools and he was of course totally ignorant of the superiority of ours; he watched our proceedings with great attention and soon saw a fine fish landed, his surprise was great but when he saw a second captured he was astounded, ran away from the spot and went into the village spreading a report that we were bewitching the fish and taking them by diabolical means. Terror seized the inhabitants and the priest was soon apprised of it, the bells rang and a crowd headed by him descended to witness our proceedings. By that time we had several fish, he came forward by himself, looked on for a little time and then requested to know how we managed [it], but which we withheld telling him as being none of his business, until he told us that unless we complied with his request he could not answer for our safety. From the excitement the people were in and as he evidently appeared in earnest, we did so and explained to him the process of fly fishing which he at once understood, but very cunningly kept it to himself and though peace and quiet was at once restored, we found on enquiry that he had not made it known, wishing as we supposed, to keep his flock from being as enlightened as himself. The miller returned to his mill but would accept of none of the fish which we offered to him.

The tricks played at times on credulous old women when an opportunity offered, created occasionally astonishment and fright in the small villages on the high road; the people having got tired of the continual passage of troops and their provisions falling short, they refused to sell anything and in anticipation of such difficulties being experienced, it was customary with many officers to carry with them portable soup cakes[67] to have recourse to in case of need, and if in humour for it and that the old woman in the cottage was unusually disobliging which often happened; she was civilly requested to put a pot with water on the fire and go into her yard and fetch a stone, clean it and put it into the pot, for rather than starve her guest was determined to see if soup could not be made from it, and being requested to obtain any vegetable she could find or purchase adding thereto a little salt; in the meantime two or three cakes of the soup during her absence were slipped into the pot which having boiled with the ingredients it contained the old lady was requested to taste it & in the instance in which I was concerned, it is difficult to describe her countenance when she had swallowed a spoonful, for it was a mixture of surprise, astonishment & fear, surprise at its goodness and fear lest some magical or other wicked expedient had been used which might be extended to her while we were under her roof, she

---

67 A block of dehydrated soup, which could be reconstituted in water.

would not be prevailed to partake of the pottage, and we left her in ignorance of the mode of making it.

Castello [Castelo] Branco having had, like every other part of the Portugal north of the Tagus, several visitations from the enemy, the inhabitants had become experienced in concealing what they could not take away when they fled even to their money, which they ingeniously disposed of in the following manner. They got a long round bar of iron made to the size of the coin, to be buried at the centre of three angles of three points such as a tree or hole in a wall &c having been ascertained in their garden or elsewhere, a hole or more was sunk with the bar to a certain depth and the money was singly dropped into it until within a foot of the surface and then the hole was filled up with mould and in making these holes care was taken to have boards to tread upon during the operation so that no trampling or displacement of ground could be perceived. For whenever the French suspected that such a concealment had taken place they threw water on the spot, and if any sinking was perceived they at once dug for the prize. This process however balked them invariably and the boast was that whenever it had been adopted success was sure to follow, and it was said to have been extensively applied from gold and silver (copper of course included) being exclusively the circulating medium & the only property beside land possessed by the inhabitants there being neither public funds, banks or other places of deposit in which capital could be invested.

The habits of the Portuguese are in general anything but cleanly both in their persons and houses and everyone in the army being billeted on them when not encamped, occupied apartments in private houses, in which it was at times impossible to avoid contamination from vermin and contagious diseases, by lying in beds which hardly had time to cool from former occupants. This fell heavily on the newcomers recently arrived from England, who had been accustomed to clean wholesome linen and who were not aware of what they had to undergo and not prepared against it, and it was exemplified in a young gentleman who had joined me as a clerk in the Commissariat from Lisbon. I perceived when busy in the office that he was constantly scratching himself & seemed most uneasy, which induced me to ask him what was the matter. He told me he was itching all over & could not account for it as he had looked at his flannel waistcoat & found nothing. Knowing from experience that vermin were cunning in their way, I advised him to go home & examine it more minutely with certain directions for his guidance and he soon returned with a joyful countenance telling me that he had found colonies of minute life in every seam, which was the cause of the torment & as the nature of the climate generated them very rapidly, had he not made the discovery, every change of linen which was not over frequent would have continued the annoyance, for being of a gross habit it was considered most favourable to the growth of such a description of companions.

4th Campaign

January 1812. English Sieges of Ciudad Rodrigo and Badajoz, Advance into Spain. Battle of Salamanca, Entrance into Madrid, Burgos and Retreat

Considerable reinforcements having arrived from England in the previous autumn, Lord Wellington from all that was going on evidently felt himself strong enough to be the aggressor and in doing so it proved the precursor of the brilliant future throughout which I was fortunate to be present with troops in the field. A battering train from the sea coast was secretly conveyed to Almeida the Portuguese frontier fortress, on the plea of its being intended to rearm that place and which being a very plausible reason created no suspicion or alarm among the French generals. Gabions[1] and fascines[2] were also silently prepared by the troops in their respective cantonments and a large force was concentrated for a forward movement. Everything having been prepared by the beginning of January 1812, Ciudad Rodrigo was at once invested and besieged with wonderful celerity and the knowledge of such a circumstance fell like a clap of thunder on the French marshals and all the peninsula.

---

1 Gabions were large wicker baskets, designed to form a defensive parapet during a siege, being filled with earth.

2 Fascines were simple bundles of brushwood or twigs tied together to be dropped into trenches or other depressions to allow infantry to cross them.

4TH CAMPAIGN

The 3rd Dragoons to which I was attached received orders to march on the 11th of the month from Castello [Castelo] Branco to join the army and we proceeded by easy marches in which nothing material occurred by Penamacor on the frontier of Portugal to Aldea [Aldeia] da Ponte which we reached on the 13th a few miles only from the besieged city and we were at once thrown in the midst of the bustle incident to such an operation. The siege was by this time much advanced and it was expected that the final stroke, the storming would soon be attempted. From a height at some distance from the village we were quartered in, we could by means of our glasses [telescopes] perceive the cannonade and by riding a further distance, the whole feature of what was taking place, such as the batteries, parallels &c was discernable, as the day and hour of the assault depended on the demolition of the walls & practicability of the breaches and was of course kept a secret & only confided to the troops concerned and in trenches. We had a rumour only of it and it was only early in the morning, finding the firing had ceased, that we learnt that the place had fallen. Seldom had a siege been undertaken at such an inclement season of the year, with the men working in the trenches knee deep in mud and a complete slough and been brought to an end in so short a time. And well it was so, for Marshal Marmont[3] under whose protection the fortress was, was already concentrating a large army to relieve it and would most likely have accomplished it had any delay occurred on our part, but providence was with us, as it was afterwards on many other occasions, for in this instance notwithstanding the gallantry of the garrison, the whole affair was unprecedentedly quicker than the usual process of attack warranted & Marmont could not it was said, account for the speedy surrender. On its success depended (it may be said) the destinies of the peninsula for it was the beginning of a great end.

Curiosity led many of us next morning to visit the town and such a scene we had never before witnessed. After wading through the

---
3 Marshal Auguste de Marmont, who had superseded Marshal Massena.

disorder of the trenches, we reached the breaches from whence the wounded were removing & dead to be buried; dead bodies mangled by wounds, broken arms, pieces of shells and bullets with broken palisades, ground torn up by explosions, masses of walls tumbled down, fatigue parties coming and going. Men returning from the town with their plunder, their faces begrimed with powder, half drunk and clothes in disorder and numbers of officers visiting the spot, produced a scene hardly to be described. In the town itself the confusion was hardly less, for the streets were encumbered with traverses as a defence, broken rafters & tiles, furniture, shot & broken shells and accumulations of every sort of rubbish exhibiting a scene of desolation & wretchedness which must have been seen to be comprehended. And in looking into the place from the top of the breaches, on the buildings in the line of our breaching batteries, the destruction was enormous, roofs smashed, walls knocked down, and everything within range and was reached by the shot, exhibited a chaos of confusion hardly to be looked upon without feelings of deep regret to see a nice town converted into a heap of ruins.

Fortunately for the garrison the thirst of [for] revenge of our men for the loss of their comrades in the assault was converted into a scramble for liquor and plunder, which so far calmed their fury that few suffered and indeed such was the confusion of our people in entering the town and dispersing in search of the objects alluded to, that had the governor made better dispositions to defend the town by keeping a strong reserve in hand & pounced with it on the marauding parties, he might have succeeded in retaking it. And this I assert on the authority of General Sir John Vandeleur,[4] who assisted in the siege and mentioned it in my presence at Malta.[5] The fact is the operation was so suddenly begun and followed up with such unceasing celerity

---

4   Major General Sir John Ormsby Vandeleur, then commanding a brigade of the Light Division.

5   This conversation occurred some 30 years after these events. Vandeleur is quoting with hindsight what actually occurred at Bergen op Zoom in 1814.

& boldness that the governor had hardly time to mature measures to made head against such energetic & desperate efforts.

Stores of every description belonging to the French army were found in the place, the most important of which was a complete Battering Train, the capture of which must have been most mortifying to Marshal Marmont who had employed it in a former siege & was his only resource, on which to calculate for the future, had he required it. As he might be expected to make an attempt to recover the place, our approaches were filled up and the defences were put in the best state which the hurry of the moment allowed, in consequence we were kept in the quarters we occupied during the siege some days longer & until every apprehension of an attack was over.

Aldea [Aldeia] da Ponte was a wretched village, quite exhausted of everything eatable, with few inhabitants and had been for months occupied by troops which we had replaced. The only comfort in it in resisting the cold weather, was that of fireplaces which the officers had constructed in a corner of their rooms with rough brick work, making a hole through the roof for the smoke to escape. And there being no such luxury as glazed windows, they had contrived frames covered with oiled paper, gloomy enough but infinitely better than being exposed to the inclemency of the weather inside as well as outside. Our horses were starving from want of hay or straw, the country around being quite exhausted and we were not much better off ourselves, having to live on bare necessaries such as biscuit and lean beef cooked with rice, no vegetable of any sort being procurable. During my stay in this delectable place I paid a visit to the fortress of Almeida, the governor of which was Colonel Le Mesurier[6] (son of Paul of Alderney[7]). He was busy repairing the place which had been so seriously injured

---

6 Lieutenant Colonel Havilland Le Mesurier who was serving with the Portuguese Army.

7 Paul Le Mesurier (1755–1805) was a Guernsey-based merchant, shipowner, director of the East India Company and Member of Parliament. The 'of Alderney' comes from the fact that the family held the hereditary title to the governorship of Alderney: his father and two of his brothers held this post.

by the explosion of the great magazine during the siege of it[8] by the French & subsequently by their garrison in successfully evading the blockade of our troops & joining their army. He received me very kindly and took the trouble of shewing me over the whole place. His garrison consisted principally of militia who were lazily working at the repairs and with which he defended, or I should say kept the place afterwards when Marmont passed by it on his entry or inroad into Portugal in the following April [1812] as a diversion to deter us from continuing the siege of Badajoz which was then nearly over. For the colonel made such demonstrations and shewed such firmness with his defences incomplete, when surrounded by the French army as deterred it from making any attempt on them; he continued for a considerable time longer in the same situation and might have held it to the end of the war, but it became too inactive for him and when in 1813 our army finally quitted Portugal, his bold and active spirit could not brook being left behind. He accordingly urgently solicited Lord Wellington to be allowed to join his Portuguese regiment and in command of it was killed at the Battle of Pamplona.[9] In his death the service experienced a loss, as he was a zealous intelligent and brave officer.

The capture of Ciudad Rodrigo, a Spanish frontier town and to us the northern door for our future entrance into that country from Portugal, electrified the whole Spanish nation and though it was prostrate under its invaders it bid it not despair, by stimulating it to renewed exertion. The regular armies were nearly annihilated, but from the wreck the guerrillas had sprung up and were becoming more and more troublesome to the French and the event I have just mentioned increased their numbers and made them bolder in the

---

8 During the French siege of Almeida on 26 August 1810, either a lucky shot or a dreadful accident caused the main powder magazine to explode, forcing the fortress to surrender the following day.

9 He commanded the 12th Portuguese Line Regiment and died of severe wounds received at the Battle of Sorauren in August 1813.

expectation that their ally would now indeed assist in freeing their country.

To our delight we received our march route on the 30 January to proceed next day in a southern direction to the small town of Fundao and neighbourhood, six leagues from Castello [Castelo] Branco on the road to Guarda, which we reached on the 3rd day and remained there until the 25 February, without any event occurring to us to disturb our quietness. Our cantonments were at the foot of one of the spurs of the Serra da Estrela (Mountains of the Stars), an immense chain which occupies so large a portion of this part of the country and were selected as affording resources of forage for the horses of the brigade which consumed large quantities of it & obliged the foraging parties to go at least 12 miles in quest of it, in every village and cultivated corner in which it could be found. The town was neater and better built than those generally met with in this province, with greater appearance of cultivation owing it was supposed to its being inhabited in great measure by a colony of converted Jews called *Cristaos Novos*, or New Christians, who apparently conformed to their new religion from fear of persecution, for they were Israelites in heart. Their commercial propensities showed themselves by more openly dealing with our troops than the Portuguese in general and they had not lost adroitness or knavery by the adoption of new principles, as several of them supplied the troops with provisions &c for which I had to pay. Opportunities presented themselves to me of going into their own apartments and in them I perceived an almost entire absence of pictures of saints on their walls & heads of their beds, which prevailed so universally in genuine Roman Catholic houses, besides which the bells of the churches did not ring so incessantly as elsewhere which confirmed the want of sincerity in their profession of Christianity & yet many generations had carried on this deceit.

While in this state of quiescence we learnt from all quarters that we should not remain much longer inactive, great preparations being in course for besieging Badajoz for the third time by bringing up from Lisbon battering trains & the immense material which such an operation needed. Besides which we learnt that the gun carriages used at Ciudad Rodrigo passed by Penamacor on the 22 February, a town nearer Spain than we were, on their way to Elvas, which is situated opposite to Badajoz & which confirmed the reports in current circulation.

On the 26 February our brigade being in an efficient state received orders to march to Villa [Vila] Viçosa in the province of Alentejo proceeding by the bridge of Villa [Vila] Velha over the Tagus by Niza [Nisa] and Borba, at which latter place we halted until the 15th of March. In this province the French had paid no visit to do much harm; we were therefore quartered in greater comfort, the towns were better built, houses well-furnished & the country more cultivated with an appearance of affluence and ease among the inhabitants not met with in the poor desolate country we had left. We got in the line of road between Lisbon, Elvas & Badajoz and saw of course much of what was passing, particularly the conveyance of the battering guns, which were drawn by long lines of miserable oxen exceeding in some instances 20 to one gun, the drawing of which would have been effectively performed by a team of four stout English horses. The [cannon]balls were conveyed on small ox carts & donkies [*sic*] and the drivers of these cattle having been forced into the service by the authorities, the work was done most unwillingly and if an opportunity offered, they deserted without caring one moment for the important object in which they were assisting. And when the difficulties are considered which we experienced from the people and their lukewarmness at moments when exertion was of the utmost importance, it is astonishing to conceive how Lord Wellington persevered and overcame every obstacle; no man less gifted could ever have prevailed.

The preparations for the siege having been at last completed, the several corps of the army concentrated in the neighbourhood of Elvas and a bridge of pontoons having been thrown over the Guadiana below

Badajoz the investment commenced, and we received orders to march, crossed the bridge and entered Spain on the 18th, and as we were a part of the covering army were at once pushed forward in the interior, to cut off all communication between the garrison and the French corps in the province. The three regiments of cavalry comprising General Le Marchant's brigade had no experience in the field and as yet had never seen an enemy, which was a material disadvantage and gave rise to odd fancies and sayings among the men, of their having to storm bridges & other improbable duties. As we advanced the few of the enemy in our front retired without awaiting our coming but we found the country stripped of every means of supply, and heavy rains having set in at the commencement of the siege and swept away the bridge over which our means of maintenance had to pass, our horses were for some days in a sad state of starvation & the soldiers fared little better, the Spaniards declaring they had nothing to give and our men not being as yet adepts in discovering concealed stores, which no doubt existed, we could be of little service to ourselves in making discoveries. It must however be acknowledged that since Badajoz had been occupied by the French, they had, to maintain the garrison with, laid constant & heavy contributions on the surrounding country. The only resource in this emergency was therefore to give the young green barley as forage for the horses, which barley contained no substance at that season, giving them little strength to go through the harassing duties they had to perform.

We pushed on by Los Santos [de Maimona], Medina de las Torres near Zafra to the foot of the Sierra Morena on the way to Seville, and the French army being expected form the neighbourhood of that latter place under Marshal Soult to disturb the operations of the siege, the utmost vigilance was necessary in watching his movements, as his approach would in a certain degree regulate the disposition of our army to oppose him in time and at the same time continue the work in hand. Patrols were therefore sent in all directions in our front for intelligence and [to] feel if he was coming. In this state of suspense it was melancholy to observe the uneasiness of the inhabitants of the towns we passed through and the deadly stillness which prevailed; they were inclined to be civil and yet they hardly knew how to shew it from the fear of being denounced & made to suffer from it on the return of the French. The officers were notwithstanding invited occasionally in a dance got up in a quiet way as tokens of hospitality, and with a wish to encourage their good feeling. A return was made by requesting the Alcalde (magistrate) to invite in our names such young ladies & their parents as were the most respectable of the place, whom we could not of course know. It was done without the least hesitation and parties were thus got up in this novel way when an opportunity occurred without the least objection being made, for then they could fairly say that they had been forced into the amusement by authority though no doubt much to their satisfaction.

As the country was a purely agricultural one and the people from their isolated situation most primitive, and with little or no intercourse with strangers, and being neither of the upper classes or highly polished, the young ladies stood on *no punctilio*[10] or etiquette in shewing us marked attention, our fair complexions they admired and as we passed their doors & windows out of which they were looking, they were heard to say in their language, what a misfortune that such fine men with such beautiful and rosy complexions should be heretics and their souls doomed to everlasting damnation.

In our peregrinations a singular custom was perceived in a large iron chain being suspended over the portico of some good houses here and there, without any apparent object or use which puzzled us until we learnt that it indicated that a king of Spain had slept there, by which the premises were exempted for ever from taxation or being used for quartering troops &c.

In our emergencies of want of forage corn, in consequence of our transport not having arrived in time from Portugal, the inhabitants of

---

10 A fine point of etiquette.

the neighbouring villages to that in which we were quartered, to our astonishment & to shew some interest in our mutual cause, volunteered to send 150 of their mules to fetch a supply and which they did to our relief. They were not however of the description usually employed, as they consisted of animals barely tamed and which could only be conducted by the muleteers with whom they were familiar. They generally went in droves of fifty without packsaddles and muzzled to prevent nibbling at their neighbour's sack when hungry, the slowest and most tractable having a bell round its neck. When about to be loaded they were driven into a yard, or enclosure and then allowed to go out one by one, and at that moment the muleteers standing by, dexterously threw a sack of corn across their back, which dividing as it were in two from being loose and being rapidly adjusted as they passed to make the weight equal, the animals were scarcely detained and joined its companions already loaded. In unloading similar dexterity took place by a jerk which threw the sack on the ground; in this way five or six men managed the whole park & the sound of the bell gave notice that the last was coming both on the journey & in other arrangements. Strangers unacquainted with these primitive customs could never have undertaken to manage these animals who, if you attempted to approach them, were most bountiful of kicks.

Salt being a royal monopoly, its conveyance was effected by large trains of bullock carts traversing the country from whence it was obtained, to where it was required. In this description of transport there was also great primitiveness, the oxen were all uniformly black & of the same wild race. They could bear no stranger to approach them, tolerating alone their own drivers, and when in file or string on the road it was impossible to pass the back of one cart & the front of the other as the heads of the cattle were close up to the one which preceded them & no effort could alter the position without a struggle & violent kicking likely to disturb the whole convoy. To their drivers only would they submit to be yoked and that must be done with celerity and yet the moment it was done they became quite manageable. These peculiarities were accounted for by being pastured in the night on the commons and isolated spots away from the haunts of men, loose but with bells on the necks of some, to ascertain that the herd was not straying too far.

We were at this time in the country which produced the famous Merino breed of sheep which were kept in immense flocks; their peregrinations were almost patriarchal for they were driven from pasture to pasture according to the seasons & almost from one end of the kingdom to the other and no one had a right to molest them; the privilege having been established from time immemorial. The shepherds and their dogs were wild looking fellows from the wandering life they led.

We also crossed Don Quixote de la Mancha's path, and heard many of his and his trusty squire Sancho Panza's sayings, now still practically in use but which in translation and ignorance of the manners & habits of the people lost in reading, all their salt and meaning. The windmills in the country were quite diminutive and could fairly be assailed by a man whose mind might not be quite right and who, in finding himself in the dark in a store w[h]ere skins containing wine, deposited there for the night, might fancy them by the feel to be a parcel of drunken fellows whom he might arouse and challenge to a fight, goading them with his true Toledo rapier and thereby finding himself in a sea of imaginary blood, much to the eventual dismay of the more rational owners of the property. The brass basin used in shaving from time immemorial was still applied to the same purpose, and in shape identical to the one the hero is represented as wearing as a helmet.

I have mentioned that we generally experienced kindly feelings on the part of the inhabitants when prosperous events favoured our mutual cause, but when the contrary happened, their lukewarmness (to give it no worse definition) shewed itself in various ways. Having oftentimes to go in search of provisions to villages away from the line of march, I went on one occasion in one on which it was reported the

French were advancing. I had with me a corporal and six dragoons to support my application and on arriving opposite the magistrate's house, he at once advised me to leave the place instanter, as there was a strong patrol of French cavalry coming in on the opposite side to which we had entered.

I doubted the truth of his assertion from having learnt a short time before at our outposts that no enemy could be near & as the country was an open plain over which we could distinguish anything that was moving by a rise of dust, I directed one of the soldiers to go up the street just out of the place, reconnoitre and see that all was clear, and I then got off my horse, went upstairs, wrote the requisition for what was required and told their unfriendly magistrate that if my demand was not complied with in so many hours, a regiment of cavalry would be sent in & quartered on them, which I knew and they themselves were aware of, would be much more troublesome than what I asked for. Under therefore the fear of such a visit I defeated his stratagem and succeeded in my object which I daresay he had before practised successfully upon others by getting rid of their importunities. I did not nevertheless feel quite comfortable until we had left the village and got on the open ground where had there been a necessity for it we could have given leg bail[11] to a stronger hostile party, as our object was anything but to seek a fight. There was however no necessity for any proceeding of that sort for no enemy showed himself.

On the 3rd of April we were still further in advance at Bienvenida near Llerena, expecting every hour to feel the advanced parties of the enemy, rumours of their approach being current. We were of course on the alert and next day as usual three squadrons of the brigade were in advance near a small village on the right of it, facing the country from whence the French were expected to make their appearance and I proceeded there to see if any provisions could be obtained. I enquired of the commanding officer if all was right in front and

---

11 To escape by flight.

he told me the patrols had just returned from scouring the country & had been nothing & that it was quite safe my going on. Captain Johnstone of the 3rd Dragoons[12] offered to go with me and we went together to the alcalde's house accompanied by a dragoon, and we were of course mounted, they on their cavalry horses and myself on a fleet mule. I at once proceeded to business and Captain J[ohnstone] being fatigued from watching all night, he went and laid on a bed and fell into a sound sleep. During the time the supplies were collecting & had been despatched, I conversed with the magistrate and took a little of his olea soup, a universal Spanish dish,[13] and while doing so, a thundering knocking was heard at the gates by which we had entered (the house being situated in a yard) and when immediately opened, another dragoon came in desiring us to come away instantly as the enemy had come on most unexpectedly and were just outside the village. No time of course was to be lost, I therefore directed the one who had come with us to bridle the horses and mule & I went myself to rouse Captain J[ohnstone]. I shook and pinched him to no purpose & as the moment admitted of no delay, I took him by the heels and tumbled him on the floor which brought him to his senses; we rushed to the door, he mounted his horse, but the man told me he could not bridle the mule & it was no use to attempt putting it on myself. I therefore got on her with the bridle in my hand and followed the captain, the dragoons bringing up the rear with their drawn swords. We sallied out and found the skirmishing had already commenced outside the village and the enemy coming into it, two or three minutes delay might have occasioned our capture and as it was we had to run for it as fast as the animals could carry us, one dragoon making use of the point of his sword to keep my mule at her full speed. We soon joined the troops and in the midst of them, was

---

12 Captain John Johnstone 3rd Dragoons had transferred into the regiment from the 21st Light Dragoons on 25 October 1810. He was Secretary to the Board of Claims at Salamanca from May to August 1812 and resigned his commission on 20 October 1813.

13 Literally 'Oil Soup'; perhaps he meant 'Aceitunas' which is a crème of olives.

near the skirmishing going on. The enemy pressed on and to check them a charge was sounded, but I am sorry to say it did not succeed for we lost by it a few men whose boldness carried them too far in the midst of the melee, for they were surrounded & made prisoners. It would however have succeeded could they have stopped in time but the enemy appearing in great strength, the retreat was sounded immediately yet too late, for we could see the poor fellows cutting & slashing away in right good earnest & the French retiring and defending themselves until they were lost sight of. I found myself in the thick of the disorder with my mule still without a bridle and after a short gallop, threes about (that is face about) was sounded, no one however apparently heard it and we continued to fall back until at last we did face about; in the midst of the run we passed my small convoy of provisions on asses running for it & dispersed, for I never saw or heard more about it. Having come to a halt & the enemy not advancing, the bridle was at last got into my mule's mouth & I proceeded to the rear and met General Le Marchant coming up with the brigade to render assistance if necessary. He took me aside & questioned me very closely about what had happened & I must say I could not give him a very satisfactory account of the affair, but after all what more could be expected from troops who had never before come in contact with an enemy whose experience had been acquired in a hundred fights. The French certainly came on in [a] bold & dashing style and as it turned out to be a reconnaissance made by the advance of Soult's army made merely to pick up information which they obtained from the prisoners, they retired for the moment and nothing further occurred during the day.

We retired however next morning on finding the enemy advancing again and proceeded to Fuente de Maestro [del Maestre] towards Badajoz. We had occasionally got information of what was going on in the progress of the siege of that place and as ground is considered to convey sound, it was customary for some officers during the stillness of the day after the march was over, to retire to a loan [sic] spot and by laying down and putting an ear to the ground the vibrations of the cannonade could be distinctly heard, but on the 7 April though we had got nearer to the place they had ceased and there was dead silence. We concluded therefore that it had either fallen by storm or the siege raised or suspended at the approach of Soult & his army. To our infinite joy and satisfaction news arrived that the former event had occurred, the Marshal [Soult] nevertheless continued to advance and we to retire until we reached the position of Albuera, the scene of a former bloody conflict and there awaited his arrival ready to give him battle in case he felt disposed to attack. In retiring, we found the news of the fall of the fortress was fast circulating through the country and General Le Marchant in one of our last marches, left in his quarters which he was likely soon to occupy, an intimation to that effect & he (Soult) must have heard it otherwise, but those channels were not likely to satisfy so able a soldier until the certainty reached him by some French dragoons whom it was currently reported had escaped during the confusion of the storm and had joined him. The bustle of preparation for the battle in the troops taking their several stations in line was soon over and it was astonishing to see Sir Thomas Graham, the hero of Barrosa,[14] afterwards Lord Lyndock [Lyndoch], then a man of sixty who commanded this the covering army, incessantly on horseback from morning to night superintending every arrangement with all the vigour of a man of 30 or 40 and in which he had been unceasingly employed in our marches since the beginning of the siege. I saw his lordship afterwards at Malta at the age of 93 where he had gone for his health and I dined in his company on the anniversary of that battle, and so clear was his intellect then that immediately on the removal of the cloth he gave us the whole account of it from first to last occupying more than half an hour, during which (not to disturb him) the glass did not circulate to the annoyance of some, and we learnt that it was his custom to do so on that day in consequence

---

14 The Battle of Barrosa was fought on 5 March 1811 near Cadiz.

of General Napier, the historian of the Peninsular War having given an erroneous account of the preliminary measures which gave rise to that event.

Marshal Soult having satisfied himself that Badajoz was lost to him, did not come to our position, but commenced his retreat and we after him with the object of harassing him if possible. A plan was formed to attack his rear guard & encircle it if possible and had the order reached the several troops in time, or been obeyed by all with the same celerity, we would have succeeded. And as it was we nearly did so on the 11th of April near Usagre,[15] and our brigade did good work on that day to retrieve the little blunder of a former day, the 5th Dragoon Guards having charged the enemy's cavalry in right good earnest and taken many prisoners, but owing to the superior speed of our horses & dashing through their ranks, most of our killed and wounded were run through the back by the Frenchmen poking at our men as they passed them. It was a stirring sight from whence I stood and I rode down immediately after the affair was over to see the prisoners which were collecting after the chase, numbering about 150 belonging to a heavy dragoon regiment. The officers wore their decorations of the Legion of Honour and all were in their fine brass helmets, with a band of tiger skin and a horse tail flowing behind, and dressed in long green coats &c. Many were wounded but yet their air was martial, one man in particular, large & stout, had received a sabre cut in the nape of the neck which must have been delivered in right good earnest, for it had gone through the helmet, tail and stock and completely laid bare the nape of the neck through a large mass of

---

15 This refers to the action of Villagarcia, where Lallemand's cavalry, covering the retreat of the rearguard, stood against Ponsonby's Brigade, each with three regiments of cavalry. However, Lallemand was unaware that Le Marchant's Brigade was marching around his flank, whilst Slade's Brigade was also coming up in rear of Ponsonby. The 5th Dragoon Guards took the French line in flank and rolled it up and the French fled to a position halfway from Villagarcia to Llerena. They were driven back to Llerena where a force of 12,000 French infantry forced the pursuit to end. The French lost 53 men killed and 136 captured; British losses were only 14 killed and 37 wounded.

flesh which was lapping on his back. Finding that I spoke French & thinking I was a surgeon he begged of me to dress the wound & sew it up; in undeceiving him I told him he must go to the rear where he at once would be attended to.

After this skirmish the French went off double quick and we in our turn retraced our steps towards Badajoz in the neighbourhood of which we arrived on the 14 April. Our curiosity was of course excited to visit the town which I hurriedly did as soon as I could. The breaches were the first attraction and we found them in nearly the same state as when the storm had occurred, with the exception that all the dead bodies that could be found had been removed, although there were some still remaining which were loosely covered and smelt offensively. The chevaux-de-frise of sword blades[16] were there in their original position towards the top of the breach and consisted of trunks of trees of about 8 inches diameter chained together and studded with the blades so thick and sharp as to render the passing them impossible. The ditches presented a chaos of debris of arms, stone walls, broken palisades, shot, shells & carcases of fireballs thrown by the garrison at the moment of attack to shew the heads of the attacking columns by a blaze of light, which must have been an awful sight, to see so many men on the brink of destruction. Beyond the breaches looking into the town, the line of fire of our batteries was defined by the destruction of the upper part of the houses, the roofs of which had been swept away, but not wishing to do more injury to the town than was avoidable, shells were not used, otherwise the mischief would have been much more considerable.

I then went to the castle situated on a hill, the ancient keep, castle or fortress of the place, the attack of which had first succeeded, though I believe little had been expected from it, but a diversion to distract the attention of those defending the breaches and such it appears

---

16 A long log of wood with sword blades protruding, used to block up a breach. They were chained into position to make it almost impossible for attackers to get past.

was entertained by its garrison, for all the guns that could bear in that direction were pointed on the breaches and their fire had been so constant that all the touch holes had I perceived, melted, being of brass. The defenders must therefore have been astonished after a short struggle to find our troops making good their footing over such high walls, for they retreated rather too suddenly down into the town and no time was given them to rally, as the gates were at once shut on them. Having obtained assistance and recovered from their panic they attempted a recapture, in which they failed & the importance of the acquisition soon settled the fate of the fortress itself. In the attempt on the castle their musketry must have been very heavy and near, for there was not a spot on the gates larger than the top of a finger which had not a musket ball embedded in them. From this elevated spot the surrounding view must have been most striking, especially on such a night, for it commanded the attack and defence and all the grandeur & horrors, but all no doubt were too occupied to look to it with any attention.

The bustle incident to the siege having died away & the tumult after the storming, the town appeared at the end of a week in melancholy dullness, for as yet little was doing to clear away rubbish and put it in a decent state of cleanliness. Few of the inhabitants had returned who had absented themselves during the siege and those who had remained were loud in their complaints of the abominable treatment they had experienced from our soldiers.

In going through the streets, I perceived that many of the locks of the doors of houses had been fired into, to force them open to get an entrance to plunder, a rough sort of knocking which could not be denied, and our men by violence had succeeded in discovering hidden stores of spirits with which they got roaring drunk and which excited them the more. Whereas the fancy of our Portuguese allies was directed towards the female population from being habitually more sober in their habits, but both in their respective pursuits conducted themselves like madmen; the plunder in money, church plate and wearing apparel &c was immense and as it was acquired in many instances in a state of intoxication, many of the more knowing ones obtained a good share of it by not even going into the town at all, remaining outside the gates & breaches & knocking down those coming out loaded with it & plundering them, and those who brought out bags of silver or plate and could strike a bargain, sold for a few ounces of gold not a twentieth part perhaps of the real value of the plundered articles, that they might return and get more. In short, the worst of human passions were doing their worst for three whole days, the officers not daring to interfere or even show themselves in the town, and these outrages were only put a stop to by the erection of a gibbet to hang those who continued refractory.

A sort of fair was held in camp afterwards (winked at by the authorities) at which numbers of Spaniards made their appearance to purchase in many instances what had been taken from them.

The French garrison were at once marched into Portugal after their surrender and Lord Wellington would not see Philippon the governor[17] from being I suppose still incensed at the immense loss he had experienced in valuable officers & men. When they got into that country the whole were put under the escort of the native Militia to take them down to Lisbon, from whom they did not, nor could they expect to receive anything like kind treatment. If a man dropt [*sic*] on the road from exhaustion, no attempt was made to render him assistance but he was either shot or left there like a dog to await a worst sort of death & this happened constantly with many other acts of the same nature which thinned their ranks considerably before they got to their journey's end.

Sir Leonard Greenwell who commanded the 45th Regiment[18] at the storm[ing] of the castle, told me afterwards that before he

---

17 General de Division Armand Philippon was captured and sent to Oswestry on parole. He escaped, breaking his parole, in July 1812 and was successfully smuggled back to France, serving with the army in Eastern Europe.

18 Then Major Leonard Greenwell of the 45th Foot.

mounted the walls he offered £10[19] to whoever would bring him the French flag [flying over the keep], but none could be found when they got in and in lieu of it he hoisted on the flagstaff the jacket of one of the soldiers who had been killed and which was of course seen as the day dawned.[20]

Many other incidents occurred of course, but as they are better recalled elsewhere I do not enter into them, having confined myself to what I saw or learnt immediately after this memorable siege which, though attended with atrocious acts on the part of our men must in great measure stand justified by the state of fury in which men must have got into, after having seen their comrades butchered by their sides, and then bursting suddenly into a place most obstinately defended, losing thereby all command over themselves and behaving like wild beasts, a result which must always be expected when the defenders of a town risk an assault when the breaches are considered practicable. The knowledge of this capture spread like lightning all over Spain and did incalculable mischief to the French cause in that country.

We were not allowed much time for rest for Marshal Marmont having made an inroad into Portugal by the way of Ciudad Rodrigo & Almeida threatening those two places on his way to distract our attention & endeavour to raise the siege of Badajoz. We proceeded from Estremos [Estremoz] (where we had been ordered) & crossed with a part of the army the Bridge of Villa [Vila] Velha on the Tagus on the way to Castello [Castelo] Branco after him, where we arrived on the 23 April, he had however retired leaving as usual, sad traces of his visit. We then recrossed that river into the Alentejo, proceeding

---

19 Equivalent to around £500 today.

20 Carey has got the story wrong. Lieutenant James Macpherson was wounded but did eventually succeed in mounting the ladders and entering the castle. Proceeding towards the flagstaff, he had the French flag removed and for want of something better, he raised his own red jacket to signify that the castle was in British hands.

by Povoa [de Rio de Moinhos], Alpalhao, to Cabeco de Vide, where we remained until the 20 May in comfortable quarters.

This short campaign had proved most injurious to the horses of our three regiments from the harassing work they performed with great scarcity of forage & it had so worn out most of them by loss of flesh and sore backs, that scarcely half of our original numbers could be brought on parade in a fit state to be mounted. Repose was therefore most needed and we had a short respite for the purpose; we where [sic] in a small retired town and nothing worth noticing from one day to the other unless it was that we were a little enlivened by the presence of the headquarters of the cavalry under Sir Stapleton Cotton, afterwards Lord Combermere,[21] who was a great fop in dress, and from being very much bedizened with gold lace and his horse richly caparisoned, was nicknamed by the soldiers the *Golden Lion*.

It was generally believed at this time that Marshal Marmont, occupying Salamanca & neighbouring provinces, was at variance with Marshal Soult whose government included the neighbourhood of Cadiz, Seville & Spanish provinces beyond Badajoz to the south of the Tagus, from the latter not having made a diversion in favour of the former while the fortress of Ciudad Rodrigo in his charge was besieged by us. And on the other hand from the diversion made by Marmont having been so slowly effected as to prove of no use in relieving Badajoz, by which apparent supineness & our rapid operations they both lost their respective frontier towns, thereby leaving those parts of Spain open to any future undertakings of ours. And Lord Wellington soon took advantage of this ill feeling and determined to keep them more apart by destroying if possible their nearest means of communication established at Almaraz on the Tagus.

An expedition under Lord Hill was accordingly plan[n]ed and executed, by which their pontoon bridge & station was destroyed,

---

21 Lieutenant General Sir Stapleton Cotton commanded the cavalry. He became Lord Combermere in 1827.

which eventually rendered it necessary for the French troops to have recourse to the bridge of Arzobispo much higher up that stream, to cross it; found greatly to impede their operations in connecting both armies from the road being [very] circuitous.[22]

We were ordered to move up in support of that operation in case of being wanted & proceeded on our way by Torre del [El] Fresno & Puebla de la Calzada, not far from Badajoz where we halted from its having already succeeded and returned to our former quarters on the 27th [May] at Cabeco de Vide. This excursion led us again a short way into Spain and for two or three days were encamped on the neutral ground between the two nations, a wild place without inhabitants (none being allowed to occupy it) consisting of large flat tracts of pasture land, interspersed with large forest trees under the shade of which we lived with plenty of fine grass, which we of course cut at discretion for our horses as the French would say, without the interference or control of anyone. Most of the cattle which grazed there in peaceable times having disappeared during the war and though a wilderness we much enjoyed it. Hares were in plenty & so tame that they would not move from their forms as the men passed them on horseback, many being killed by being thrust through with the sword. From this encampment our march was effected through Campo Mayor [Maior] and Assumar, a different road to the one we had come.

From the arrangements which were in progress to complete the efficiency of all arms, a general impression existed in the army that Lord Wellington was meditating an aggressive movement into Spain. He had now tried the Portuguese troops and acquired confidence in them, and being incorporated with our own he found himself at the head of a more formidable army than he had yet commanded and with which the

---

22 The pontoon bridge and two small forts protecting it were captured by Hill's corps on 18–19 May 1812. The country at the nearest bridge at Arzobispo was stated by the historian William Napier to be impassable to the south for cavalry or artillery and therefore a greater detour via Toledo was necessary, adding 435 miles (700km) to the journey.

celebrated campaign of 1812 was achieved. Our brigade accordingly got their route and we commenced our march on the 1st of June for the north of Portugal proceeding by Niza [Nisa], over the pontoon bridge at Villa [Vila] Velha on the Tagus to Castello [Castelo] Branco, and here an officer of the 3rd Dragoons with which I was serving, informed me that by a register kept by him, the extent of our peregrinations during the past three months had not been less than 1,200 miles [1,930km] which however was subject to a certain degree of uncertainty from distances between places, particularly in Portugal, being regulated in a very preposterous manner and not by a measured standard. For there were several descriptions of leagues, each nominally of three miles but which varied from 2½ to 5 miles according to hills to be ascended or descended and the time consumed, an hour being supposed to be a league on the average, but by no means an invariable rule. For these irregular leagues had in the Portuguese language several definitions such as, a small league, a league, a long league & very great league, and lastly a devil's own league. When tired at night and anxious to reach our destination, on enquiring the distance to it, it was at times necessary from bad roads on which to go at night, to ascertain which of the leagues it was. Otherwise the disappointment & inconvenience was annoying on finding no end to the journey, if it turned out to be one of the latter description which the inhabitants of one village were not always desirous of defining, hoping that we might be induced to go on and not trouble them by quartering ourselves on them until morning, an occurrence which often happened to small detachments.

Since marching from Cabeço de Vide the troops were bivouac[k]ed, that is encamped in the open air; the weather having become extremely sultry and dry and the nights warm, a mode of living which continued almost uninterruptedly (three or four instances excepted) until the end of the campaign in November. A tree or hedge & that not always to be had, becoming our only protection under the canopy of heaven which was found in Portugal infinitely preferable to occupying houses often without inhabitants and half unroofed. But not so in Spain where the people had been better treated by the French, with whom they became more familiarised and had preserved their houses, farms &c by heavy periodical contributions to which they submitted no doubt with silent murmurs & execrations & which they smothered to avoid worse consequences, for when we again appeared among them they seemed to be worn down by continued oppression but not sufficient to force them from their homes.

On the 5th of June we resumed our march to Alpedrinha at the foot of the Estrela Mountains, Caria, Casteleiro, on the 8th to [Ribeira da] Nave, 9th Villa [Vila] Boa, 10th Quinta de Aguilla & on the 11th encamped in the neighbourhood of Ciudad Rodrigo without the occurrence of anything material excepting great professional activity & exertion which absorbed from every other object my time and attention. The army was clustering in all directions round that fortress for the grand movement expected to take place on Salamanca and it commenced on the 13th. It was a most animating scene to see the imposing appearance of the masses intermingled and moving on in the highest spirits in another endeavour to shake the power of the French in the peninsula, which was in some measure compromised by Buonaparte withdrawing some of his best soldiers to accompany him in his grand eruption into Russia. We took three days in our march to the environs of Salamanca, passing through a wooded flat country without much interest and meeting with no enemy, though moving forward with the necessary caution to prevent surprise in case of falling in with him from one moment to the other. And this was done by sending out patrols (consisting of an officer & a few of the best mounted men) of cavalry in front & flanks, who scoured the country for information, and the columns were preceded first by two or three men with their carbines ready to be discharged, then two or three others at a short distance behind at regular distances, then a small detachment and after it the same process repeated with additional numbers & followed by the main bodies, by which a surprise was intended to be avoided in a close country.

In this cautious manner we proceeded until the 16th when the enemy's cavalry were perceived crowning a height which prevented our seeing anything beyond it. It being however Lord Wellington's object to get on it, to see more of the country, a skirmish commenced to drive them back, the light cavalry taking the lead and we the heavies supporting them, and quite near. The extended line of skirmishers commenced firing & advanced, then grouped together and charged, the supporters gradually closing up, and thus with a short struggle the affair was soon over by the enemy retreating, and though a good deal of firing took place on both sides there was little harm done which rather surprised me considering how close the men were to each other, but being in extended order there was plenty of room for the shot to pass between.

Immediately after, everyone who could do so rode up to the eminence from which the city of Salamanca, so famous for its university was perceived in the distance, picturesquely crowning a hill with the River Tormes winding at its base, still occupied by the enemy. We encamped for the night near where we were and then advanced next day towards the city which was found evacuated. The inhabitants appeared transported at our presence & received us with every demonstration of joy. Their enthusiasm was sincere and at its height evincing their having suffered much by continued oppression.

As it was there was still a thorn in their side, for the French had fortified two [three] convents in the city and left garrisons in them, which were at once invested & their sieges commenced.[23] Our brigade with other troops crossed the river by a ford above the town and marched beyond it on[to] some heights to cover the operation. The French army having only retired a short distance awaiting for reinforcements & having been joined by them, it came on again either to assist or withdraw their comrades in the convents and took

---

23 The three convents which had been converted into fortresses were named San Vincent, San Cayetano and La Merced.

up ground opposite to us and so near that the line of sentries were within a hundred yards of each other in an open country without even an hedge to separate them or anything else. Though so near all was calm & still & having rode with an officer to the advanced sentries it happened that some mounted French officers were doing the same and I could distinctly hear them speak to their men which appeared strange, enemies as we were and so near without coming to any act of hostility. Such however was the good understanding (if it may be so termed) which existed between us not to harass or disturb the advanced posts and it was a common occurrence when the main bodies were in a state of quiescence and that no advantage could be gained by it. Being encamped outside the town curiosity led us occasionally into it to ascertain the progress of the siege and get a glimpse of it if possible. Fortunately I did so early & got into the tower of the cathedral (which was not permitted afterwards) from whence many of the details could be seen from its completely overlooking the fortifications of the convent's glacis, and our approaches. The firing was going on and the glacis being the site of houses demolished round about and rudely levelled, our riflemen were seen ensconced as near the walls as they could reach without being exposed and popping away whenever an embrasure was opened to run the gun out to fire it, by which they annoyed the gunners who in revenge fired grapeshot at them occasionally, which in striking the stones behind which they lay, rose [sic] a cloud of dust apparently doing little harm. While in the tower, a shot was fired at it or most likely at the window or loophole from which we were looking, the shock of the ball being most perceptible & it having been afterwards repeated after we left & before it, an order was subsequently issued to prevent anyone but those on service to ascend it. From this height the extent of the wanton destruction of buildings to complete the fortifications of this stronghold which took a whole year to complete could be perceived, amounting it was said to hundreds of private dwellings and public edifices which must have led to much individual loss and suffering.

FEEDING WELLINGTON'S ARMY IN THE PENINSULA

This city in times of yore & previous to its occupation by the French must have been one of the first in Spain, its university, edifices & convents of friars & nuns were very numerous but they now lay in ruins, the inmates having been ejected by their rapacious enemies and their great revenues derived from lands &c appropriated to the pay & subsistence of their army, for they had a mortal antipathy to drones[24] of that description & the wood work of these immense piles of building[s] were applied by the soldiers to cook their victuals with.

I understood that the cathedral was only preserved in consideration of great pecuniary sacrifices made by the priesthood & inhabitants for that special object. It was a Gothic pile and the great altarpiece was in my opinion truly magnificent, part of it consisting of silver angels round a glory upon a dark ground of velvet. It was not however the moment for examining it attentively, and it was probably incomplete from many valuable parts having been removed no doubt to a place of greater security.

An attempt [was] made to storm the forts [but] unfortunately failed, and in the meantime the enemy attacked the right of our covering position on the heights of St Christoval [San Cristobal] to communicate if possible with their garrison by signals, but it was not successful, which manoeuvring for the purpose Lord Wellington was there on the watch seated on the ground from whence he could observe all that was passing & surrounded by his Staff. The heat was great & no cover or shade from the sun, a blanket was therefore brought & fixed up as well as it could be done to shelter him, and in that position, with an enemy endeavouring to find a good opportunity to give him battle and another contending in his rear in the city, he wrote a long & laboured despatch on Portuguese finance, full of ability, thus showing a wonderful command of mind in embracing at the same time two such opposite objects.

---

24 Loafers.

4TH CAMPAIGN

Our brigade was in support of the troops engaged, and during the cannonade lost three horses by a cannon shot taking them in file and passing through their flanks without injury to the riders who merely felt the animals sinking under them as if going to lay down.

Lord Wellington having had an imperfect account of the strength of the forts and not [having] brought up sufficient guns or ammunition to continue the siege to its termination, it became necessary to send for a further supply to Ciudad Rodrigo which occasioned a delay, during which the French army continued manoeuvring to annoy us and received reinforcements, but it was kept in check. The siege was then resumed and the forts capitulated in the midst of the attack & when in flames by our bombardment; the garrison being marched off prisoners of war towards Lisbon after a defence which lasted ten days.

Marshal Marmont was speedily informed of the event, and decamped on the 27 June, to take a position on the northern side of the Duero and we the next day went in pursuit halting at Villares [de la Reina] and the following day at Nava del Rey near that river. The French force being immediately on the other bank & held the bridge over it at Tordesillas with a tête de pont[25] which gave them the power of passage whenever it felt powerful enough to undertake it.

The duty assigned to the corps to which we belonged appeared to me to be to watch a ford at Pollos on our left flank of which the enemy seemed jealous of & resisted our ascertaining its practicability. An attempt was notwithstanding made, of which we had a complete view from our side, being very high ground and the other a low flat on which a line of infantry and four guns in advance were stationed to prevent us. Our infantry soon plunged into the stream in skirmishing order & the enemy's guns opened upon them striking the water and dashing the spray over them. They continued to advance but it at once appearing that they would be seriously opposed, two guns of

---

25 A fortified bridgehead.

ours were instantly dispatched down the hill to their support and having taken a commanding position opened their fire. The first shot passed over the artillery and made a hole or gap in the line of infantry by killing one file (three men), those on each side being seen to recoil and then close up to fill the blank, the second shot had the same effect which induced the commandant to withdraw the infantry, our men continued to advance through the water to find where it was most shallow, and in the meantime the artillery fired at each other. Our third shot plunged into their opponents and evidently disordered one of their guns and our practice continued so successful that it obliged them also to retire at a distance, with apparently two of their guns hors de combat; on our side the artillery remained untouched and only a man or two of the infantry got hurt. The ford however was found so deep that though some got across, it was considered impracticable. We had the vantage ground on this occasion for our guns in being well directed could hardly fail doing mischief, bowling as the shot did along the level & sweeping everything in their way, whereas those of the enemy plunged into the water or bank at once. They evidently did not like their position and fired too quickly to take good aim, for though many spectators crowned the heights on our side within range, no attempt was made to throw a shot among us.

The heat of the weather was intense at this time as it was nearly throughout the greatest part of the campaign and our exertions were incessant night and day. I had been toiling all the morning of the 1 July in the broiling sun on horseback to obtain supplies, the regiment was encamped on a plain partly cultivated and partly fallow, without a tree for shelter and though not a breath of air was perceptible the pole of the tent (a soldier's bell tent) was risen on a box, thereby elevating the body of it to catch if possible under it the slightest breeze it being unbearably hot. I was exhausted and parched with thirst and had just laid down to get rest when I received a peremptory order to go forthwith to headquarters, a distance of some miles to wait on the Commissary General and when I got there I found it to

4TH CAMPAIGN

be on some trivial matter which could have been just as well attended to by directions in the letter I received as by my presence. Such was the mode of annoyance resorted to when anything went unavoidably wrong and I shall never forget it as a wanton act of unnecessary tyranny, for had the exertion been required for a good purpose and even doubled, it would have been submitted to and cheerfully performed as unavoidable for the public service, it being a common occurrence to submit to every sort of inconvenience and drudgery at all times, but more particularly when the armies were in presence of each other. Extraordinary efforts should therefore have been reserved for useful purposes and at that moment such was the case, as we were in an exhausted country drained by the French Army and our own to the very dregs, and therefore requiring every exertion to obtain any subsistence from it. Bread which before our arrival was sold for a penny a pound could not be had for less than four pence and wine which ordinarily sold for a half penny a pint was charged four pence and both particularly the former could only be procured in trifling quantities compared to our wants, which obliged us to depend in great measure on biscuit brought all the way from the coast of Portugal by the mule & other transport attached to the army, although Castile in which we then were is considered the granary of Spain, but then the harvest was only reaping & all others had been consumed & wasted.

Our army necessarily remained inactive for some days on the watch, expecting the enemy to be the assailants but the excitement in it to move was very great and a similar feeling was reported to exist in the French army, the strength of which was daily increasing, in short there was a desire for a fight in both sides.

From the heights in our vicinity we soon perceived that something was in agitation for the enemy were perceived in movement and on the 15th of July strong corps were seen in motion to their right, apparently with the intention of crossing the river in that direction at Toro, but by a masterly manoeuvre effected during the night of retracing their steps to their left, Marshal Marmont succeeded in deceiving Lord

Wellington and passed his whole force by the bridge of Tordesillas before he could be effectively opposed and took us unawares by turning our right flank. Our brigade was among the troops which gave him a check and a cavalry affair & a very serious one for the infantry took place in which the French General Charrier [Carrie] was taken prisoner.[26] I was not up at the time, but immediately after his charger was brought where I was, a great grey lanky beast apparently done up by the work he had gone through.

On this day the French horsemen were particularly bold and insolent, a small party of them followed a squadron of the 11th [12th] Hussars commanded by Captain Geytrick[27] which was retiring and dashed among them heedless of the disparity of numbers and the only way of getting rid of them as they would not surrender, was by cutting them down. They must have been heated with liquor, the captain killed one himself and while the fellow was in the act of falling he cut at the captain & struck him across the face just under his nose and above his teeth, by which they were loosened and his first act was to spit five or six of them with the blood which was accumulating in his mouth. He came in with his head bound, got leave of absence to England and I often afterwards saw him with a slight mark on his lip, and a good row of teeth, so that there was no great disfigurement in his face.

The object of Marmont was now to force us back to Portugal by turning our right flank or bringing on an action and in this manner the two armies manoeuvred every day in parallel lines quite near and opposite to each other on the road leading back to Salamanca. It was a beautiful sight to observe these two great bodies marching and watching each other, as they could be plainly perceived from the

---

26 This describes the Action of Castrillo on 18 July 1812. Brigadier General Carrie commanded the cavalry brigade involved.

27 Actually Lieutenant John Gitterick 12th Light Dragoons who was wounded on 18 July 1812. The action involved a squadron each of the 11th and the 12th and it is easy to see how Carey confused which regiment Gitterick was in.

open nature of the country, in this manner until we again occupied the heights of St Cristoval [San Cristobal] in front of Salamanca on the 20th, and there we awaited to see what the French general would do, and he soon took his determination of crossing the River Tormes to force us still further back towards Ciudad Rodrigo. We followed him, he taking one ford and we the other, leaving our 3rd Division of infantry behind in case he retrograded and seized Salamanca before we could prevent him. He however, did not make the attempt and after a harassing march we took ground at night near where the battle was fought. Next day the enemy being as usual near us, at night the weather became stormy and a most violent thunderstorm broke over us, killed several horses of the 5th Dragoon Guards (part of our brigade) the others breaking loose from their pickets, to which they were fastened as usual in rows, galloping over the men in all directions, creating such a hubbub and indescribable confusion as can hardly be conceived. The colonel (Ponsonby) lost his best charger which with several others strayed in[to] the French camp & on which French officers were afterwards seen riding.

Next day, the eventful one of the battle, commenced as usual by manoeuvres, in the course of which we occupied one of the Arapiles,[28] from whence much that was doing by the French army could be perceived, but we neglected to occupy in time the other next to it which the enemy seized. These hills are peculiar in their formation, being conical & table hills, the cone being cut off at about two thirds of its height & there was a large plateau or tableland at top, perfectly flat; these two hills were considered the keys of the position and the French & Spanish name the action by their name.[29]

At one time of the day, it was more than doubtful if an action would take place, but as a precautionary measure all the baggage

---

28 The battlefield of Salamanca is dominated by two heights known as the Greater and Lesser Arapiles.

29 In France and Spain it is known as the Battle of the Arapiles.

& stores of every description were peremptorily ordered to the rear that the roads might be kept clear in case of emergency, or being intercepted by the enemy.

Having done my part in this duty I was left to act as I pleased, provided I was not too distant from the troops I was attached to in case of being wanted. I therefore wandered about and first went into Salamanca, the streets of which were deserted & gloomy in the state of suspense in which the poor inhabitants found themselves, whether or not they should again fall in[to] the enemy's hands, it depending on the result of the operations of the armies that day. Our wounded (who could move or be moved) in the skirmishing that was going on, were almost the only people to be seen and there I met a young acquaintance in the 61st Regiment who had had a ball through the fleshy part of his thigh and had succeeded to reach the great square of the city; he had not however been seated many minutes before he found himself unable to get up or walk, his wound having got cold & stiffened the limb to such a degree as rendered it necessary to have him carried to his billet or lodging.[30]

At about one o'clock I then left the town and rode about the field for some time undetermined what to do until I decided to get to a point where I could best see what was going on and I got on a spot of the Arapiles from which I could see to the right & left of them in the rear of our position among the troops in reserve and for some time in company of Colonel Halkett[31] (afterwards Sir Colin) whose acquaintance I had made when in Guernsey and who at the moment commanded a light battalion in the King's Hanoverian Legion with our army. From thence much that was passing could be observed, the French in our front were cannonading our troops from their own Arapiles and we could distinctly see the [allied] shells pitching among

---

30 It has proven impossible to identify this officer with any certainty, although Ensign Robert Singleton is a possibility.

31 Brevet Colonel Colin Halket commanded the 2nd Light Battalion, King's German Legion, but at this time was commanding a brigade in the 7th Division.

them or exploding in the air over their heads. To our left the right of the French army was apparently taking ground & encamping for the day, while the infantry of their left wing were marching in large bodies along the frill of wooded heights to our right opening their guns as they advanced and making apparently for a hill on which they intended to establish their left flank to complete their day's work. The bulk of our army were marching parallel with them on the plain and as the ground I then occupied was much above them, our view embraced all their evolutions and I could with my glass perceive my brigade which was all that was necessary for me to do.

It was a most interesting and at the same time anxious scene and the suspense continued for a long while, during which doubts existed of a serious action taking place which had it not occurred would have most probably obliged us to retire again into Portugal & this feeling was evidently experienced in the French army from the circumstances I have mentioned, that their right had already encamped & would not be required.

In the midst of their uncertainty, at about four or five o'clock, the French had crowned the hill alluded to and Lord Wellington, perceiving with his eagle eye that they had weakened their left centre, instantly resolved on an attack, and under that probability he had stealthily withdrawn the 3rd Division (of upwards of 6,000 bayonets) left on the other side of Salamanca and unperceived by the enemy brought it up through the sinuosities of the valleys to his assistance, and as the French marshal conceived that he saw the whole of our disposable force in the plain, he (it was supposed) judged his movement to be a safe one.

The evolutions made appeared as on a map, the troops were seen advancing in beautiful order with the division alluded to simultaneously attacking the hill, our men swarming up it like a cloud & the French crowning its summit & firing down on their assailants. It was the work of a few minutes to capture it and in the meantime a whirlwind arose which with the dust and smoke completely enshrouded the contending armies and completely hid everything from our view making it an awful prelude to this great struggle.

Not to be too distant from my brigade, I made for an eminence on our right in the neighbourhood of which I thought they were and while doing so the French left had been turned and overwhelmed and columns of prisoners were already coming to the rear. There they were in whole battalions without arms of course, with their officers at their head distinguishable by their epaulettes and decorations, left almost unguarded. One of the officers came up to me & asked me what he and his men were to do and when he found I spoke French he seized me by the hand and would not let me go, offering me his purse for protection and I soon perceived their cause of alarm was occasioned by the appearance of the Spanish troops under Don Carlos de Espana[32] who began to insult them. As I could not stay or go with them, I handed my new acquaintance & his people to a sergeant of the 3rd Dragoons who with a party was to escort them to the rear. He equally laid hold of his hand and I daresay the purse was not refused a second time. It amounted almost to regret to see so many thousands of brave men[33] humbled as they appeared, and yet it was a moment of great exultation to behold them as prisoners.

Though the battle was raging in all its fury, the Spanish general was indolently conversing with the French officers instead of advancing in support as he was required to do. A Staff officer rode up to him & in no measured language desired him to press forward without delay & it was fortunately done for the defenceless Frenchmen, as the Spanish soldiers were beginning to leave their ranks to plunder & ill-use them, they were then marched to Salamanca under escort as they could collect them and were shut up in several large yards for the night, separate from the officers and shortly after proceeded

---

32 Roger Bernard Charles Espagnac was a French-born general in the Spanish army. He commanded a division of Spanish troops at the Battle of Salamanca.

33 French prisoners numbered some 7,000 at Salamanca, most being captured during the destructive charge of the heavy cavalry.

on to Portugal & Lisbon under the tender care of their irritated enemies, who could not be expected to be over kind to them but much to the contrary and many in consequence never reached their destination.

I ventured some little way in advance where the action was continuing to our left, to endeavour to learn particulars of what was going on, but as all was in the greatest confusion with more prisoners and war wounded coming from the front and night approaching, I rode to the rear with stragglers of the 3rd Dragoons to where I understood the quartermaster & some others of the corps were collected with the provisions intended for the day, and which I immediately sent up to the regiment on the chance of finding it, and having succeeded fortunately, it was acknowledged to me many years after in a letter I received from Lieutenant Colonel Clowes who then commanded & who wrote to me about the Peninsular medal, it was as follows:

> 'I have much pleasure in having brought to my remembrance the gratification felt and expressed at the time by the regiment and myself at your exertions in supplying us with our rations at 11 o'clock at night on entering our bivouac after the battle of Salamanca & thus enabling me to distribute a double ration after the fatigues of that memorable day.'

I soon learnt with much sorrow and regret that General Le Marchant had been killed at the head of our brigade in charging the enemy, for in him I lost a kind and valuable friend as in being under his immediate eye he was constantly kind and it endeared him to me. We were related,[34] he was a noble soldier of powerful frame and a capital swordsman and in the act of gallantly leading his men received three musket balls in his body. His death was a loss to the country for he

---

34 John Le Marchant had married Mary Carey, a distant cousin.

was without doubt one of the best cavalry officers with the army. Had it been in my power, I should have gone [to] where he lay, but I had professional duties and arrangements to attend to and I was very much fatigued from the exertions of the day. I sent however by an orderly a message to his son who was with the body, offering any assistance in my power, and the orderly brought me word back that the general had been buried wrapped up in his cloak. Having been on intimate terms with that son, Carey Le Marchant,[35] who died in 1813 [1814], he wrote me occasionally and in one of his letters he says:

> 'I must return you my best thanks for offering me your assistance on the melancholy night of the 22 July; consolation is in vain and we must resign ourselves with humble resignation to the divine will. You who were so well acquainted with my poor father must be aware how I feel his loss, I believe no parent was fonder of his children and no person ever made more sacrifices for them, how then ought we not to mourn his loss. It is some consolation to know that he died most gloriously and I shall ever regret that I was not with him when he received the fatal wound, no officer was near, indeed the confusion was great'.

The fact was, which I ascertained from the men who were in action with the brigade, that they found the enemy in line and rode over them, then another line presented itself and a third and when they had galloped over the first, these turned and fired back at them which placed them between two fires and so on with the second and third lines which occasioned the greatest confusion and the dispersion of many of our men. The enemy were however so disordered by the charge that they became an easy prey to the troops coming up, and it

---

35 His son Carey Le Marchant was then an Ensign in the 1st Foot Guards. He was an aide de camp to his father but was absent when he was killed. He died of wounds suffered at the Nive on 12 March 1814.

led to nearly the whole of their left flank being cut off, by having been too much extended and these were the men I afterwards met coming to the rear. The facts thus related of this great victory I either saw myself or they were related to me during the night or shortly afterwards, for of what happened to our left in other parts of the field is described in the despatches &c and did not come under my immediate notice.[36]

We stopped for the night in the open country about a mile in the rear of the field of battle & near Salamanca and lay down in one of the primitive open threshing floors of the country on chopped straw, wrapped up in a blanket to get a little sleep if possible after the existing great excitement, and before dawn were again up and were surrounded by some of the melancholy results of the action and sufferings of poor humanity, the road was thronged with mules, donkeys &c and their drivers fetching the wounded who could not walk, some of whom had crept as far as they could during the night lying exhausted and crying for water round about us; among them were groups of Frenchmen who had been plundered and ill used by the peasantry even to stripping off their clothes and had kept together in hopes of affording each other protection. As the Spaniards passed them they insulted them, and until every one of our men had been collected and brought to the hospitals, they would not attend to their most pressing solicitations. This sad scene continued until we passed the field of battle which bore evidence by the number of the dead, of the determination of the struggle.

Next morning before break of day, the troops were in pursuit & had it not been for the Spanish general withdrawing without orders, a detachment which guarded the bridge of Alba de Tormes over which the French army had a possibility alone of escaping, the greatest part must have laid down their arms, for as it was our advance overtook their rearguard and captured three battalions of infantry. Having been obliged professionally to remain on the road several hours I was not up at the moment of the encounter but

---

36 The charge of Le Marchant's cavalry is steeped in mystery as we have few first-hand accounts, so Carey's comments although second-hand are therefore very useful.

arrived in time to see the prisoners and the spot where the gallant charge of the heavy Germans under Baron Bock had been so successful.[37] The dead & wounded were still on the ground and the arms of the French were still piled ready to be carried away. The events of the previous day had evidently disheartened them for they did not behave in their usual determined manner. After this rencontre the enemy's retreat became a run and we found it hopeless to follow them in expectation of doing them further mischief, it being left to some of the light troops to push them further and the bulk of the army halted to get some rest.

We subsequently advanced on to the city of Valladolid and passed through it, the inhabitants receiving us with slight demonstrations of joy which was not to be wondered at as they had become accustomed to the French whom they expected again to see shortly, our advance being considered but temporary.

The heat had become truly oppressive & the sun scorching in the open air now our constant residence, to the extent that it burnt the skin of our faces & lips producing scabs, to go therefore into a house or church was a delightful sensation from the comparative coolness existing in them, especially in the latter which being objects of curiosity were usually entered if time or opportunity permitted.

The cathedral of Valladolid is a huge pile as yet unfinished,[38] rather a characteristic of the Spanish nation, the prevailing disposition of

---

37 At Garcia Hernandez, Major General Eberhardt von Bock's cavalry brigade, consisting of the 1st and 2nd Dragoons KGL, came up on the French rearguard. The French cavalry retired rapidly, leaving eight battalions of French infantry to defend themselves on a hill, where they formed squares. The dragoons charged the first square (a battalion of the 6th Light Infantry). The French held their volley too long and although a number of horses were mortally wounded, their impetus brought them into contact with the square, creating a gap through which the dragoons followed and the infantry were forced to surrender. A second square was frightened by the scenes they had witnessed and simply broke when charged. French losses were 200 killed and wounded and 1,400 prisoners. The Dragoons lost fifty-four killed and sixty-two wounded.

38 The construction of Valladolid cathedral began when the city was the de facto capital and was designed to be the greatest cathedral in Spain. However, the decision to move the capital to Madrid left it unfinished and it remains in this state today.

which is to form grand designs beyond their power or means & which are begun but never completed, it being put off to 'tomorrow' their national proverb; which was further exemplified by a magnificent canal which we crossed at this time & which was intended to communicate between Madrid & Bilbao, but left unfinished on its reaching the foot of the mountain range over hanging the latter place & which would have proved [an] incalculable benefit to Castile and every other province it traversed.[39]

I went into the cathedral above alluded to and was struck with the solemn gloomy stillness which prevailed [&] contrasted with the bustle outside. Few persons were then at prayers and some of these were evidently devotees & others were performing vows of penitence, the former on their knees or crouched to the ground and the latter kneeling with extended arms like a cross silently and earnestly looking up to their titular saint for intercession and endeavouring to remain in that position as long as their strength permitted. These acts of duty prevailed in every church we visited throughout our campaigns and was most strikingly observable when the regular services were over and when the building was occupied by those only whose obligations were imperative or who were more religiously disposed than the rest of the community.

Lord Wellington (as will have been perceived) having struck a momentous blow at the French power in the north of Spain, contemplated another which he at once put into execution, for having for a time at least crippled the army opposed to him, he determined on menacing the capital and we accordingly received orders to retrograde & march in the direction of that city. Not that we were told of his intentions, but suspected them, as he was most secret and never communicated even to his generals his resolves, so that the French

---

39 The Canal de Castilla was begun in the late seventeenth century with the aim of enabling wheat grown in the Tierra de Campos region around Valladolid to be easily transported to Santander. After a hundred years of building, the railways made it redundant and the canal never reached the coast.

never could ascertain them in time to give them a check until they were carried into execution.

We moved by easy marches on Segovia, encamping in the neighbourhood of small villages, the inhabitants of which were occupied in reaping and threshing their corn quite illustrative of the mode alluded to in the scriptures. There was the floor and the cattle treading out the grain in ear, the animals being however muzzled, some tied in a row held by a cord walking round a man in a circle and others drawing a sort of sledge in which a man sat with a boarded bottom studded with sharp flints which cut the straw after it was threshed to serve as forage, no hay being made in the country.

While the corn was still standing, the mode of supplying the cavalry with forage was simple but oppressive and was thus effected. As we approached the intended place of encampment, a field of barley as contiguous to the road as possible was looked for, selected and enquiries made for the proprietor. If he made his appearance he was told of what was to take place, but if not found it was all the same, the men then got off their horses and with their sickles, cut as much as they thought the animals would eat for the night, after which they remounted with their bundle & proceeded to their ground. The Commissariat officer then calculated what the regimental rations amounted to, in pounds weight of corn in the ear, and gave his receipt for it to whoever claimed it, either on the spot, or where the troops halted, which receipt was afterwards paid by the Commissary General. But the owner was never fully indemnified as there was much waste although it was far preferable to getting nothing for their crops, for which the French never paid a farthing.

When the season advanced and the corn had been threshed & winnowed & lay in heaps on the threshing floors outside the villages, the alcalde (the local magistrate) was required to furnish from them what was necessary and then the business was transacted with more regularity, though the owners parted unwillingly with his or their winter store; such were some of the miseries attendant on a state of war.

With respect to bread, it was usually obtained by paying for it in ready money, even then it was not always to be obtained in sufficient quantities. For such a gormandiser as a concentrated army is found to be, by the part of the country subject to its consumption. Meat was also an object of difficulty, but being a moveable article of subsistence in the shape of an ox or sheep, it could be brought from afar or seized upon when met in the neighbourhood of the camp, or searched after where it was ascertained to be concealed & as the Commissariat was understood to pay for what was consumed on the spot, provided always that adequate pecuniary resources existed, which was seldom the case; the officers of the department were furnished with small sums of money to pay only for what was absolutely indispensable and could not be extorted from the holders who had safely secreted the articles wanted. This money was a source of great anxiety to the holder, from the difficulty of securing it properly in a tent in the mist of the soldiery who knew of its existence, and the army having many loose characters in it the temptation to plunder it was great and it happened that while the brigade of cavalry was within two days march of Segovia my brother Commissary[40] attached to the 5th Dragoon Guards had this money amounting to 1,500 dollars, in silver, equal to £330 sterling,[41] carried off most cleverly. The box containing it was under his pillow with the top nailed down, the robbers notwithstanding managed to remove it without his waking, carried it outside, broke it open and replaced it under him, and it was only on his going to make a payment next morning that the loss was discovered, of which loss he was only exonerated after much trouble & investigation.

---

40 I have failed to find a General Order identifying the Commissary of the 5th Dragoon Guards. It appears that the Commissary also avoided a court martial.

41 Equivalent to about £16,000 today.

I was equally provided with a sum, but fortunately my bed was a patent one contained in an iron bound box the frame of which drew out on which to lay the mattress, my pillow being over the empty part in which the money was secured, so that it was impossible to reach it without moving me bodily, which could hardly have been done without my awaking. There was no doubt that the robbery was committed by the men of his regiment.

On the 7th of August we encamped in the neighbourhood of Segovia, a famous old town in old Castile so celebrated in Spanish romance, but into which I could only peep for an hour or two & it well repaid my curiosity. The Alcazar is a magnificent pile or fortress of Moorish architecture[42] majestically situated at the extreme point of a bluff rocky cliff, on a knoll overlooking a river torrent winding round it, the sides of which knoll are bold, deep and savage. It was used as a prison being cut off from the town by a ditch &c. The town itself had much the appearance of those already visited, with narrow streets to keep the sun out. In proceeding to our encampment we passed under the famous Roman aqueduct consisting of two sets of arches, one above the other, over or by which the water is still conveyed across a valley into the city; its solidity appeared to ensure its lasting for ever, requiring no repairs, the only perceptible indication of its antiquity being that the sharp angles of the stones were rounded by time. Over the lower centre arch there was a niche in which an inscription had originally been put, but it had disappeared and the period of its erection could not be ascertained in our hasty enquiries. The Emperor Trajan is however the reputed author of it;[43] the water comes from the adjacent mountains, dividing Old & New Castile.

On the 8th we encamped near Valsaín in the neighbourhood of San Ildefonso the summer residence of the Royal family, beautifully

---

42 The Alcazar was the ancient fortress of the Kings of Castile.

43 The latest archaeology supports a date around the time of Emperor Trajan (r. AD 98–177) or just afterwards.

situated in an isolated spot at the foot of the northern side of the Guadarrama mountains on the high road from Madrid to the north of the kingdom. The mansion or palace is small, but the gardens are magnificent with shrubberies & lime trees feathering up to the top of the hills (a treat in Spain) and most extensive water works which, with fresh breezes from the mountains, produces a most delightful coolness not to be found elsewhere within the same distance from the capital.

We had a day's halt while the army was concentrating which gave us the opportunity of seeing this Elysium[44] & being present when Lord Wellington with his numerous Staff visited it. The concourse of officers & inhabitants was great and on so exhilarating an occasion all the water works played in succession consisting of fountains, cascades, jets &c intermixed with statuary producing such striking effect as to be considered equal to those of Versailles. Some of the regimental bands played & the evening went off to the gratification of all present particularly of the natives, whose joy seemed to know no bounds at being freed from an oppressive yoke. One of the works consisted of a jet & basin surrounded by a walk & beyond it by a hedge of evergreens trimmed like a wall & so closely matted as to prevent its being passed through except at two or three openings; this jet had a secret spring which when touched threw the water in every direction like a shower of rain and being near one of these openings his Lordship was put in the secret, and having placed his foot on it step[ped] quickly out of the circle, leaving all those that followed him to escape as they could. The rush was great and excited much merriment, those caught in the trap being however more frightened than hurt. It was a capital practical joke and no doubt had often amused royalty long before. The water which fed these water works is obtained from reservoirs constructed by the damming of valleys or ravines in the mountains through which streams or runs of water pass

---

44 Paradise.

and being high up, the jets are propelled to a great height. Charles the 4th[45] hunted in these mountains and the mode of proceeding consisted of batteries by which the game was concentrated in one spot and it was said his majesty fired at the concourse of animals with mountain guns carried on mules, a folly not to be wondered at from a man considered half an idiot, and who left his country to be governed by the favourites of his immoral queen.

On the 10th our march commenced by ascending the mountain road beautifully constructed & zigzagging as we proceeded up the picturesque passes, rendered more interesting at every turn by the dense masses of our troops, which passes had they been defended, would have given us some employment, but no enemy appeared and we gradually arrived at the summit or col of the pass. In our descent on the reverse side the plain of new Castile burst upon us, but it appeared arid and only relieved by the city of Madrid, perceptible at a long distance like an oasis in the desert and distinguishable with our glasses by its public buildings with little or no other feature of beauty. The Escurial [El Escorial] celebrated as the 8th wonder of the world in the estimation of the Spaniards being discernible to the right at the foot of the range of mountains just passed by us extending in that direction. It was a moment of exultation and of proud feeling to see so near an object we all had long been desirous to visit and we beheld it as conquerors who had well-earned such a gratification.

We had however next day a mishap to undergo before we reached it. The brigade of cavalry to which I was attached preceded as usual the infantry on the plain & after the march we encamped on the 11th in a ravine off the road with an advanced guard of Portuguese dragoons with a brigade of horse artillery. Being in the second line with the heavy German cavalry in our front we were allowed to unsaddle, but always in readiness to move in support when required and being

---

45 King Charles IV of Spain had been forced to abdicate to his son Ferdinand VII who was also forced to abdicate by Napoleon in lieu of his brother Joseph.

in a hollow as described, we remained in a state of quiescence and could see no distance around us. Cooking was going on quietly when all at once an officer of ours, Major Hutchins[46] who in his zeal had fortunately pushed on to the front, came to the edge of the ravine bellowing at the top of his voice to 'saddle, bridle, and form as soon as possible as the enemy was advancing'. The scene of bustle & confusion which ensued at such a moment can hardly be described; everyone scrambling to get ready in various ways, some to pack the baggage and others to leap on their horses, and by twos and threes ascend on the plain and there form up as they arrived. The brigade then moved forward & soon came to the rescue; we found however the affray just over, but saw the Portuguese dragoons in great confusion, disperse and flying in all directions and many of the poor Germans laying dead. The cause of the uproar was as follows. The French who had been reported as about to retire from the city, unexpectedly delayed their departure and made a dash with a body of cavalry at our advance & fell on the Portuguese dragoons with such impetuosity that they at once routed them & no stand was made. Our artillery seeing that, were obliged from want of support to fly also, but as they could not get over the ground quick enough, were obliged to abandon three of their guns which were found next day with the carriages burnt. No time was allowed to alarm the second or supporting line & the enemy fell on the heavy Germans unprepared; they were therefore obliged to get on their horses half clothed, fighting at great disadvantage, lost many men & were roughly handled just before we had come up. They notwithstanding, succeeded in driving back the enemy who probably did not intend to come further, for had they pushed on they might have done much mischief or got themselves into a scrape. I am afraid we were too confident at the moment, under the impression that they were in full retreat; had the Portuguese made a common

---

46 Actually Captain Thomas Hutchins was Brigade Major, he became a Major on 10 December 1812.

stand & restrained the enemy by skirmishing & a charge, we could have come up in time but the fact is they were taken with a panic & bolted at once leaving everything exposed. The affair being over, after alarming the whole army, we returned to our encampment with no chance of dinner & the night was passed in feverish excitement.[47]

Next morning the 12th of August, it was ascertained that the enemy had actually evacuated Madrid accompanied it was said, by King Joseph and forty thousand inhabitants in his interests, called Afrancesados and that the city was occupied by the various bands of guerrillas which had usually hovered about it. Orders were soon received for our marching into it and the cavalry formed the advance with our infantry swarming behind us, filling up the road for several miles. On arriving near it we found the guerrillas all mounted & lining both sides of the road to bid us welcome, exhibiting a motley assembly clothed in every variety of Spanish & French costume, many of them having on the uniform of their enemies whom they had killed and despoiled. They sounded their trumpets as we advanced and now began one of the most interesting as well as amusing scenes it was possible to witness. It was indeed a triumphant march before which the oppressors had fled and relieved the oppressed from a thraldom of four long years duration and joyfully did the latter evince

---

47 This refers to the action at Majadahonda. Lieutenant Colonel Benjamin D'Urban commanding a Portuguese cavalry brigade of about 700 men and escorted by Macdonald's horse artillery troop, had spent the morning, leisurely driving back the rearguard of the French army. Reaching this village he ordered his troops to cook and rest during the intense heat of the afternoon. Unfortunately, King Joseph had ordered a cavalry reconnaissance in strength under General Treillard and his force of over 2,000 sabres now descended on the Portuguese. D'Urban sent messages to call up the brigade of KGL dragoons in his rear and deployed his Portuguese cavalry ready to fight, although outnumbered three to one. D'Urban ordered his men to charge, but the Portuguese cavalry turned just before they crossed swords and fled in confusion. A small party of about twenty KGL dragoons had joined the fight and sought to protect the retreat of three cannon but were cut to pieces and the guns captured. The whole were driven back on the village of Las Rozas, where the KGL troops were, so quickly in fact that many of the German dragoons fought half-dressed or without a saddle. The Germans fought bravely, but numbers overwhelmed them and they were forced to retreat slowly, until Ponsonby's Brigade arrived, when the French retired in haste, leaving the captured guns behind.

their feelings of gratitude on the occasion. As we proceeded on, the whole population rich and poor appeared to have come out dressed in their best to receive us and the streets were so encumbered with the masses that it became necessary to halt occasionally to clear the way. In these halts the enthusiasm of the people knew no bounds, men & women, ladies & gentlemen embraced our legs, shook hands with us, offered us wine & provisions and in many instances pulled us off our horses to kiss us, and it was done indiscriminately to the officers & soldiers. The cheers & acclamations mingled with the trumpets & regimental bands were deafening, occasioning an uproar difficult to be described. Thus we advanced with a succession of these animating scenes, which instead of calming, increased until we reached the main street (the broad Alcala[48]) the fronts of the houses of which were all decorated (as on their greatest Holy day) with hangings of silks and satins & the balconies filled with inhabitants in their best attire waving their handkerchiefs and producing a perspective view, including our troops filling the street in dense masses, which must have been seen to be conceived, and the exultation of feeling to be appreciated. In short, everyone seemed to have lost their sense in delirium of joy and when it was necessary afterwards to occupy our billets or lodgings in the various parts of the city and [we] had to go on foot for that & other purposes, we were so constantly waylaid by all classes either to shake hands or embrace us, that for two or three days in the height of the excitement it became so great a nuisance that many officers remained indoors to avoid it. For although many a pretty young woman paid us the compliment, many less desirable were equally importunate.

On going to the municipality for my billet with the officer charged with that duty, I was asked if I understood French, which having answered in the affirmative, an order was given me on a very superior house to that which I was entitled, with an intimation that I was sent

---

48 Calle de Alcala.

there to protect the family who were in the French interest, as unless it was thus occupied an apprehension was entertained that it might be sacked & burnt with its inmates by the populace exasperated against anything French. I was of course received with open arms by the family and allotted a suite of apartments fit for a prince and when the aide de camp of the general commanding the cavalry came to me on business, he remarked that I was better accommodated than his chief which I found it necessary to explain, to avoid my being turned out. I was therefore left in peace to enjoy for a few days a luxurious residence in which I fared sumptuously at no expense, the lady of the mansion providing my meals and sending to know every morning what I liked best for dinner. I had however little intercourse with her or hers, as my presence with my guard of four dragoons, though a protection was anything but gratifying to her, her husband having fled with the intrusive king with whom he unfortunately sided.

Having made good my quarters and shaken off the accumulation of dust from off my person & washed my face, which was absolutely covered with dust & perspiration, the march having been so dusty as to prevent our seeing each other, though elbows almost touched. I ventured into the street on business and saw that everyone was still enjoying himself, and I may in a few words say that this jubilee continued for several days without interruption and no wonder, for in the time of French dominion no assemblage was tolerated. In the evening the Constitution which had been adopted by the Junta at Cadiz[49] was proclaimed on a stage erected purposely in the Plaza Mayor [Maior] (or Great Square), but I regretted to see shortly after this solemn announcement, a bolero danced upon that very stage, in which dance the people apparently took more interest than in the former ceremony, evincing thereby their indifference to being

---

49 The Junta or Government of Spain had resided in Cadiz as one of the last areas of Spain free from French domination.

politically emancipated from the ancient tyranny of their kings to which they had been accustomed for so many centuries.

In the midst of this universal joy there was however one drawback which appeared unheeded by the inhabitants, but which required immediate attention on our part & that was from a French garrison having been injudiciously left in a fortified palace, the Retiro situated on the Prado or public walk, just outside the city wall, the guns & mortars of which might be expected to fire from one moment to the other & could have done immense mischief to the city.[50] Preparations were therefore made to besiege it and curiosity having led me to get a glimpse of the place, the Prince of Orange aide de camp[51] to Lord Wellington passed me on his way to have a parley with its commandant, at the end of a wall which projected on the Prado, under or behind which we were protected from the advanced sentries of the enemy, an iron balustrade extended completely open to their fire. The prince took out his pocket handkerchief, advanced some paces waving it and called out that he wished to speak to an officer. A dead silence ensued and then an officer came forward, and after a short conversation which no one person present could hear but themselves, they separated and everything continued as before, until the place was taken. We could of course hardly be considered as quietly in possession of Madrid & therefore decided steps were taken for its possession. After driving the garrison within its inner line of defence, offers of capitulation were made and accepted, and the garrison marched out with the honours or war, that is in being allowed to

---

50 When the French left Madrid, King Joseph left a garrison of 2,000 men under the command of General Lafon Blaniac in the Retiro fortifications. Napoleon had ordered the Retiro heights to be fortified in 1808. A field fortification of earth banks had been constructed with ten bastions and within this was a star fort as a final defence. However, once the outer defences had fallen easily, the French sought terms and surrendered. A huge number of cannon and other military stores were captured including the two Eagles of the 51st Ligne and 13th Dragoons.

51 Colonel Prince William of Orange, the son of the current Stadtholder, served on Wellington's Staff as an extra aide de camp.

appear on the glacis[52] with their arms. They then grounded them and at once commenced their long and I may say perilous journey towards Lisbon, through a population most inimical to them. They were a fine body of infantry 2,000 strong besides followers, but such was the exasperation of the populace against them that it was not considered safe to pass them through the city. They were therefore taken round it, passing through a double row of our troops for their protection, and as there was an immense crowd of inhabitants to witness the scene, the poor defenceless fellows were received with loud imprecations and threats which were followed by attempts made to assassinate them with the knife, the use of which is so well understood by Spaniards & which were brandished in their faces by the more furious of the people who could hardly be restrained by our men. One fellow near where I stood succeeded in getting through and had he not been seized at once murder would have been committed, and I am convinced had not unusual precautions been taken, every man of them would have been destroyed in a few minutes. As it was many eventually fell victims on the road, especially such as [those] knocked up on the march, or the English escort could not be conveniently sent with them beyond a short distance from the city, and they were then handed over to the precarious mercy of Spanish and Portuguese soldiery.

The defences of this fortified palace had been in course of erection a year or two & when surrendered was found to contain an arsenal full of guns, muskets (many of English manufacture taken by the French from the Spanish armies) ammunition & materials of all sorts, and when it was taken possession of all the mounted guns & mortars in battery were found loaded & pointed towards the city, which had they been fired would have, as I said before, done much mischief. When we were afterwards obliged to evacuate this part of the country a great portion of this arsenal was unavoidably destroyed by us by breaking the stocks of the muskets & placing the mouths of the guns

---

52 The outer earthen slope.

facing each other & firing them into each other which disabled them. It turned out a piece of great folly in leaving this fine garrison behind for they were unnecessarily sacrificed, it being impossible for them to make a defence long enough to be relieved or extricated in time, but the fact is that our advance was so sudden that no measures could be matured by the French before we were on their backs.

After this serious business had been settled the joy of the people continued; the Prado (the great public walk) became the lounge to which Lord Wellington & many of the officers resorted every evening but he was so much made of & it may be said so worried with kindness that it evidently annoyed him.

A bull fight was exhibited by the magistrates, at which an immense concourse assisted, but as such a scene is described by every traveller who has ever visited Spain, it is needless for me to enter into its details & all I shall say is that the horses on which the picadors were mounted were such miserable animals that they hardly showed strength enough to exert themselves in advancing on, or retreating from the fiery bulls; several were consequently gored & killed without a fair chance of doing their duty. Of course, the men were wonderfully agile and performed their respective parts with great coolness & bravery and no wonder as they are brought up to the profession and are quite accustomed to it from long practice, travelling for the purpose about the country where required. The bulls were magnificent animals, half wild and as fleet as horses with beautiful shaped horns & in some instances the dewlap[53] & neck was one mass of curl; they were in high condition and quite a contrast to the poor horses against which they were pitted. Consequently, there is no comparison between them & the heavy corpulent English bull & when they first made their appearance in the arena they looked truly formidable, fought most gallantly in most cases and it was with regret that at last they fell at the feet of the matador after unavailing

---

53 The projection of skin that hangs down from a cow's neck.

efforts to preserve life and fight it out to the last. The Spaniards both men and women appeared in raptures at this national pastime and were astonished at the little interest we comparatively took in it, in almost regretting the destruction of such noble animals.

After the enthusiasm of our presence had a little subsided, we visited the town in many of its details. It appeared extremely small for the capital of so vast a country, having no suburbs and I easily walked round it in three or four hours. We found the women very handsome, but the generality had decayed teeth from it was said, an immoderate use of sweetmeats, which defect in great measure spoiled their beauty. Notwithstanding its smallness we found the city well built & having the advantage over Lisbon in the breadth of its streets & the uncommon number of good houses of the nobility &c. The King's palace is an immense & superb pile of building vieing [*sic*] with anything I had before seen, but there was not a church suitable in grandeur to correspond with the other public edifices of a place which at that time was a mere shadow of what it had been previous to the oppression it had suffered. In point of curiosities, none existed that we could learn at the time; the French with their usual habits of plunder having removed or carried away everything they could lay hands on to add to the Napoleon Museum[54] at Paris. There were however some paintings in the municipality (as we were told) on the walls, representing King Joseph's exploits in forcing the Sierra Morena mountains & capture of Seville, which before our entrance had been covered over with coloured wax, and remained so until his [future] return, when no doubt they were again exposed to view. This was not publicly known to [the] Spaniards but it was mentioned to us under the impression that no advantage would be taken of it, and therefore the walls looked as if they were merely painted in panels which to a common observer had all the appearance of permanency.

---

54 The Louvre was temporarily renamed the Napoleon Museum during his reign.

4TH CAMPAIGN

A river was said to flow on one side of the city & there were bridges over its bed, but the stream hardly flowed at the time,[55] though we were told that in winter it often overflowed its banks, which appeared anything but picturesque, the wonder being that a capital city should have been placed on so barren a spot, without any visible advantage whatever but that of being in the centre of the kingdom.

The occupation of it by us after the battle of Salamanca electrified the peninsula and had the energies of the lower classes been properly directed, the French might have been expelled from the kingdom, but unfortunately the administration of affairs was entrusted to men who either were corrupt, or imbecile, for those entrusted with military commands were incapable of conducting them and those directing the general government were equally deficient. The precious moments for energetic measures were therefore frittered away in needless matters and the only consequence which followed so splendid an achievement was the raising of the siege of Cadiz by Marshal Soult and evacuation of Andalusia followed by the concentration of [the] French armies with the view of again driving us out of Spain into Portugal.

Our hold of the capital appeared therefore but temporary, and having the acquaintance of General Alava,[56] a noble & active Spaniard on the personal Staff of Lord Wellington, he also expressed to me his doubts of our being able to keep long our advanced position in the face of the overwhelming force likely to be brought in a month or two from all directions against us. The moral effect of doing so far as was practicable was however deemed indispensable to stimulate if possible, the nation to exertion in all quarters, of which there might be a fair chance when it was known that the capital was free.

The first symptoms of our having to keep the enemy in check was in the north, in the neighbourhood of Valladolid; to face the army which after having been thrashed by us, was again advancing after

---

55 The River Manzanares.

56 General Miguel Alava was the Spanish Military Attaché to the Duke of Wellington.

receiving reinforcements; and as a preparatory measure the brigade to which I continued to be attached, now under the command of Colonel Ponsonby[57] afterwards killed at Waterloo, received orders with other troops to return to San Ildefonso on the 21 August, where we arrived on the 23rd recrossing in the march the Guadarama Mountains, our horses occupied the stables & the officers & men the quarters usually occupied by the Spanish Guards when in attendance on the king whilst in seclusion here enjoying a cool climate comparatively. As the troops were marching detached in great measure & not in concentrated masses at the moment, we were alone in the town and found it dull with few inhabitants, its filling or occupation being dependent on the arrival of the court or on such an occasion as the one on which we recently passed through on our advance to the capital; the gardens were our lounge or I should say that of the officers, as I myself had little leisure, unless it was for an hour in the evening to make a little exploration in the cool, during which I found nothing new to mention.

Fresh orders arrived in a few days to continue our progress northward & we commenced our march on the 29th, by Segovia to Coca on the road to Valladolid during which we met with other troops in the way, one division of infantry of which had been at the Escurial [Escorial] (seen only by us at a distance); the officers spoke of its immensity by mentioning that a corps of the army consisting of at least 14,000 men, besides animals of all sorts, when ordered to occupy it, marched into one of its courts and in an incredible short time disappeared in its numerous corridors & stables, without confusion & with hardly any appearance of so great an increase in its population.

The country we were traversing consisted of immense flats & plains bounded by noble ranges of mountains seen at great distances, and from the tower of the village church in the neighbourhood of which

---

57 Brevet Colonel the Honourable William Ponsonby.

we were encamped, the one to which we were proceeding the next day could be distinctly seen, indeed before the cutting of the corn had taken place the appearance all around was like the sea there being no hedges or detached buildings to disturb the evenness or uniformity of the landscape, the church towers only appearing by the mirage as so many ships under sail; there was therefore little to interest us except in the inhabitants who hitherto had seen little of us and were dressed more peculiarly than had come under our observation before. Having in the course of my duty to go in quest of supplies out of the line of march I occasionally visited isolated villages the inhabitants of which until then had not seen English soldiers & being accompanied by three dragoons, when we neared the place and were perceived, the excitement among the people was very amusing, the bells of the church were put in motion, everyone came to their doors looking at us with apparent astonishment and as our guide (who mentioned who we were) was leading us to the magistrate's house (the alcalde) we were followed to his door by the crowd desirous of beholding Englishmen & heretics, for our name was synonymous to the other in the opinion of the bigots & as a common saying when points on religion were mooted by these simple people, many of whom had been made to believe by their priesthood that we had tails like the evil one. I could hardly get off my horse when we stopped, as numbers began examining our swords, saddles & bridles &c, particularly the dragoons whose thighs they pinched to ascertain if possible that we were really like themselves; such were the strange notions they had between a Roman Catholic & a Protestant. The men remained on horseback until my interview with the peasant magistrate was over, during which I was requested to show myself at the balcony for the gratification of the curious; we were then asked to eat something and our horses put up to feed & while that took place we were almost worried by the curiosity of these good people in their coming in & going out, for probably they had not even seen a French soldier, for the troops of that nation could only go in large bodies, whilst we could go even singly without the least danger or molestation & might reckon on kind treatment.

On the 4 September we left Coca and encamped near Alcasaren [Alcazaren], this march was through a pinewood in company with a regiment of German hussars & took place between 3 & 8 o'clock of the morning to avoid as usual the great heat of the day. As we proceeded along & only the tread of the horses feet was heard with not a breath of air stirring & the day just dawning with a most delightful freshness, suddenly a fine melodious voice was heard, then another and more in succession until most of the German regiment added their efforts to this novel entertainment, the effect at such a time & place was grand & most pleasurable, for the performance was sung in parts and the chorus so correctly, that even the horses seemed animated with it. We were therefore loth to part with such amusing 'companions de voyage' for though going the same way we were too large a body of horse to be accommodated without necessity at the same place, and thus we parted at the end of the march. In going through this and other pine woods we perceived the simple way in which the turpentine was extracted from the trees, by a scoop or flute being cut in the body of the trunk six or seven feet in height, an inch deep & a foot or less broad from the surface of which the liquid exuded & trickled down into the sandy soil forming a cake which was taken up at stated times & another scoop made round the stem, a mode which appeared to us anything but economical, being wasteful and slovenly.

On the 7 September we crossed the Duero and again entered Valladolid shortly after the enemy had evacuated it, encamping as usual in its neighbourhood. The inhabitants received us without enthusiasm apparently indifferent as to whom they should be subject to. We were now in chase of the French army and saw their retiring columns every day apparently disposed to fight but it seemed as if Lord Wellington was more inclined to drive them before him than try his strength. He accordingly turned the positions on which they

4TH CAMPAIGN

offered battle by flank movements for several days in succession & we progressively advanced by Duenas on the 12th, Cordovilla [la Real] 13th near the position of Celada del Camino which they occupied to cover if possible Burgos, but a Spanish army having reinforced us, they retired through that city leaving a numerous & chosen garrison in the castle which had been strongly fortified. The road we had taken for the last few days was very picturesque abounding in valley & mountain intersected by ravines & small rivers and rich in produce, by which the two armies were well supplied with provisions &c although at the cost of the inhabitants.

Arrangements were at once made to dislodge the enemy if possible from their stronghold but it unhappily failed in the end. We came up in support of other troops, and had crowded the high road which was lined with rows of trees when the enemy suddenly unmasked some guns commanding it & opened their fire down it upon us; several of the cavalry were knocked down at once, but orders having been immediately given to open right and left & get in the adjacent fields no further injury occurred, the shots subsequently fired bowling down harmlessly. The troops remained in still & solemn silence while a reconnaissance was going on by His Lordship & in the meantime the enemy withdrew from our front and we found we were at the foot of the heights of St Michael [San Miguel], on which an advanced work [hornwork] was situated, nothing was done at that moment and we bivouacked for the night during which the infantry attacked and carried it,[58] driving the enemy within the defences of the castle, the siege of which was at once commenced. But as cavalry is not employed on such a duty, being kept in reserve to act in the front against an advancing foe & cover otherwise operations in case of need, became mere spectators of what was going on & were quartered in a small hamlet called

---

58 The hornwork was assaulted on 19 September with a loss to Wellington's forces of 421 killed and wounded.

Villayerno [-Morquillas] between two or three miles from the scene of action.

From a height near our village we could with our spyglasses distinctly see the operations of the siege, the battering train was found totally inadequate to the undertaking, consisting of only 3 iron eighteen pounders and five or six brass howitzers, which we had brought with us to batter down such block houses as might have crossed our path, for as the French correspondence, owing to the guerrillas, could only be kept up by strong relays of escorts they had fortified houses on the road at every stage in which garrisons were stationed & it was possible that some might have unexpectedly impeded our march had we not been provided with proper artillery to reduce them. But they were not intended for a regular siege and their inferiority soon manifested itself, for they had hardly been put in battery when the enemy's superior fire broke the trunnion of one & another shot disabled the second by striking it in the muzzle, leaving the third to perform alone its gigantic work of breaching, viz that of knocking down the facing wall of the enemy's defences, and it was rumoured that this solitary gun had become unruly by capsizing frequently when a little warm. The siege therefore progressed but slowly and it was soon found a hopeless case to continue this mode of attack and recourse was had to sapping, mining by which a series of attacks occurred and ground was gained only foot by foot with great loss of life on our side. Most of these operations took place at night and in witnessing some of them (when aware of their going to happen, as they were kept a secret as much as possible) the only thing perceptible from our look-out resembled, as far as it could be described, more a grand firework than anything else, but the comparison was of a melancholy nature, aware as we were of the destruction which was occurring in our ranks. On one occasion the affair occurred in the afternoon by a mine being sprung, which threw up a cloud of smoke & earth with portions of walls of outworks and was immediately succeeded by storming parties advancing, among whom the 24th Regiment was conspicuous. We saw them running up and enter the work, but almost instantaneously all was shrouded in smoke by the fire of the enemy and our own, and nothing more could be seen. The cannonade continued & was distinctly heard rendering us aware that the work of death was not over.

The tediousness of the siege and obstacles encountered began to tell on the spirits of the men, discontent followed with bad weather, which made them careless and in many instances the proportion of work allotted in the trenches to working parties for the night was not completed, but by the detachments of the Guards and no wonder as the trenches were knee deep in mud, and the usual annoyances which the garrison should have been subject to and kept in check, by shells and other destructive measures could not be applied from not having them to make use of. It therefore emboldened the besieged in the opposite degree that it damped the ardour of the besiegers, which had it much longer continued, might have become serious to the subordination of the army.

Some of the officers of the regiment of cavalry (3rd Dragoons) to which I was attached, visited the trenches from curiosity but they were glad to make an early retreat from the dreadful wet state they were in and though protected by the mounds of earth thrown up, the French marksmen had become so expert that a hat put on a stick and raised just above them, was instantly perforated by bullets. In going myself near enough to see the details of things distinctly through a glass [telescope], I perceived this destructive fire came from narrow interstices between boxes filled with earth ranged along the parapets of the walls behind which the most deliberate aim could be taken, and which would not have been permitted if an efficient battering train &c had existed. It was a great oversight on the part of Lord Wellington to attempt this siege without adequate means of that nature and it will, it is to be feared, ever be a blot on his brilliant career both on account of its failure and the great loss of life it occasioned. It is supposed that he expected by his recent successes to impose on the French commander to surrender the fortress, but it would not do & he caught a tartar.

The city of Burgos lay from us on the other side of the citadel & just below it; it was almost deserted by the inhabitants and was no attraction for us. I nevertheless went in on several occasions to see it and the cathedral. The approach to it was partly under the enemy's fire but which they never directed against individuals unless an attempt was made to go over the bridge which was directly within the range of shot and was the shortest way in from the English camp and cantonments; even then many ventured to pass and were not molested, yet it was unnecessarily hazardous. We found as we might expect, the streets gloomy & solitary and the square being partly exposed, had a curious appearance on the first entering it. To see on one side the shops shut & totally deserted & not a person walking by and the other with our loungers & various other people carrying on business. A newcomer would at times venture to peep to get a sight of the French sentries, but he was immediately warned back. The cathedral is a magnificent specimen of florid Gothic architecture, rich in ornament both inside and outside and being well described in most books of travels, any account I was enabled to give would be superfluous. All I will mention is that in going into it under the circumstances of the moment the solemn silence which existed produced a melancholy reflection which could not fail to create an impression on every mind, of regret that the destruction of so splendid a building might occur from one moment to the other.

This unfortunate siege continued in its tedious course for days & weeks, disheartening everybody and making but slow progress from the inadequacy of the means alluded to, yet it must have succeeded at last, had there been time allowed to follow the slow though sure process of sap & mine by which we would have at last bored under the principal work & blown it up had not the garrison surrendered.

Events were however occurring in other parts of Spain which did not permit it and accordingly on the 20th of October the Commissariat attached to the troops received a circular on immediate service directing them to move all provisions & stores to the rear on the road to Valladolid with the exception of a supply for three days, indicating thereby that we were about retiring from the neighbourhood of a place we had vainly endeavoured to capture. It was a serious check to our hitherto victorious campaign and must have greatly mortified Lord Wellington in having failed before a third-rate fortress, but it no doubt proved a salutary lesson to him which may have been of use afterwards.

The order to retire followed immediately and was effected during the night of the 21st in perfect silence for the garrison not to disturb us; as the infantry to gain time, had to pass the bridge over the Arlanzon which I have before described as being under fire of the place, the guns used in [the] siege were buried & everything else which could not be carried off was destroyed, but as our means had been of the most scanty nature, the enemy could not boast of any great trophy.

By some stupidity of the Spanish guerrillas, the French suspected that something was going on & fired on the bridge, as they could not however ascertain the actual course & were not able to point their guns a second time with certainty in the dark, no great harm followed & the passage was effected. The cavalry I was with, crossed the river by fords & did so of course unmolested.

Our retreat therefore commenced and no time was lost in continuing it, for it was surmised that nearly the whole of the French armies in Spain were assembling to annihilate us if possible. The enemy's force immediately opposed to us soon followed and began pressing us in trying to turn our flanks and preventing us from blowing up the bridges on the Pisuerga and other rivers we were crossing; in some instances we succeeded in doing so & in others failed.

At Torrequemada situated on a high hill & overlooking the plain on which the army was retiring & the French at our heels, the manoeuvring on both sides was distinctly seen, producing a scene both beautiful and animated of actual warfare. In one direction the French cavalry in imposing numbers were sweeping onwards &

driving ours back, when all at once two small battalions of the Kings German Legion commanded by Colonel Halkett (now Sir Colin) apparently unheeded by both, appeared between them as if left to their fate, the French cavalry charged them at once but were received so warmly and lost so many men & horses before the squares as obliged them to rein in & retire. They came on again, but with no better success being gallantly repelled. In the meantime our cavalry having reformed, came on afresh & relieved the gallant band from their perilous situation in which they gained the greatest credit by their noble conduct. In other parts of the plain masses of infantry following each other, their firelocks & bayonets flashing in the sun, while other corps were engaged, among whom the Spaniards were conspicuous, not for similar conduct as the Germans, but the contrary, and Lord Wellington who was looking on at the time was so angry at it, that he broke out against them to General Alava the Spanish general on horseback by his side, who without being perceived rode down and tried to rally his countrymen and in doing so got severely wounded.[59]

The day passed in this manner, and the troops encamped for the night; the hill on which Torrequemada is situated is a honeycomb of wine cellars perforated in the rock and the troops having discovered & broken into them, a dreadful scene of drunkenness occurred which I am afraid led to many of the men being taken prisoners the next day.

Next morning the retreat continued and the enemy as usual in pursuit until we got behind the Duero on the 29 October, which being a large river was expected to keep him in check for a day or two at least, but practicable fords defeated that expectation and we had to take another position a little in the rear near Rueda for some days, where we halted and were joined by Sir Ro[w]land Hill (afterwards Lord Hill) with that part of the army which had been left to cover

---

59 General Alava was wounded in the groin at the Action of Villamuriel on 25 October 1812.

4TH CAMPAIGN

Madrid, from which he was obliged to retire by the advance on the capital of a superior French force commanded by King Joseph and Marshal Soult who were following him slowly, so that we were in great measure getting encircled on both flanks by armies denominated of the north, centre & south of Spain, very considerably more numerous in the aggregate than we were.

We could not it was evident, remain long stationary and we accordingly fell further back on the 6 November towards Portugal, halting on the 8th in the neighbourhood of Salamanca. These three French armies formed their junction and their commander in chief was evidently determined to bring on a general action or force us still further back and the opinion in our camp for a day or two was that we should accept the former alternative.

About the 13th, on the same ground on which we had gained the last victory but a great deal [of] manoeuvring taking place & the enemy having made a movement to our right by which our communications with Portugal were endangered & could not be effectually prevented, Lord Wellington decided on retreating, by which we were forced to leave the poor city of Salamanca again to its fate. It was quite sad & melancholy to pass through it; the inhabitants looked miserable and dejected and quite aware of the misfortunes which awaited them.

On the 10th I received an order from the Commissary General to give up my duty with the 3rd Dragoons & did so some days afterwards & was directed to join the 4th Division of infantry under the command of Lieutenant General Sir Lowry Cole,[60] a service of much greater importance than my previous one, there being eleven battalions in it viz [1/]7th Fusiliers, 20th Regiment & [1/]23rd Fusiliers with a company of the [5/]60th Rifles being the left brigade; the [3/]27th, [1/]40th, [1/]48th & a provisional battalion of the 2nd & 53rd Regiments with a company of Brunswick light

---

60 Sir Lowry Cole was a Major General in 1812, being promoted to Lieutenant General in June 1813.

infantry, composed the right brigade,[61] all British excepting the latter company; and the 11th & 23rd Portuguese regiments of the line & the 5th [7th] Regiment of cacadores were the centre brigade[62] as they stood when formed together into line, with a brigade of German artillery consisting of 5 nine pounders & a howitzer (six guns in all), a large family to maintain but which with my increased rank, I was to expect, and I am happy & proud to say I remained with that noble division throughout the succeeding campaigns of 1813 & 1814 to the conclusion of the war.

I was extremely sorry to leave the 3rd Dragoons, for I was on the best of terms with every officer in it & the men knew and liked me, and I got on very well with everyone both high & low & it was gratifying to hear afterwards that my absence was regretted, my successor not being found so accommodating in many ways in which the convenience of the corps could be attended to without detriment to the service. To be transferred at a moment when the armies were in presence of each other & the greatest bustle going on was indeed a trial of no little moment, for I had a great deal to learn & undertake & to set to rights when there was neither leisure [n]or opportunity to do it.

Hitherto the weather had been fine and owing thereto, the previous part of the retreat had not been accompanied by uncomforts [sic] which wet weather produces, but unluckily all of a sudden a change took place on the very day the army began its march towards Ciudad Rodrigo. Fortunately the greatest part of the infantry had time to strike its tents, disentangle itself from its position of battle and get on the line of march before it commenced, the cavalry remaining in the rear to protect or cover the remainder of the army. The enemy soon discovered the movement & followed up & though the rain was

---

61 Oman is in agreement, except that he places the 5/60th company and the Brunswick company in the opposite brigades.

62 Known as Stubb's Portuguese Brigade. Carey seems to have made a mistake here, Moises Gaudencio and Robert Burnham's *Fighting Cocks*, and many other sources have the 7th Cacadores in this brigade.

pouring in torrents, it was beautiful to see the plain covered with the cavalry of both armies manoeuvring & watching the one to make an attack & the other to repel it. An inconsiderable affair took place to our right but where I was, we got to our wet bivouac without anything of moment occurring.

Our encampment without any cover whatever for the night, was in a wood of evergreen oaks in which large herds of black swine were feeding on acorns, a temptation too strong to be resisted by the troops, who though they had received their rations were hungry enough for more after a long march, more particularly for such a luxury as fresh pork. The poor animals were assailed in all directions and shot wherever found in or out of the camp and it happening in the dark it was dangerous to move about or even remain in the tent, the whistling of shots being heard frequently. I therefore made a sort of embankment on each side of me with boxes of papers and baggage and slept between them as well as I could but the disorder lasted a good part of the night and for a time occasioned some alarm at Lord Wellington's headquarters, as it was apprehended that a night attack had, or was taking place, the enemy not being far distant.

Next morning before the day had even dawned & in a pouring rain, preparations were made for the march and in leaving the camp soon after, the sad results of the preceding night's slaughter of the pigs were seen as we issued from the forest to get on the road, for portions of them, here half a one, there a quarter, were left in a mangled state, the men who had shot them having helped themselves to what they could carry away & eat, leaving the remainder of the carcass on the spot, a proof of the wanton disorders and waste which had occurred.

The country we were retiring through was flat & wooded & the whole plain soon became swampy, making the march most embarrassing to officers & men who were wet to the skin with mud halfway up the knees and in this plight the march continued, followed & harassed by the enemy. In the afternoon an attack being expected the baggage was ordered to the rear, so that no one had the comfort of it during the night which was most trying for all were obliged to take rest as they could under torrents of rain without the slightest shelter but that which trees afforded, this was born with patience, but being repeated the next day, the troops got savage & disheartened & beginning to straggle, might have become the forerunner of disorganisation.

The army marched in several columns on lateral roads and as the troops fell in, two hours before day break and in pitch darkness, the greatest difficulty was felt to get on the line of march before dawn, every rivulet and indeed the whole country was then flooded, so as to embarrass every step and I may say for a good half hour I followed the living stream without being able to perceive where we were going. During that day the French cavalry increased in boldness & dashed between the columns & carried off the second in command, Sir Edward Paget[63] & it became dangerous to cross from one to the other. The deluge continued and in the evening when the troops had taken their position for the night, the French were upon us & commenced a cannonade to our great annoyance until it was dark, when they could no longer point their guns.

During the evening I had occasion to go to the front on duty and being joined by other commissaries, one of whom rode a white horse, we were mistaken for a General Officer & Staff and fired upon, the shot coming bowling down the road which rendered it necessary to disperse. That night I by accident fortunately found a part of my baggage, my tent being pitched I managed to get a night's rest, but as the canvas was not impervious to the rain and the ground underfoot was in a soak, I got some dust from a neighbouring sawmill, which being dry I laid upon it, wrapped in my cloak, not thinking it advisable to unpack my bed in case of having to make a start in the night. The day following the soldiers straggled in search of provisions & plunder; others laid down exhausted by fatigue & could not be moved & it was

---

63 Lieutenant General Sir Edward Paget was captured on 17 November 1812, remaining a prisoner of war until the end of the war in April 1814.

frightful to see the plight in which the army was marching, sodden with wet which had now lasted more than three days. All looked dejected and hardly keeping their ranks, especially the Portuguese whose woeful countenances shewed what they were enduring; many had their handkerchief or anything else at hand, partly stuffed under their caps & the remainder hanging down their backs to prevent the trickling of the rain into their collars; others had cut a hole in the centre of their blankets through which they popped their heads, keeping by that means the wet off, though adding to the weight they had to carry & this was also adopted by the mounted officers which had a singular appearance, every one endeavouring to shelter themselves by every available expedient, added to which the roads grew worse from being so much trampled upon, and provisions had become scarce. Fortunately, it was the last day of the retreat, for had it continued two or three days longer with similar weather the army would undoubtedly have become a wreck.

The enemy having given up the pursuit we reached the neighbourhood of Ciudad Rodrigo, a fortress in our possession & encamped there & when it was ascertained satisfactorily that they had retired, parties were sent back to assist the sick and knocked up on the road, as well as to collect the stragglers who for plunder &c had left their ranks, many were relieved and brought back but many were found stripped and laying on the ground, the sad consequences of war in the worst of its features.

On the 19th we had a most brilliant day, the troops halted and the whole camp appeared as a vast drying ground; every description of wearing apparel, blankets &c being hung on the trees and bushes exposed to the rays of the sun which had not been seen for the four preceding days, and it was astonishing to see how soon annoyances & privations were forgot and good humour prevailed among those who had gone through them in safety.

Lord Wellington did not however recover his spirits so rapidly, for he immediately issued a most caustic General Order in which he reproved the officers in no measured terms for their negligence in not having kept their men in more order. It was conceived at the time to be a very harsh step which was not deserved to the extent he conceived, as the army had gone through immense exertions from the beginning of the campaign, had suffered greatly by intense heat, long marches, battles, sieges and every casualty of war and though last not least had been exposed during the four last days of the past retreat to excessive November rains, night and day, which greatly exhausted and reduced its ranks.

As an instance of it the regiment of cavalry (3rd heavy Dragoons) to which I was attached during the time (and their casualties were not considered excessive), when I joined them a year before consisted of 450 officers and men & 546 horses, had been reinforced with men and remounts of horses during the time and on my quitting them at Salamanca before the latter part of the retreat they were reduced to 340 of the former and 320 of the latter. The losses of the infantry were however infinitely greater and sickness prevailed to a great extent among them after the excitement of activity was over and they got into quiet quarters, the deaths resulting from which should be added to the loss experienced in the field. One consolation however was that we had done good work and freed a third of Spain from the French yoke and shaken the foundation of its hold on that country.

Being unable for the present to do more offensively & the winter having now set in, we moved on the 20 November to the village of Villar de Ciervo preparatory to our going into winter quarters in Portugal, and the arrangements for the distribution of the army in various parts of the country being soon complete, we commenced our march on the 28th, and on the 4 December arrived at our destination St Juan de [Sao Joao da] Pesquiera, situated on the River Douro twenty two leagues from Oporto; the division occupying that small town & all the circumjacent villages at and within the distance of twelve miles. And happy were we all in the anticipation of some repose, for as there was a probability of our remaining in these cantonments for at least three months everyone endeavoured to make themselves as comfortable as very limited means allowed. We were quartered in private houses as usual and though the accommodation was indifferent, yet on a comparison with that of other troops, we had no reason to be dissatisfied.

Our little town (or village I should say) the one I have mentioned and in which I took up my residence, was situated on high ground a short distance from the river, which river ran its course encased as it were between hills of great height, on the sides of which the vineyards producing port wine were in terraces from their base to their tops. The surrounding country was extremely wild & mountainous and being immediately in the vicinity of the province of Tras-os-Montes, the most mountainous in all Portugal, views of the greatest extent surrounded us in every direction. At the distance of a mile from our residence, a convent was most romantically situated on a nearly perpendicular crag overhanging the river with a corresponding one on the opposite side, the stream flowing at their feet sixteen hundred feet below, having apparently forced its way between them by some violent disruption which had, as it were, rent the mountain asunder, it being seen from above foaming & tearing its way over masses of rocks which had fallen in its bed & impeded its progress particularly for mercantile purposes. From this projecting and elevated situation the river was seen pursuing its course downwards and appeared like a pale thread and as boats could come up thus far, they seemed like dots on it although some of them were of a size to carry one hundred pipes of wine.[64] The flight of eagles which we had disturbed on our approach, soaring about us in various directions as we stood contemplating the scene, added greatly to its loneliness and grandeur and so interesting was it that we often went on the spot to enjoy a sight of its solitude & beauty away from the busy cares of our mode of life.

---

64 A pipe or butt of wine contained 126 gallons (573 litres).

This impediment in the channel of the river having been found of great inconvenience in supplying the army on the frontier between Portugal and Spain by water carriage, our engineers were subsequently employed in blasting the principal rock in the chasm by the removal of which boats loaded with provisions &c were enabled to go much higher than before. The reason given for not having before opened this communication was to prevent a Spanish invasion which thereby might have been facilitated in the conveyance on it of warlike stores &c, the consequence was that this noble stream was rendered almost useless as a means of conveyance between the two countries.

On the other side of the river to that we occupied, the country appeared still bolder in its features, mountain topping mountain as far as the eye could reach, and having to ride at times on business at break of day, it was curious to watch the rising sun progressively dissipating the mists which overhung the earth & made it appear like a sea, immediately after the peaks of the several mountains gradually uncovered, as so many islands increasing by degrees & producing the most diversified views which changed every minute & appearing sometimes as rivers meandering along until the illusion dispersed and the country returned to its natural state. Where those mists continued longest in the deep valleys, the ague prevailed & we were obliged in consequence to remove detachments which had been sent to occupy houses down on the river side from that disease having broken out among them and knocked down almost every man of them. The people among whom we lived were unpolished and rugged as their country; all peasantry with only a very few of the superior classes, land proprietors and wholesale wine sellers who, the former especially, were either absent with their families or kept aloof from us, so that our society was mostly among ourselves.

I and my Commissariat subordinates had plenty of occupation in making up the accounts of the previous campaign and attending to the supply of the troops as well as many other miscellaneous duties, which hardly left us a moment idle. But how the officers could beguile the time in this sort of banishment was most surprising to me, for with the exception of a few newspapers containing much of their own proceedings, they were deprived of almost every other resource; shooting excepted, for there were neither libraries, billiard tables, lounges, promenades or any other sort of amusement to occupy the long winter evenings in such an out of the way place. Drills & parades in the day & the table & cheap wine in the night were their only solace & such was the scarcity of literary resource to employ the mind even among the greatest of us, that in my usual official visits to the general officer under whom I was serving, I found him & his Staff frequently amusing themselves at battledore & shuttlecock.

In this state of idleness however, military duties were not neglected; the regiments were filling their ranks rapidly from the hospitals and by reinforcements from England. Drilling and marching was attended to and the army was organising on improved principles to meet the contemplated campaign which it was rumoured was to open in the following spring. The regiments marched in succession towards the coast for their new clothing which could not be brought up to them, as conveyance in this poor country could not be obtained to carry it, and it was curious to see them depart with their clothes ragged & patched up with every available piece of cloth whatever colour it might be and many of their caps perforated with musket balls, returning with everything quite new like young soldiers, their bronzed faces excepted which soon dispelled the illusion as they drew near.

The spirits of the army were improving daily and the dreadful result of Buonaparte's Russian campaign being known, hopes of the most sanguine nature were entertained that the next effort of ours into Spain would prove more fortunate than former ones. The time however for the final start was supposed to be still far distant.

In allusion to a better organisation of the army which experience suggested, I may mention one feature of it which was found of the utmost convenience, for hitherto the cooking of each regimental company was made in large weighty iron camp kettles, carried on a public mule provided for the purpose. Instead of which a small portable tin kettle sufficient for the cooking of six men was substituted to be carried alternately by them and the mule was employed in carrying three bell tents for the company's accommodation, which sheltered them from much bad weather and made the encampments much more picturesque.

It was doubtful for a time if I should remain long in my present duties in consequence of the violent temper of Sir Lowry Cole, the lieutenant [major] general commanding the division, who was constantly urging me to apply to be removed. I told him as often that it was [for] him to do so, if he was dissatisfied with me and the fact was I neither wished to take the initiative. I had two masters to serve, both exacting impossibilities in different ways and in endeavouring to please both, I failed as a matter of course. The general wished me to dedicate the whole of my time in attending exclusively to the immediate wants of the troops and the Commissary General was at the same time urging me most peremptorily to make up & send in without loss of time, the voluminous accounts of the last campaign which had unavoidably got behind-hand & which in their compilation engrossed every disposable moment of my time. I was therefore most dreadfully badgered for a while, but feeling that I was doing my duty to the utmost of my power, I bore every reproach cast on me with calmness and such was its effect with the general that he treated me with civility, though apparently with smothered anger. In one instance I was sent for by him under great irritation at something that had happened and before going into his room the aide de camp (Captain Wade[65]) told me to be prepared for a reprimand. I went in and saw at once that he was in passion, I calmly heard all he had to say on the subject for which I was sent and in reply gave him the best explanation I could at the moment. It did not appear to satisfy him but I left the room without a reproof; the matter was of no importance

---

65 Captain Thomas Wade, 42nd Foot, aide de camp to Sir Lowry Cole,

& did not concern me individually although it had irritated his fiery temper. Next day the aide de camp informed me that on going to him after the occurrence, the general told him that he could not rebuke me, my manner was so gentlemanly & mild (such were the words) as to disarm him of his anger. This gave me confidence, and I remained at my post and having waded through the multiplicity of business which had been the source of contention & the bar to active exertion, we got on better together and it ended in my continuing under his command to the conclusion of the war, and he afterwards became to me a steadfast friend.

Being on the banks of the Duero and in the immediate neighbourhood of the vineyards which produced the port wine, I availed myself of the opportunity to see how it was manufactured, and one of the principal quintas (Quinta dos Carvalhos) or country houses in which it was prepared being in our occupation as a depot of provisions, I obtained a great deal of information about it. The vineyards, as I have before mentioned, were arranged in terraces from the bottom or river bank to the summit of the high hills between which the stream flowed, the best wine being produced from those immediately next the river, in a south aspect and decreasing in quality as they increased in elevation and singular it is that the wine produced over the hills & beyond them on their reverse side was port no longer, being vin ordinaire. The superior quality exuded without pressure of the grape and was kept separate, there being from the circumstances mentioned on each estate graduations of goodness, the whole being deposited in huge casks or vats containing from 20 to 40 pipes each in stores immediately near the bank of the river for the facility of conveyance in regular casks to Oporto by water, where it was prepared and doctored to the taste of the several countries importing it. The exhalations & fogs from the river are supposed to impart the excellence to the wine, for the grapes appeared the same on the river as elsewhere, large & coarse. Many officers were at great pains to purchase the very genuine article without adulteration, but when bottled at home & kept the usual time, it was found comparatively tasteless & unpalatable. The fact is that on its arrival at Oporto it is strengthened with brandy and other ingredients added, which gives it the flavour port wine has when drank [*sic*].

This wine being principally intended for the British market, the English factory at Oporto monopolised it in former times under the conditions of a treaty, but having abused the privilege by reducing the prices paid to the grower, the Portuguese government established a company in opposition, which had the right of purchasing the article before any other competitor and then fixing the value, by which it was intended to defeat the injustice alluded to, but intrigue and corruption being a prevailing evil in the country, the remedy was soon found to be worse than the disease, and though the system apparently continued, it became of non-effect.

A very good description of this wine could be obtained by the officers and men in our present cantonments for two pence[66] a pint, and that quantity being issued daily as a ration to the soldier, he could easily double that portion by purchase without much expense and enjoy himself; its cheapness & that of spirits was a great temptation & led to scenes of drunkenness which did great injury to the soldiers' health.

1813

In this lonely part of the world we passed our Christmas (1812) and New Year's Day of 1813 of course without relations or friends with whom to participate in the usual festivities of the season, or to whom could be personally expressed the kindly congratulations of mutual esteem. Yet good cheer was not wanting on the occasion to commemorate those anniversaries, for our foragers were successful in their endeavours to procure something out of our common fare, such as turkeys, Lamego hams, famous for their quality & other

---

66 Approximately 40p today!

4TH CAMPAIGN

delicacies which, though enjoyed with thankfulness and good feeling could not be compared to the family circle at such a time and I can say there were many among us homesick who felt the privation.

As the month of January progressed to its termination, the division increased rapidly in numbers & we were joined by Colonel Skerrett[67] who had distinguished himself in the defence of Tarifa near Gibraltar & who was afterwards killed in the unsuccessful assault of Bergen op Zoom in the Netherlands in 1814. He took the temporary command of the Fusilier Brigade quartered in our village & being a kind & good natured man, I became well acquainted with him as well as with his successor, Major General Ross,[68] who subsequently fell in action on the coast of the United States in the same year.

February came and saw us still in quiet and it gave us hopes that we might remain undisturbed for two or three months longer, aware as we were that any change would be towards the frontier & for the worst decidedly in point of comfort, but our expectations were soon cut short, for on the 27th our Route unexpectedly arrived directing us to proceed towards the Coa River on the frontier of Portugal. It may perhaps prove amusing if I annex the march route as I received it from Lieutenant Colonel Brooke [Broke] our Assistant Quarter Master General[69] and who was brother to Captain Brooke [Broke] RN[70] who in command of the *Shannon*[71] captured the *Chesapeake*[72] American frigate.

Immediately after the retreat in November 1812, the strength of the division in the aggregate was 5,864 officers & men and on

---

67 Brevet Colonel John Skerrett commanded a brigade of the 4th Division until June 1813.

68 Major General Robert Ross took command of the brigade in July 1813 and commanded it until the end of the war. He was killed at Baltimore in September 1814.

69 Brevet Lieutenant Colonel Charles Broke 5th Foot, Assistant Quartermaster General.

70 Captain Philip Broke RN.

71 HMS *Shannon* of 38 guns.

72 USS *Chesapeake* of 38 guns.

commencing this march we had increased our numbers to upwards of 8,000 & before our grand & final eruption into Spain in [the] May following, we mustered above 9,000, such had been the numerous reinforcements we had received before the celebrated struggle of ejecting the French armies out of that country.

Our march only lasted four days over a wild country & bad roads without incident or moment having happened worth notice. The infantry forded the Coa, a small turbulent river flowing over a rocky bed deeply sunk between craggy hills, but the artillery was under the necessity of making a detour as a matter of precaution to join the former, by the bridge near Almeida, from the possibility of that river swelling & interfering with the movement in which the guns might have been the obstacle; as we expected, the change of quarters was much for the worst.

We occupied Figuera [de Castelo Rodrigo], a small town or village (more properly) in a part of the country which had been immediately in the neighbourhood of the seat of war for some years, which had so worried & molested the inhabitants that most of them had forsaken their houses & left us in quiet possession. My quarter or lodging was the house of the apothecary, with his shop on the ground floor, containing nothing but empty shelves, broken bottles & other wrecks of his trade, which were swept away for the accommodation of a small guard of Portuguese soldiers attached to me & kept over a sum of public money in my possession. And as the room I occupied was immediately over this guardroom, having between us a floor without ceiling & full of chinks, their incessant conversation was overheard in the day & their snoring at night with the usual effluvia arising from such occupants; such was the description of accommodation we put up with from there being no other & in it we managed to vegetate for two months, complaint being useless and was therefore submitted to with the best possible grace. It might have been for a few days only, as by this time we were led to consider ourselves on the wing and liable to be called to march at a few hours' notice, according to circumstances; it however turned out that we were mistaken in our calculations as we had often been before & afterwards.

The monotony of life was much the same as it had been before, but being within a long ride from Lord Wellington's headquarters at Vilar Formoso, immediately near the frontier of Spain, I occasionally took a trip there either for business, novelty or to pick up the news of the day and I usually started just before day dawn to avoid the heat of the day which began to be felt, though it was rather a matter of danger, for being in a wild country with forests here and there it was infested with wolves and in my progress invariably crossed their path in their return from the low country (where they had been in search of prey) to their fortresses in the hills, and as the high road on which I was travelling intersected their track I often passed them within thirty or forty yards & others at greater distances. They appeared like large grizzly dogs & looked at me in a surly manner, without increasing or altering their pace but as my horse might have got frightened had they growled and perhaps become unmanageable had we remained in each other's immediate presence, I found that a shot from my pistol holster made them speedily understand that they had better be off and which they did without further hesitation. They are a solitary animal only herding together when they require each other's assistance & in times of scarcity & unusual cold they become very savage & dangerous, their depredations on the cattle then become most destructive and it becomes necessary to invade their haunts by an organised battue,[73] accordingly all the villages combine for the purpose and the whole of the able men & boys surround the spot known as their place of refuge, the most expert of them are armed with guns and the others with long poles which they handle with great dexterity & other offensive weapons. The circle being formed they move progressively to a common centre driving everything before them, the animals retiring before them, consisting

---

73 A beat to drive them out of cover.

of wolves, foxes & hares, and as the space becomes more confined & no outlet left for escape or shelter for concealment, an occasional rush of the boldest takes place, a fight ensues which becomes more animated until the whole becomes a scene of indescribable confusion during which some of the men get at times severely bit in personal conflicts with the more savage of the animals, who are slaughtered in great numbers, the skins of which being valuable at times amount to several cartloads & the law requiring that this description of hunt should occasionally take place & no excuse admitted, they are always well attended, indeed the loss of sheep, calves & cattle is such before they are resorted to, that all turn out with alacrity.

A batch of convalescent soldiers from our hospitals in the rear, joined us in the month of April under the command of an officer who was accompanied by a *chère amie*, a Portuguese lady whose flight with him occasioned considerable disturbance on the road and in our cantonments. He (a son of the Emerald Isle, handsome as he was heedless) had served as acting aide de camp to Major General Ponsonby who commanded our right brigade and was quartered in the house of a fidalgo (a nobleman) in our former station and having become intimate with the family which had further time to increase by his having remained behind with the sick that could not march, he so ingratiated himself in the heart of the handsomest of the daughters as to prevail on her to elope and accordingly when the detachment marched she followed him. So soon as her absence from home was discovered the mother proceeded in pursuit with several of her people boiling with indignation and offended pride and soon came up with the runaways, and having stirred up the inhabitants of the several villages on the road in her behalf, it was with the greatest difficulty that he succeeded in reaching his destination after several attempts at a rescue and nearly bringing about a collision between the soldiers & the peasantry who felt incensed at such an attempt. In this plight they arrived and sought protection in the house of his friend, a Commissariat Officer, Mr Howie[74] serving under my orders, who came to me to know what he was to do in his dilemma, as the mother had already arrived & was creating a disturbance. I told him that as they were now under his roof without invitation from him, there they should remain for the present & no blame could be attached to him. The old lady applied for redress to the general officers but as her daughter was of age & acted voluntarily they did not interfere, she remained however in the village walking about in a frantic manner with a dagger in her hand threatening to kill her daughter and haranguing the Portuguese soldiery in the hope of inducing them to assist her in the rescue, but not succeeding in her object she at last proceeded to Lord Wellington's headquarters & having made her complaint, which was supported by a representative from the authorities in Lisbon, an order came from His Lordship to Lieutenant Thompson of the 27th Regiment,[75] the culprit, either to give up the girl or marry her, as the keeping with him of a woman of her quality & standing in society was highly objectionable and likely to create a bad feeling in the country among the influential class. He accordingly married her and I met her oftentimes afterwards on the line of march riding on a donkey the only conveyance he could afford; she appeared however, gay & reconciled to the mode of living. She poor thing followed him to Ireland but I know not what afterwards became of her. The family finding every endeavour ineffectual of recovering their daughter gave her up as dead & having disgraced them by such

---

74 Clerk Thomas Howie. Challis shows him only arriving in the Peninsula in February 1814, but Carey makes it clear that he was there in early 1813. He was appointed as Deputy Assistant Commissary General in May 1814.

75 It is certain that Carey has identified the wrong man as Lieutenant Alexis Thompson, 27th Foot, died in September 1812. It has proven impossible to discover the true identity of this young officer. Lieutenant Braithwaite Christie, 5th Dragoon Guards, was an extra aide de camp to General William Ponsonby for most of this period, but he was of Scottish descent and died at Bath in 1824. I cannot find any reference to him marrying in the Peninsula. Major Arthur Helsham Gordon, 5th Dragoon Guards, was aide de camp to William Ponsonby and was indeed Irish, but again there is no record of a Peninsular marriage, as he married Anne Bilton in York in July 1820.

a union, they had recourse to a curious expedient to blot her from their genealogy by the performance of a funeral service committing her to the grave (in effigy I presume) a proceeding dictated by pride which among the Portuguese nobility is carried to an excess little understood elsewhere. It certainly was a disgraceful proceeding on the part of the officer, though the arising intimacy should have been perceived & guarded against in a country in which morals & education are not of the highest standard & in which jealousy for females is carried to an extent savouring of their Moorish descent.

To enliven if possible our mode of living, an attempt was made to get up a dance at the headquarters of the Portuguese brigade, commanded by an Englishman & the officers being mostly natives, they succeeded in collecting a few young ladies (accompanied by their mothers) of the neighbourhood, who had returned to their homes & who with the wives of the officers made up a sort of party, but the male part being more than three to one of the other sex, the chance of dancing was so little that I preferred looking on from not being an adept in waltzing or their country dance. It took place in the best house of the place called a Quinta & the refreshments in that exhausted country were as might be expected of the most simple kind which did not however damp the gaiety of the entertainment which passed off to the apparent satisfaction of all present. What struck me most before quitting the house occurred by accident in mistaking one door for another & walking into the bedroom of a part of the family which had not joined in the amusements of the evening; they had been doubled up to make room & consisted of the very young & old & were laying asleep as far as I could judge (in the hurry of the visit) more than a dozen in one large bed with pillows at top & bottom, one half one way and the other half opposite, their feet meeting in the centre apparently dovetailed and being in profound repose which I fortunately did not disturb, I retreated as quickly [&] silently as I could, and on mentioning what had happened, I learnt this mode of sleeping was not unusual in ordinary times or circumstances.

A curious instance of itinerant preaching occurred while in our present quarters owing to the village Roman Catholic priesthood not being usually in the habit of addressing their congregations in sermons, in consequence of which the most eloquent of the clergy both regular & secular are appointed for the purpose & perambulate periodically certain districts; the individual who on this occasion visited our village to administer spiritual information to the few Portuguese who were among us was a friar in whose train a small cask came loaded with large rollers resembling geographical charts and when he ascended the pulpit a few hours after to preach, they appeared laying on each side of him. I went to the church on the recommendation of my Portuguese servants and was particularly struck at the mode adopted by him in the operation of his subject; it was on the crucifixion and after he had reasoned sometime thereon, he commenced illustrating every circumstance by unrolling one by one the supposed charts which represented in a series of paintings the progressive events from the betrayal, judgment hall, to Mount Calvary, handing to a man below each painting as he had done with it and having worked up his congregation to a state of great excitement by overdrawn & terrific details they one and all began crying and wailing, apparently in despair at what had occurred, and it was some time before the sensation calmed down and I verily believe that had a Jew been discovered at the moment among them, he would have been torn to pieces in revenge, this preacher certainly knew how to work up his auditory and impress them with the subject being evidently an adept in his calling. He spoke extempore and no doubt repeated the same occurrence in the different towns & villages through which he peregrinated.

The month of March expired & no move, but we began to be on the tip toe of expectation for the march forward which we conceived would work some good to Spain, in which country we hoped to pass the next winter, but in the midst of these sapient cogitations several officers & artificers of the Royal Staff Corps came unexpectedly &

established themselves in the neighbouring Convent of Aquiar[76] and commenced building an extensive range of buildings called Pese huts intended for hospitals in case we should have to return after the campaign, and it having become a part of my duty to be paymaster of the workmen in addition to the multiplicity of other matters I had previously to attend to, I was well informed of the object of their erection. It was certainly a damper to the sanguine expectations entertained of our future operations and gave rise to many reports especially in our division in which the 7th Fusiliers, the officers of which became most expert in fabricating rumours for the amusement of the remainder of the army, and being old soldiers the information they circulated was so plausible and possible that they obtained the greatest credit, and it was only after reaching headquarters that they were found to be without foundation. This continued until we finally moved and for a time proved an annoyance to many who wished for any other thing than what these reports stated as likely to take place, and actually disturbed many a private arrangement of those weak & silly enough to believe them.

The realities however of the service were daily taking place during the month of April, in the reinforcements which arrived, completion of field equipments, keeping a reserve of provisions & live cattle and every other arrangement indicative of the march of events & individually we all were better prepared for privations likely to occur. I added to my establishment a tent, two English horses for the saddle and another servant, a portable table & two chairs which folded, besides other etceteras which rendered me quite independent when encamped, for as soon as we commenced moving the probability was that we should not see the interior of a house (to occupy it) for some time to come & it was of consequence that we should soon be stirring, for the country around us was becoming totally exhausted. Almost

---

[76] The Convent of Saint Mary of Aguiar is about 1 mile south-east of Figueira de Castelo Rodrigo.

4TH CAMPAIGN

every head of cattle had been purchased and consumed wherever it could be found far or near, to such an extent that an apprehension was entertained that there was not a sufficiency left to restock Portugal, every stack of hay or store of straw had disappeared and for months no wheat for bread, barley or Indian corn for the horses or mules could be obtained locally, all supplies of that description including biscuit, rice &c being obtained from America[77] & other countries by sea & brought up to the army on the several rivers or other communications, the expense of which to England was enormous.

As a specimen of the outlay in one single article of consumption of essential necessity, every pound of meat actually given to the soldiers was calculated not to cost less than 2/6d[78] & in many instances more from the number of cattle after purchase which died, reduced in weight by marching, strayed or stolen and which never came to the slaughter, and I may add from knowing it as a fact, that every other article required for the subsistence of the army could only be obtained at the same exorbitant price, from which the effort we were making may be inferred, but as it was a struggle for political life or death and whether or not we should succumb to the power of Buonaparte the pecuniary sacrifice was well worth making.

In the beginning of May the 4th Division was complete in strength and the Marquis inspected it. It was never more efficient in every way, the brigade of artillery consisting of six guns, (5 nine pounders and 1 howitzer to throw shells), looked remarkably well, as well as the two brigades of British infantry, and the Portuguese brigade was a strong and splendid body of men, with British officers at their head and the men with their swarthy features, their grenadiers wearing black moustaches contrasted with effect to their fairer & smoother chins and upper lips of their brothers in arms. The whole mustered

---

[77] These food supplies from America continued throughout the war despite the United States and Britain being then at war with each other.

[78] About £6 per pound at today's values.

above 8,000 men under arms so that including followers allowed rations, the aggregate strength exceeded 9,000 persons, a number never before attained.

The commander in chief appeared with a small Staff, and was simply dressed as usual in a grey surtout coat, white neckcloth and low cocked hat edged with a small frill of ostrich feathers, indicative of his being a general officer. Nothing material occurred on the field beyond the usual routine, but immediately after it, a hare rose in front of the troops & being a fair object of pursuit it was followed by several mounted officers among whom was one of the young Commissariat officers under my orders of the name of Beverley[79] who actually run it down after a long chase & this I mention to shew that there was an energy among us all fit for any undertaking.

Another review by his Lordship of a more imposing character took place almost immediately after, indicating very decidedly that the move forward would not be much longer delayed, and as it occurred in our neighbourhood I could not resist the temptation of seeing it. It consisted of all the regiments of cavalry of our army which could be collected together in one spot, numbering eighteen or upwards, and I never before had seen such a grand spectacle of mounted horsemen from our shores, both men and horses in the highest order & condition which could not have been surpassed in Europe numbers excepted.

The memorable events which had succeeded the destruction of the French army in Russia in the latter end of the past year forced the Emperor Napoleon to order drafts of his best soldiers to join him in the north of Germany, from Spain, Italy & wherever they could be obtained to assist in the organisation of another army to oppose the advance of the Russians & the rising defection of the Prussians, Austrians &c which step in addition to existing circumstances could not but produce a disheartening effect on the French army in Spain.

---

79 Clerk Charles Beverley was appointed a Deputy Assistant Commissary General on 15 January 1814.

4TH CAMPAIGN

And as every day added strength both to ourselves & the Spanish Corps in cooperation & about to take the field, the Marquis of Wellington did not stir apparently until every arrangement was complete to ensure his striking an important blow with every chance of success. Of his dispositions no one of us had the slightest conception for they were clothed in impenetrable secrecy & not one of his generals or other officers were presumed to be in his confidence, unless it was his Quarter Master General, Colonel Murray (afterwards Sir George)[80] through whom all the movements of the army were unavoidably communicated & arranged, and such was the precaution taken to prevent the enemy from ascertaining them in time to counteract them, that the business of his office was exclusively conducted by commissioned officers in whom of course every reliance could be placed. Even Sir Lowry Cole who commanded our division was invariably (I was fully satisfied) quite in the dark as to what was in contemplation, for I seldom went to headquarters without his enquiring from me for any information I might have picked up in the several offices in which I had transacted business.

Just before the commencement of the campaign the French armies opposed to us occupied various positions in connexion with each other, extending in our front from Madrid to Valladolid, Toro, Zamora & to the Esla more northward, with advanced posts in front of Salamanca &c. Whether we should make a dash at Madrid to our right, or in the centre towards Salamanca & Valladolid, or to our left towards the Esla & Zamora, was the question which no one could answer, as our troops were so disposed as easily to take either & it completely puzzled the French generals until they were unexpectedly undeceived by the sudden eruption we made in adopting the latter of the three moves by which we endangered their communications with France.

To be Continued . . .

---

80 Major General Sir George Murray was the Quartermaster General.

Index

1st Division xvi, 10, 119 fn, 122 fn
1st Dragoons KGL 202 fn
2nd Division xii, 78 fn, 85
2nd Dragoons KGL 202 fn
2nd Foot 227
3rd Division 194, 197
3rd Dragoons 153, 156, 165, 176, 186, 198, 199 fn, 223, 227, 228
3rd Foot 51 fn
4th Division 95, 227, 239 fn, 247
4th Dragoons 153
5th Cacadores 228
5th Dragoon Guards 153, 179, 195, 205, 243 fn
6th French Light Infantry 202 fn
7th Cacadores 228
7th Division 196 fn
7th Foot 227, 246
10th Hussars 7 fn
11th Light Dragoons 194
11th Portuguese Line Batt 228
12th Light Dragoons 194
13th French Dragoons 213 fn
13th Light Dragoons 117, 213 fn

14th Foot 3 fn, 95 fn
15th Hussars 7 fn
16th Light Dragoons 127 fn
20th Foot 33, 227
23rd Foot 3 fn, 95 fn, 227
23rd Portuguese Line Batt 228
24th Foot 67
27th Foot 99, 227, 243
40th Foot 227
43rd Foot 80
48th Foot 227
50th Foot 120, 121, 131
52nd Foot 80
53rd Foot 227
59th Foot 3 fn
60th Foot 3 fn
61st Foot 196
71st Foot 120, 131
81st Foot 3 fn
92nd Foot 120
95th Foot 3 fn, 14, 80

Abrantes 55, 57, 99, 147, 149, 156
Alava, General Miguel 217, 226

INDEX

Alba de Tormes 201
Albuera 108 fn, 146, 178
Alcantara 55 fn
Aldeia da Ponte 165, 167
Almada 40
Almaraz 184
Almeida xvi, 108, 110, 112, 115, 146, 150, 164, 167, 168 fn, 183, 240
Alpalhao 184
Alpedrinha 187
Alten, Brigadier General Charles Count 22 fn
Arlanzon 225
Arronches 99
Arroyomolinos 155
Arzobispo, El puente de 81, 83, 84, 185
Assumar 185
Audit, Board of 113
Audit Office 29
Auditor General 36 fn
Aveiro 49fn

Badajoz x, xv, xvi, 85, 86, 88, 89–90, 93, 95, 96, 97, 99, 100 fn, 146, 164, 168, 169, 170, 171, 177, 179, 180, 183, 184, 185
Bagenal, Lieutenant John, 87th Foot 83 fn
Bainbrigge, Colonel John 33 fn, 34

Baird, Lieutenant General Sir David xv, xxviii
Baltimore, Battle of 33 fn, 239 fn
Bandeira, Jacinto Fernandes da Costa, merchant 143
Barrosa, Battle of 178
Becket, Mr John, banker 147
Beresford, Marshal William Carr 108, 146
Berlengas Islands 40 fn
Beverley, DACG Charles 248
Blaniac, General Lafon 213 fn
Bock, Major General Eberhardt von 202
Bogue, Captain RHA 34 fn
Bonaparte, Joseph 95, 208 fn, 210, 213 fn, 216, 227
Bonaparte, Napoleon ix, x, 125, 208 fn, 213 fn, 248
Boulogne-Billancourt 114
Briscall, Rev Samuel 96 fn
Brock, Mr William Henry 67
Broke, Lieutenant Colonel Charles, 5th Foot AQMG 239
Broke, Captain Philip RN 239
Brotherton, Major, 14th Light Dragoons 95 fn
Brunswick Light Infantry 227
Buenos Aries 64
Burgos xvi, 221, 224

Busaco 116
Buxton, Paymaster Isaac, 24th Foot, 68 fn

Cabeco de Montachique 125
Cabeco de Vide 184, 185, 186
Cadiz 74 fn, 75, 92, 178 fn, 184, 212, 217
Cadogan, Lieutenant Colonel Hon Henry, 71st Foot 131
Campbell, Brigadier General Alexander 76
Cape of Good Hope 94
Carey, Elizabeth xxi, 135 fn
Carey, Isaac xx, xxi, xxvi
Carey, Mary xxi
Caria 187
Carrie, Brigadier 194
Cartaxo 129, 132
Castelo Branco xvi, 57, 58
Castrillo 194 fn
Chesapeake, USS 239
Christie, Lieutenant Braithwaite, 5th Dragoon Guards 243 fn
Cintra, Convention of 1
Ciudad Rodrigo x, xvi, 110, 115, 150, 154, 164, 168, 170, 183, 184, 187, 191, 195, 228, 231
Clinton, Lieutenant General Sir Henry xii
Clowes, Major William, 3rd Dragoons 156, 199

Coimbra xv, 43, 46, 47, 55, 99, 100, 101, 103, 105, 116, 145
Cole, Lieutenant General Sir Lowry xvi, 227, 236, 249
Condeixa-a-Velha 99
Constantia *see* Punhete
Cooper, DCG xv
Coria 63
Corunna xv, xxviii fn, 2, 7, 10, 17 fn, 21, 25, 26, 29, 30, 31, 32, 33, 35, 42
Cotton, Lieutenant General Sir Stapleton 184
Craddock, General John 41
Craufurd, Brigadier General Robert 10, 21 fn, 80
Cuesta, General Gregorio 69, 72, 76

Dalrymple, General Sir Hew 1 fn
Daniel, Commissary John xii
Dobree, DACG John 145
Downie, ACG John 74
Doyle, Lieutenant General Sir John xv, xxvii, xxviii
Duenas 221
Dumaresque, ACG Thomas 150
D'Urban, Lieutenant Colonel Benjamin, Portuguese service 210 fn

El Escorial 11 fn, 208, 218
Elvas xv, 85, 86, 88, 149, 170

INDEX

Erskine, Commissary General xv
Erskine, Major General Sir William xvi, 119
Espagnac, Don Carlos 198
Espinhal xvi, 116, 117, 130
Estremoz 183

Factory, The British 54, 238
Falmouth xxi, 1, 26, 27, 28, 35
Ferreira, Alvers, clerk 160
Field Train Department, the xviii
Forster, Albert 135
Framingham, Lieutenant Colonel Hoylet RA 50 fn
Franceschi, General 49 fn
Frere, John Hookham, diplomat 29, 82

Gafete 99
Garcia Hernandez 202 fn
Gavaio 99
General Hospital xv, 6, 65, 79, 81, 82, 85, 86, 87, 140, 150, 201, 235, 242, 246
Gillespie, DACG Joseph 159 fn
Girard, General 155 fn
Gitterick, Lieutenant John, 12th Light Dragoons 194 fn
Golega 118, 119, 128, 148
Gordon, Major Arthur, 5th Dragoon Guards 243 fn
Gordon, Lieutenant Colonel James Willoughby xxviii

Graham, General Sir Thomas 178
Graham, Commissary William xii
Greenwell, Major Leonard, 45th Foot 182
Guarda 169
Guards, the 3 fn, 51, 52 fn, 90, 96, 102, 223
Guernsey xiv, xx–xxi, xxiii, xxvi, xxvii fn, 2, 7, 33 fn, 37, 64, 67, 68, 145, 158, 159, 167 fn, 196

Halkett, Colonel Colin, 2nd Light Batt KGL 196
Head, DACG George xix fn, 100, 102, 104 fn, 153
Henegan, Richard, AC Field Train xii
Hill, General Sir Rowland 49 fn, 78, 103, 116, 155, 184, 185 fn, 226
Howie, DACG Thomas 243
Howorth, Major General Sir Edward xv, 44, 94
Hutchins, Captain Thomas 3rd Dragoons 209

Imaz, General 146 fn

Johnstone, Captain John, 3rd Dragoons 176
Junot, General Jean-Andoche 1 fn, 143, 156

253

Kettles camp 235
King's German Legion, the
   22, 226

La Lippe, Fort 88
La Serre, Ensign Nicholas, 87th
   Foot 64, 76
Laidley, DACG John 115
Lallemand 179 fn
Lawson, Captain RA 53 fn, 114
Le Marchant, Ensign Carey 1st
   Foot Guards 200
Le Marchant, Major General John
   Gaspard xvi, 153, 158, 171,
   177, 178, 179 fn, 199, 201 fn
Le Mesurier, Lieutenant Colonel
   Haviland, 12th Portuguese
   Line Batt 167
Le Mesurier, Paul, merchant
   167 fn
Lefebvre-Desnouettes, General
   Charles 28
Leiria 42, 55, 99
Light Brigade, the 21, 80 fn
Lisbon xvi, xxvi fn, xxvii fn, 33,
   37, 39, 40 fn, 42, 43, 49, 55,
   58, 82, 87, 88, 89, 92, 101,
   107, 108, 110, 111, 116, 117,
   119, 122, 124, 125, 130, 133,
   134, 135, 137, 140, 141, 144,
   145, 147, 148, 149, 150, 153,
   154, 157, 163, 170, 182, 191,
   199, 214, 216, 243

Llerena 175, 179 fn
Lugo 29, 30
Lutyens, DCG Charles 107

Mackenzie, Major General
   John 55 fn
Mackinnon, Lieutenant &
   Captain Daniel, Coldstream
   Guards 92
Mackinnon, Colonel Henry
   Coldstream Guards 87
MacPherson, Lieutenant James,
   45th Foot 183 fn
Madrid ix, xvi, 29 fn, 56, 58,
   72, 91, 202 fn, 203, 207, 208,
   210, 213, 227, 249
Mafra 39
Marmont, Marshal Auguste
   165, 167, 168, 183, 184, 191,
   193, 194
Massena, Marshal André 113,
   123, 165 fn
McCrea, Captain Rawdon 87th
   Foot 64
McNaughton, DACG
   Alexander 95
Medical Department, the 6, 30,
   85, 151
Merida 85
Military Chest, the 30, 66
Militia, the Guernsey xx, 67
Militia, the Portuguese 53, 130,
   168, 182

INDEX

Miranda, Sebastian de 74
Moore, Lieutenant General
   Sir John x, xv, xvi, 7, 17 fn,
   24, 29, 33, 41 fn, 56, 83, 85,
   86, 88, 89–90, 93, 95, 96, 97,
   99, 100 fn, 146, 164, 168,
   169, 170, 171, 177, 179, 180,
   183, 184, 185
Morrogh, merchants 42 fn
Murray, Major General Sir
   George QMG 249
Murray, Commissary General
   John xv, 37

Napier, Major William 179, 185 fn
Nava del Rey 191
Nisa 57, 170, 186

Oporto 40, 43, 48, 50, 51, 52 fn,
   53, 54, 58, 67, 232, 237, 238
Orange, Colonel William, Prince
   of 213
Ordenanza, the 130
Ordnance Department, the xviii,
   6, 66, 78
Oropesa 69, 78
Ourense xv, 7, 12 fn, 14, 15, 18,
   21, 22

Paget, Lieutenant General
   Sir Edward 230
Paget, Lieutenant General Lord
   Henry 7, 15, 28, 31 fn

Penamacor 165, 170
Pero Negro 122 fn
Petkin, DACG William 114
Philippon, General de Division
   Armand 182
Pinhancos xvi, 109, 113, 114,
   116, 130
Plasencia 63, 65
Pollos 191
Ponsonby, Colonel William,
   5th Dragoon Guards 179 fn,
   195, 210 fn, 218, 242, 243 fn
Pontevedra 18
Portalegre xvi, 99, 149
Portsmouth xxviii, 28, 35, 38
Punhete 99

Rawlings, ACG Philip xiv, xxvi,
   xxvii
Retiro, the 213
Reynaud, Brigadier
   General 154
Rob, Lieutenant Colonel
   William, RA 44, 46, 50 fn
Romana, Don Pedro Marquis of
   xv, 21, 132
Ross, Lieutenant Colonel
   Robert, 20th Foot 33,
   34, 239
Royal Engineers, the 6, 52,
   66, 234
Royal Staff Corps, the 52, 65,
   66, 245

Sahagun 17 fn, 28
Saint Croix, Brigadier General Charles 126
Salamanca xi, xvi, 153 fn, 176 fn, 184, 187, 188, 194, 195, 196, 197, 198, 199, 201, 217, 227, 232, 249
Sampaio, Henriqu,e 1st Conde de Pavoa 144 fn
San Cristobal 190
Sanchez, Don Julian 154
Sandeman, Mr George, merchant xiii, 41, 135
Santarem 128, 129, 148
Santiago de Compostella 9, 12
Sao Jao da Pesquiera 232
Sao Julian, Fort 40, 124
Saumarez, Admiral James 33
Saumarez, Surgeon Richard 33
Schaumann, DACG August xii
Sealy, Mr Richard, merchant 42, 135
Segovia 204, 205, 206, 218
Seia 109
Seville 56, 74 fn, 75, 81, 82, 92, 171, 184, 216
Shannon, HMS 239
Singleton, Ensign Robert, 61st Foot 196

Skerrett, Colonel John 239
Sobral de Monte Agraco 120, 122
Sorauren, Battle of 168
Soult, Marshal Jean-de-Dieu 53, 82, 146 fn, 171, 177, 178, 179, 184, 217, 227
Stewart, Lieutenant Colonel Charles, 50th Foot 131
Stott, Paymaster Thomas, 29th Foot 78 fn

Talavera, Battle of xi, xiii, xv, 64 fn, 76, 79, 83 fn, 111
Talavera de la Reyna 68, 71, 72, 82
Tarifa 239
tents 77, 228, 236
Thompson, Paymaster Alexander, 53rd Foot 78 fn
Thompson, Lieutenant Alexis, 27th Foot 243
Toledo 174, 185 fn
Tomar 99, 117
Tordesillas 191, 194
Toro 193, 249
Torrequemada 225, 226
Torres Vedras xvi, 133
Treasury Clerk 38

INDEX

Treillard, General 210 fn
Trujillo 74, 85

Usagre 179

Valladolid 202, 203 fn, 217, 218, 220, 225, 249
Vandeleur, Major General Sir John 166
Vaux, DCG John xvi, 134
Victor, Marshal Claude 55
Vigo xv, 15, 17, 18, 21, 22 fn, 23, 25, 26, 27
Vila Velha de Rodao 57, 58
Vilafranca de Xira 126 fn, 133, 147
Vilar Formoso 241

Villagarcia 179 fn
Villamuriel 226 fn

Wade, Captain Thomas, 42nd Foot 236
Waters, Colonel John 51 fn
Whitelock, Lieutenant General John 64
Wight, Isle of 1, 38

York, Duke of 107

Zafra 171
Zamora 249
Zarza la Mayor 61
Zebreira 59